P9-DMD-249

by
Stanley C. Vance
H. T. Miner Professor of Business Administration
Head of Personnel and Industrial
Management Department of the
University of Oregon.

Over 100 directors and chief executives of our largest corporations were interviewed by the author in developing this significant volume.

THE CORPORATE DIRECTOR focuses attention upon and analyzes the inner workings of the board of directors—the top decision-making component of our industrial society. It is filled with facts about how directors are picked and how effective boards function, and presents a number of pertinent case studies.

Among the corporate giants who contributed actively in building this book are Armstrong Cork Company, Continental Can Company, Ford Motor Company, General Foods Corporation, The B. F. Goodrich Company, H. J. Heinz Company, The National Cash Register Company, Radio Corporation of America, Sears, Roebuck and Company, Standard Oil Company (New Jersey) and Westinghouse Electric Corporation, to name just a few.

THE CORPORATE DIRECTOR is "must" reading for every executive and member of the board.

DISCARD

BETHA
COLLEGE
LIBRARY

# The Corporate Director
A CRITICAL EVALUATION

# The
# Corporate
# Director
## A CRITICAL EVALUATION

STANLEY C. VANCE, Ph.D.

H. T. Miner Professor and Head of the
Department of Personnel and
  Industrial Management
University of Oregon

1968
DOW JONES-IRWIN, INC.
Homewood, Illinois

DOW JONES-IRWIN, INC., 1968

All rights reserved. No part of this publication may be reproduced, stored in a retrieval system, or transmitted, in any form or by any means, electronic, mechanical, photocopying, recording, or otherwise, without the prior written permission of the publisher.

*First Printing, September, 1968*

Library of Congress Catalog Card No. 68–23341

*Printed in the United States of America*

# Acknowledgment

More than 200 top-ranking executives and directors contributed to the development of this study. The list of contributors is much too long to detail. However, special recognition must be given to the following major corporations:

1. Aluminum Company of America
2. Anaconda Company
3. Armstrong Cork Company
4. Bethlehem Steel Corporation
5. Caterpillar Tractor Company
6. Cclanese Corporation
7. Continental Can Company
8. Corn Products Company
9. Deere & Co.
10. E. I. du Pont de Nemours & Co.
11. FMC Corporation
12. Ford Motor Company
13. General Foods Corporation
14. General Tire & Rubber Company
15. The B. F. Goodrich Company
16. W. R. Grace & Co.
17. Gulf Oil Corporation
18. H. J. Heinz Company
19. Hoover Company
20. International Business Machines Corporation
21. International Telephone and Telegraph Corporation
22. Kennecott Copper Corporation
23. Mobil Oil Corporation
24. National Cash Register Company
25. Owens-Illinois, Inc.
26. J. C. Penney Company
27. Radio Corporation of America
28. Sears, Roebuck and Co.
29. Singer Company
30. Standard Oil Company of California
31. Standard Oil Company (New Jersey)
32. Standard Oil Company (Ohio)
33. Union Carbide Corporation
34. United States Steel Corporation
35. Westinghouse Electric Corporation

v

658.42
V277c

77365

In each of these instances two or more of the company's top-policy makers—chairman, president, vice president or director—participated in an interview process. The combined interview time dedicated by key executives of these firms was in excess of 600 man-hours. The views expressed in these interviews provide an empirical base for the analytical process.

Yet it should be emphasized that the inferences and conclusions expressed in the following pages are entirely those of the author. A conscientious attempt has been made to keep in the strictest confidence information which, if quoted, might result in embarrassment to the cooperating individual or his firm. In every instance where individuals, companies, or episodes are identifiable, the facts are founded in a public source and were in no way elicited from any of the interviews.

Finally, I wish to express my deepest appreciation to Standard Oil Company (New Jersey)—particularly to the secretary of the corporation, John O. Larson; and to the assistant secretary, C. Fred Lindsley. Much of the study's field work was accomplished during a sabbatical leave from the University of Oregon made possible by financial assistance from Standard Oil Company (New Jersey). In addition, Mr. Larson, then president of the American Society of Corporate Secretaries, facilitated contact-making with representatives of the cooperating firms. Mr. Lindsley gave unsparingly of his time, assisting in all phases of the study. To them and to the many individuals from other firms who helped make this work a reality, I wish to express my gratitude. Hopefully this analysis will give the interested reader a new and better perspective of the role of the director in modern large-scale industrial enterprise.

*July, 1968*                                        Stanley C. Vance

# Table of contents

## Part I.   The Background

# Part II.   Analysis Examples

# Part III.   Conclusions

# Appendix

# Recommended Reading

# Indexes

# Part I
## THE BACKGROUND

# THE BOARD-ROOM MYSTIQUE

To most Americans, a directors' board room—while it might be just around the corner physically—is as far distant as the furthest reaches of space. The only board-room meeting most of us can expect to attend, even if we are fairly substantial investors in a company, is the formality of the annual meeting, but at these rituals there is virtually nothing a stockholder can see or learn about how a board of directors performs during the rest of the year. (Sidney Weinberg, perhaps the best-known of all professional directors, is said to have referred to corporate annual meetings as "circuses."[1] )

The typical investor does not even know how often a given board of directors meets. Nor does he know which directors attend regularly and which appear only now and then. Nor is there a meaningful transcript of board minutes which he might peruse (supposing he is a conscientious and discriminating investor) to see which directors seem alert, which lackadaisical. And it is an extremely rare investor who can even name three or four of the directors on any fourteen- or fifteen-man board. In short, the American public's knowledge of the meaning of and the need for boards of directors approaches zero.

In theory, a company's board of directors is supposed to manage, rule, or guide that company's affairs. This is how a dictionary would define a board's prime function. In turn, managing, ruling, or guiding means taking a fairly active interest in company affairs; and an active interest implies a depth of knowledge, a high degree

1/ *Wall Street Journal,* "Readings in Business," May 26, 1965.

of competency, and a pervasive attendance to detail. But in to-day's highly technical and intensively competitive economy, even the most dedicated company officer finds it difficult to keep abreast of developments, and this difficulty will in all probability be compounded as the concept of the conglomerate firm increasingly makes industry classification meaningless. The difficulty will be even further exaggerated as virtually every major company in the world sheds its regional or national characteristics and becomes truly multinational.

It is an anomaly that at a time when there seems to be an intensified need for knowledgeable directors, many companies are adding directors to their boards from outside the company. In a sense, this would seem a contradiction. In only the rarest instances do outside directors have even the faintest idea of the technical processes, the competitive strains, or the real financial status of the host company. But from the pinnacles of industry we hear the rebuttal loud and clear: Our major corporations do not need or seek directors who are intimately conversant with the host company; they seek rather (so it is said), men of character, sound judgment, intuition, poise, statesmanship, wisdom, sophistication, economic integrity, and similar lofty—but nonetheless intangible—traits. Visualizing what the typical corporate chief executive hopes to find in a director-candidate, one could almost conclude that a new Age of Angels or at least of Supermen is upon us.

That corporate chief executives need assistance if they are to guide their company effectively is a truism. Setting stringent specifications for selection of their board-room associates is certainly in order. But when it comes to finding candidates who meet those specifications, corroborating evidence is seldom if ever demanded. It too often appears that a director-candidate is wise, sage, sophisticated, and otherwise qualified on the say-so of one or, at the most, of only a few key individuals. A company's entire board must, of course, pass on the acceptance of every candidate and, ultimately, the stockholders must ratify or reject each nominee at designated annual meetings. But, as every student of the proxy system knows, the presumably democratic right of ratification is simply the right to acquiesce; the typical 98 percent or higher vote in favor of the management-selected slate of candidates for a given board indicates a voter regimentation more rigid than that found in any totalitarian regime. Of course, there are strong arguments for such regimentation. Some contend that just as dual unionism is harmful to unions, so, too, setting up a rival slate of director-candidates would be disruptive to companies. Others argue that the typical investor knows so little about the needs of a given company and the availability of directorate talent that he could only cause harm by intruding into the director-selection process. For these and many other reasons—debatable as they may be—today's stockholder is quite effectively disenfranchised.

Because of the uncertainty, the confusion, and the contradiction shrouding the board of directors and its members, we have the board-room mystique. It is no one man's invention. It is simply an accident of our times.

Historically, this aura of mystery has a logical base. Just a generation or two ago, many—if not most—of our major enterprises were owned and operated by one man or by a relatively small group of associates. The typically small investor was completely overshadowed, overpowered, and overawed by the giants of our Age of Enterprise. Both the finance-oriented and the product-oriented entrepreneur ran his firm in the manner of a satrap. For the most part no one questioned his authority or behavior, and only in a very few cases of flagrant disregard for the law was corrective action taken. But since it is a characteristic of our society that no single sector or component exists completely independent of other sectors, it seems logical to predict that within the very near future the board-room mystique must begin to shed some of its mystery. There are some very powerful forces which cannot tolerate the haziness and uncertainty that are part of that mystique. Among these forces are:

1) The progressively more intimate association of government and business. This association will intensify as national defense becomes more and more a matter of technology. Government's widening sphere of influence in areas such as social welfare, education, and finance also makes its closer alliance with business almost a necessity.

2) The phenomenal increase in the number of individual owners of corporate stock. Within the past twenty years, the number of stockholders in the United States, conservatively estimated, has about trebled—to more than 24 million. This vast number of own-

ers of American business increases by about 1,000,000 each year.

3) The rise of large-scale institutional investors. Today institutions own about one fourth of the shares listed on the stock exchange. Considering that the Big Board alone lists about 1,300 companies with 11 billion shares valued at nearly $600 billion, an institution's right to know what a board of directors does or is supposed to do cannot long be ignored.

All three forces—government, 24 million stockholders, and strong institutional investors—are gradually but very definitely taking a keener interest in corporate actions and problems. Even the general public is becoming much more literate about corporate matters. Under such circumstances it is inevitable that the board-room mystique give way to a more rational explanation of directorate functions.

Concomitant with these three forces for change are:

1) The increased democratization of all segments of our society, a trend noticeable not only in politics but also—perhaps especially —in religion, in education, and in our social pursuits.

2) The continuing stress on professionalization. This trend, so noticeable in practically every facet of life, must ultimately be felt in the corporate board room. We expect corporate officers to acquire the attributes assumed to be part of professional management. By kindred reasoning, corporate directors will eventually be required to meet a set of stringent professional requirements.

One basic reason for the general public's mystification about what goes on in corporate board rooms is the extreme sensitivity and defensiveness of some industrial leaders. For example, two perennial disrupters of the tranquility of annual meetings, Wilma Soss and Beatrice Kelekian, representing the Federation of Women Shareholders in American Business, Inc. (FWSAB), introduced the following shareholders' proposal at the 1966 American Telephone and Telegraph annual meeting:

Resolved that stockholders of American Telephone and Telegraph Company hereby request our Board of Directors to take such steps as may be necessary to provide that in the future all nominees for AT&T directors shall disclose in the AT&T proxy statement any and all directorships which they hold in business corporations in addition to their major occupations when standing for election or reelection to the Board of American Telephone & Telegraph Company.[2]

In an accompanying statement, these shareholders noted that the company did make available a booklet containing such information—but that despite the fact that the company had about 3 million shareowners representing more than 4¼ million people, it printed only 240,000 of the booklets.[3] The proposers of the resolution objected to the company's policy of forcing interested stockholders to write and request such information. (Actually, the knowing stockholder could have looked up such information in *Poor's Register of Corporations, Directors and Executives.*)

The directors of AT&T recommended a vote *against* the FWSAB proposal, because:

> Your company gladly volunteers information about the directors, including their directorships in other companies and makes it readily available. New shareholders receive our leaflet entitled, "Directors of AT&T and Chairmen & Presidents of Bell System Companies," which lists the positions the Directors hold in various industrial, financial, civic and governmental organizations. We also advised all shareholders in the 1965 proxy material that they might obtain this leaflet on request. However, out of more than 2,850,000 shareholders, only about 1,000 have asked for it—hardly more than one shareholder in 3,000. This tends to confirm our view that there should not be a requirement, as proposed, to publish information of this kind in the proxy material repeatedly, year after year, with little change each year.[4]

The company also pointed out that the 1966 resolution was substantially the same as one introduced in 1965 which was "overwhelmingly defeated by over 96% of the votes cast." In typical proxy fashion, the shareholders placidly accepted the board's recommendation and in the 1966 meeting once again defeated the proposal by a close-to-unanimous vote.

In their plea for the very pertinent information about the direc-

2/ American Telephone and Telegraph Company, *Proxy Statement*, March 16, 1966, pp. 3 to 4.
3/ AT&T, *1966 Annual Report*, p. 23.
4/ AT&T *Proxy Statement, op. cit.*, p. 4.

tors' outside connections and endeavors, the petitioners had pointed out that, "IT&T, RCA, IBM, General Electric, General Motors, U.S. Steel, and Std. Oil of N.J. voluntarily disclose these [interlocks]."[5] It is difficult to interpret the reluctance of AT&T's board to make such information more readily available. Perhaps the company felt that such disclosures in its proxy statement would focus attention upon the part-time character of its board. Or perhaps the extremely high incidence of interlocking among its directors at the very highest levels of all sectors of our society was the chief reason. Congressman Emanuel Celler's Committee on the Judiciary report, *Interlocks in Corporate Management,* pointed out that in 1964, "All told, there were 104 corporate interlocks between the directors and officers of AT&T and other corporations. This was the largest number of corporate interrelationships found in any of the 29 corporations included in the industrial category of the sample."[6]

The directors of AT&T continue to have considerable other interests outside the company, and the company's board is one of the leading examples of absentee directorship: AT&T's directors have a combined total of 23 major bank directorships, 13 top insurance directorships, and 32 major industrial directorships. In addition, there are six members of AT&T's board who are members of the President's prestigious Business Council. Its directors are also policymakers in a great variety of educational, professional, religious, governmental, and charitable organizations. (It should be noted, however, that the latter offices, while an indication of interlock, are also one index of a dynamic and high-image group of directors.)

In terms of board-room mystique, it is precisely the kind of action followed by AT&T in its proxy statements that assumes and perpetuates stockholder lack of interest and knowledge about corporate affairs. Instead of trying to enlighten their shareholders, companies much too often assume that either their stockholders do not care or that they are incapable of comprehending.

Surprisingly enough, in its following year's proxy statement (1967) American Telephone and Telegraph included the very ma-

5/ *Ibid.*
6/ Committee on the Judiciary, House of Representatives, *Interlocks in Corporate Management,* March 12, 1965, U.S. Government Printing Office, Wash., D.C., p. 157.

terial voted unnecessary at its 1966 meeting: in the 1967 proxy
statement, each of the directors' major directorships, in addition
to his AT&T membership, were listed.[7] There is no reference to
the past two years' rejection—by holders of nearly 540 million
shares of the company's stock—of the proposals requesting precisely this sort of information. In a sense, then, we have an example of unilateral company action, repudiating overwhelming
votes of the stockholders. We also have an implied judgment of the
worth of the proxy system. But most significantly, AT&T's action
is an example of how both a company and its stockholders perpetuate the notion that the board of directors is a mystical, sancti-
fied institution. The very fact that in previous years less than one
in 3,000 stockholders had taken the trouble to request pertinent
information attests to the apathy of most AT&T (and other) owners of voting stock. Both stockholder apathy and management's
overpowering emphasis on prerogatives, however, tend to perpetuate the board-room mystique.

Radio Corporation of America provides a comparable yet quite
different illustration. At its 1966 annual meeting, which was attended by 2,200 shareholders, a resolution setting age 72 as a
mandatory limit for individuals serving as directors was defeated
by a 93.17 percent vote of the stockholders. But despite the fact
that at the May 3, 1966, meeting there were 41,029,965 votes cast
supporting management's position *against* the setting of any age
limit, and only 3,046,151 for it, the company's board reversed
itself just one month later, on June 3, 1966, when it amended the
bylaws of the corporation to provide "that no person who had
attained the age of 72 would be eligible for election as a director."[8]

Neither the AT&T nor the RCA illustrations should be interpreted as indictments of those companies; they are used simply to
cast some light upon why we have permitted a board-room mystique to grow and flourish in the corporate policymaking sphere in
an era otherwise characterized by a rejection of blind faith and of
placid acceptance. There are, however, rumblings of discontent,

7/ American Telephone and Telegraph Company, *Proxy Statement*, March 15,
1967, pp. 2 to 3.
8/ Radio Corporation of America Forty-Seventh Annual Meeting of Shareholders,
May 3, 1966, *Order of Business*, p. 24.

and in a sense the small group of chronic disrupters at some major annual meeting can be viewed as a positive force. Quite understandably, most managements consider long-talking intruders into the ritual as troublemakers. Yet, under the trusteeship concept, the owners have a right to ask questions—once a year. (One of the best summaries of these intrusions upon an otherwise placid corporate scene is the annual publication of the Gilberts. The Gilbert brothers have for more than a quarter of a century been campaigning for what they term shareholder democracy.)[9] There are, in addition, other and increasing manifestations that the boardroom mystique is being found wanting and even objectionable in other sectors of society.

## Government

There is probably no better example of a top-level control mystique than that surrounding Great Britain's government. Despite many democratic trappings, Britain has continued to adhere to relatively aristocratic patterns in most sectors of its society. In the sphere of government, for example, such patterns are fairly abundant, and they resolutely resist change.

On December 16, 1966, the House of Commons, by a vote of 264 to 177, decided to hold morning sessions on Mondays and Wednesdays at 10 o'clock. To most Americans this would certainly not seem a momentous decision. But viewed in the context of traditional British patterns, it is a rather vital move, signifying a shift toward professionalism at the Parliamentary level, a breakaway from the part-time politician toward full-time professionals.

For generations the assumption has been that the attributes essential for top-level decision-making are a sort of birthright handed down from father to son. This notion has been perpetuated and strengthened by Britain's exclusive "public" school system. Competency for top-level decision-making posts in government, business, and all other phases of British life has generally been assumed rather than proven. But some change has obviously taken place. As Richard Crossman, the Labour party leader in the

9/ See Lewis D. Gilbert and John J. Gilbert, *Twenty-Seventh Annual Report of Stockholder Activities at Corporation Meetings During 1966* (published privately).

House, put it, "The country gentleman disappeared long ago as the dominant element in the House and now the predominance of financial and learned professions has been challenged by the arrival of members who had to abandon their jobs when they entered Parliament."[10]

Another significant step in relegating the aura of mystery at top government levels to eventual oblivion was the 1966 agreement by the House to set up two special committees—one on science and technology, the other on agriculture. In the United States Congress there is perhaps an overabundance of such committees, but British tradition, nurturing what may be termed the officialdom mystique, has found such specialization antithetical. By definition, however, specialization implies measurable or at least observable abilities, and, consequently, acceptance of specialized personnel violates the precept of the aristocratic generalist. Thus, the increasing stress on specialized competency, the growing need for demonstrable attributes, intensifies the erosion of the officialdom mystique.

## Hospital administration

*The medical board.* The aristocratic pattern of an elite and super-exclusive top governing body (coupled with an organization of "worker-doers") is of course not restricted to other lands. In this country there are many comparable instances. During 1966 there was a rash of disturbances in many of our hospitals caused by strikes and threats of strikes by the nursing staff. A very obvious cause for much of this discontent was the relatively low pay nurses receive. Another less obvious but probably more significant factor was the almost complete exclusion of nurses from top policymaking posts in our larger hospitals. It is still generally assumed that the nursing function is strictly a "doing," or operational, task. Nurses are considered as line-operatives lacking any real decision-making function—or capacity.

One tangible result of the 1966 strike threats has been, in most instances, a noticeable improvement in working conditions and in

10/ *New York Times,* "Commons to Hold Morning Sessions," Dec. 17, 1966.

pay. In far fewer instances has the deeper-rooted causal factor been given notice. One seeming exception is in the city of New York. There, according to the *New York Times:*

> Dr. Howard J. Brown, the City Health Services Administrator, announced yesterday that registered nurses would be added to the boards that supervise the medical affairs of municipal hospitals.
>
> The appointment of nurses to our medical boards signifies a revolutionary reorganization of our hospitals that is the only answer to our critical nursing shortage.
>
> New York nurses are going to be recognized professionals; they will no longer be a doctor's handmaiden, but will be his professional partner.
>
> Dr. Brown said that the first appointment of a nurse to a medical board would be made at Bellevue Hospital.[11]

This is a momentous step, and could be the beginning of serious modifications in the medical-board mystique. There is no question about the relatively high-level technical competency of most medical boards. There is, however, some question as to the adequacy of medical boards as presently constituted to solve current problems. The incidence and seriousness of nurses' revolts attest to the seriousness of the question.

*The board of trustees.* It is not putting it too strongly to say that radical reforms are long overdue in the sphere of top-level policymaking in our larger hospitals. The astronomic rise in average daily-per-patient costs from about $9.39 in 1946 to $57.93 in September, 1967, is one sure index of trouble ahead, representing as it does a skyrocketing increase of more than 500 percent over the 20-year period.

It would obviously be quite unfair to indict hospital boards of trustees for this phenomenal rise in costs. Technological advances have more than proportionately been translated into higher costs, and labor costs have outpaced average daily-per-patient cost increases. That there is real justification for the upward changes in both these cost categories is not the question. Hospital help, including nurses and interns, has been notoriously underpaid, and a

11/ *New York Times,* "City to Add Nurses to Medical Boards," Aug. 2, 1966.

major portion of the cost increase is the result of terminating this subsidization of patients by hospital personnel. This is a most laudable and long overdue rectification of a serious inequity.

But hospital costs are also moving upward as a consequence of a startling rise in the patient-room-use factor. Where in the past the hospital was considered virtually a last recourse measure, it is today used for a great variety of previously home-treated ills. The obstetrics section, for example, once a very minor component of a hospital, today constitutes a world of its own. Medicare, too, has served to transform not only our philosophy of health care but also the plant layout and utilization practices of many of our hospital facilities.

Most of these changes reflect an improved standard of living and a step forward in our attitude toward the ailing and afflicted. What is less obvious is the fact that these changes have also necessitated a restructuring in hospital administration. This has led to the evolutionary development of a new type of manager, the professional hospital administrator. Currently, there are at least 14,000 such administrators. "For decades, especially before World War II, hospital administrators were a catch-as-catch-can conglomerate of head nurses and doctors who didn't want the job, and an assortment of bankrupt businessmen, elevator operators, retired ministers, and butchers' helpers who often gave hospital administration a bad name."[1][2] Today, nearly one third of all hospital administrators are specialists who have earned advanced degrees in hospital administration.

It is this group of technicians which is given the task of keeping hospital costs contained. Their responsibility, however, is rarely balanced with commensurate authority, and in almost no instance does the hospital administrator sit on the board of trustees. The typical hospital organization at the trustees' level is shown diagrammatically in Figure 1.

There are strong arguments for the arrangement shown in Figure 1. Hospitals, like most other eleemosynary organizations, have traditionally been considered as almost exclusively community-service, non-profit endeavors primarily concerned with local sociological problems. They had need for a board of trustees quite

12/ *Business Week,* "Hospitals Get a New Specialist," Oct. 10, 1964, p. 70.

different from a business-type board of directors. Consequently, prominent and affluent local citizens constituted their prime components. Till recently, this was a workable arrangement. But today, with our radically changed approach to health and hospitalization, the old organization structure seems wanting—it abounds with "mystique." Socially prominent and/or affluent trustees today provide only an incidental portion of hospital revenues, and vested interest groups such as unions and churches have a steadily decreasing role in our larger hospitals. Thus it becomes progressively more difficult to explain why specific individuals are appointed to hospital boards.

FIGURE 1.  Typical hospital organization chart

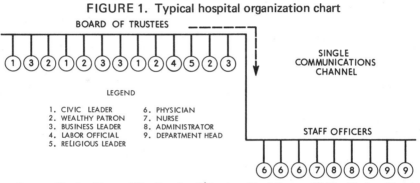

Source: Stanley Vance, "Do Boards of Trustees Need Surgery?" *The Modern Hospital,* June 1965.

The attendant mystery, while still tolerated, will almost certainly become more and more an irritant to those who are vitally and daily concerned with running the hospital. Some of these individuals, such as the physician deeply immersed in his professional problems, will undoubtedly sublimate their irritations. For the most part, however, physicians, department heads, nursing supervisors, and especially hospital administrators will seek more meaningful guidance from the trustees. Because this is happening, or will happen, most hospital boards need radical restructuring. Every single appointment to the trustee's post must be justified in terms of individual competency and hospital needs. It can be hoped that this change will be evolutionary and imperceptible.

One tangible result of an abandonment of the medical mystique will be a significant shift toward inclusion of more functional experts on the board. Hypothetically, tomorrow's hospital boards

FIGURE 2. Proposed hospital organization chart

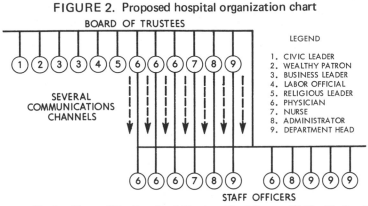

Source: Stanley Vance, "Do Boards of Trustees Need Surgery?" *The Modern Hospital,* June 1965.

of trustees will approximate the pattern shown in Figure 2, a radical departure from the organization diagram shown in Figure 1.

## Religion

With the exception of totalitarian regimes and the military, the Roman Catholic Church has probably the most rigid top-level structuring of any large organization. The concept of infallibility on *ex cathedra* pronouncements gives the Pope a decision-making power rarely found in any other organization, and even outside the concept of infallibility the Pope's decisions are generally universally accepted by officials and members of the faith.

In recent years, particularly in the many sessions of the Vatican Council, there has been ample evidence of restiveness on the part of the laity, priests, and even bishops. Serious questions have been raised concerning many of the presumed prerogatives. The following instance stresses the radically changing concept of control by the Church over its higher-education facilities.

In April, 1967, the 22-member faculty of the School of Sacred Theology at Catholic University of America voted to go on strike. The issue in question was the dismissal by the university's board of trustees of Reverend Charles E. Curran. The board found fault with some of Reverend Curran's publications and pronouncements and he was summarily fired. The School of Sacred Theology's decision to strike precipitated a boycott by practically all the

600-member faculty and the 6,600-member student body and a resolution was passed

> in which the faculty called the board's actions an "unusual exercise of administrative power [which] is tantamount to a rejection and a repudiation of the entire faculty of the school and its teaching. . . . We've got to stop the meddling of the trustees . . . this interference by the religious side on academic matters. . . . We've sent notes of protest to the board during the past 10 years."[13]

Reverend Curran was offered a hearing before the board of trustees. He rejected this offer, stating that he did "not want a hearing in which only the board would sit. He said he wants members of the faculty of the School of Sacred Theology to sit with the board."[14] In a sense, this was a rejection of the ultimate authority assumed to rest with any board of trustees.

The astounding aspect of this revolt is the serious questioning of one of the most prestigious boards of trustees in the entire world. Catholic University's board consists "of all five United States cardinals, 22 archbishops, six other bishops, eleven laymen, and [was] chaired by New York's Francis Cardinal Spellman."[15]

As the dispute continued, there were signs of capitulation on the part of the trustees: "Boston's Richard Cardinal Cushing announced that he would not condemn Curran. 'He must teach all sides. It makes no sense to appoint people to a university board who know absolutely nothing about running a university.' "[16]

This last comment has a special significance, reflecting as it does a rapidly growing sentiment even in the Catholic hierarchy that the members of a governing board of a university—call them trustees, directors, regents, overseers, what you will—should possess certain readily identifiable competencies. If this is so, then the notion that a director becomes fully qualified by the very act of designation is becoming a minority opinion.

There is some evidence of such a change. For example, in late spring of 1967, "Ownership and control of University of Portland

13/ *The Oregonian,* Portland, Ore., April 21, 1967.
14/ *Ibid.*
15/ *Time,* April 28, 1967, p. 62.
16/ *Ibid.*

was transferred from the congregation of Holy Cross to a non-church-related board of regents. . . . The change-over agreement stipulates that the university will be under full control of the independent board, but a program of Catholic theology and activity will be continued. Five priests will be members of the board."[17] Since there are forty members on the university's board, this modification reduces the previously dominant group to a minority.

In May of 1967, Washington's other Catholic university, Georgetown, named three laymen to its fourteen-man governing board which formerly consisted entirely of Jesuits. On November 14, 1967, Catholic University of America itself capitulated. The university's board of trustees agreed to reconstitute itself as a body of thirty members of whom fifteen must be laymen.[18]

While these and comparable changes are certainly not a repudiation of previous leadership, some inferences can be made, the most obvious being that governing boards within the Catholic Church are being redesigned to meet changing needs and circumstances. The aura of mysticism associated with most governing boards, and especially those in the religious sphere, is giving way to a more rational and more functional structuring.

## Education

The changing attitudes in the Roman Catholic Church and in Catholic institutions of higher learning are equal only to a gentle swell when compared to the tidal wave of change sweeping across governing boards in public education. In some instances, such as the 1964 University of California at Berkeley episodes, the desire for change becomes outright revolt.

Presumably, most of the student and faculty resentments are focused upon imperfections in our educational system, and obviously no board of higher education can mandate perfection. Nevertheless, it is the responsibility of the board to determine courses of action. Practically all boards of higher education consist of appointees. As a rule, these are outstanding members of the community. Their services are gratis—but also part-time. Relatively few

17/ *The Oregonian,* April 21, 1967.
18/ *The Oregonian,* Nov. 15, 1967, p. 10.

board members have any technical acquaintance with educational aspirations or problems and, thus, the board usually becomes a ratifying agency, seconding the proposals of its one or two educator members. There are, of course, some constraints. Prevailing practices and trends must be considered, and more and more federal and state mandates must be observed. On occasion, community sentiment is listened to. There is even an occasional response to taxpayers' sentiments. On the whole, however, despite the theoretically superb checks-and-balances system built into boards of trustees for education, policymaking tends to gravitate into the hands of the one or two technicians on the board. In this respect, education boards are very similar to industrial boards of directors which have a predominantly outside membership.

The natural concomitant of such board structuring is, bluntly put, a dictatorial control. In the realm of higher education this means that the faculty and student body can express their views through only one channel—the university's representative on the board. There is no question as to the dedication and integrity of most such inside representation on the boards of educational institutions. The problems stem, rather, from the drastic limitation of the communications flow through a single person—sometimes two persons. Invariably, such a restricted communications flow is colored and conditioned by the administrative attitude; it is definitely staff-oriented as opposed to line-oriented. Yet, in theory at least, the line (or students and faculty at the university level) constitutes a self-policing, self-governing community of scholars.

These problems are not unique to higher education. At the local level the situation is just as acute, perhaps more so. The increasing incidence of teacher strikes and the growing acceptance of unionism by teachers is one index. At a national seminar in New York on "Who Controls American Education" (sponsored by the Joint Committee of the National Educational Association and the Magazine Publisher's Association), Mrs. Elizabeth D. Koontz, speaking on "Why Teachers Are Militant" stated:

At the risk of oversimplification, I would suggest that it is simply the resultant determination of teachers *to share in the determination of policy* that can make the difference between successful teaching and learning and the frustrated frenzied activity that teachers are forced to become involved in that really allows little time for teaching. . . . The attitude that teachers must wait until the most widespread array of self-appointed judges decide that they deserve conditions under which they can do the job is in direct opposition to the premises underlying every other facet of professional activity, business, government or industry.[19]

*Time* magazine in a pertinent article, comments on the teachers' demand for

a bigger voice in the establishment of education goals. There is some justice in the teachers' claim to power. Those now in charge of the schools, particularly in the big cities, have failed miserably. [But] if school boards lack technical knowledge and administrators get buried in bureaucracy, are teachers organizations the best hope? Not necessarily. The trouble with many union groups is that they are dominated not by the best teachers but by mediocre time-servers primarily worried about job-security and self-benefits.[20]

Whatever the causes of educator unrest, and no matter what corrective actions will ultimately be taken, it does seem evident that some significant changes are coming at the top levels. In the near future, family connections, local prominence, political position, wealth, or repute will not be enough alone to qualify a person to serve on an education board. Mystique in education boards, just as mystiques in every other area of human cooperation involving organized endeavor, seems on its way out.

19/ *Wall Street Journal,* "Notable and Quotable," May, 1967.
20/ *Time,* Oct. 13, 1967, p. 64.

# THE INFORMATION VOID AND
# BOARD-ROOM MYSTIQUE

The attitudes, historical accidents, and philosophical justifications of governing boards in various sectors of society have been referred to as *mystiques,* the implication being that the structures and functions of governing boards are accepted as an article of faith, that in some respects the established order is viewed as preordained. Yet it is equally assumed that if our society is to continue its dynamic thrust, there should be no sanctuary, especially in the board room, for the mysterious and unexplainable.

We will now attempt to analyze what can and should be done to minimize the mystery that shrouds our top-level policymaking boards, confining the scope of the analysis basically to large-scale manufacturing industry. (When feasible, allied areas such as banking or merchandising will be included.) The prime purpose of this undertaking is to note how much logic, and what kind of logic, presently underlies the structuring of industrial boards of directors.

A basic premise in this investigation is that the directors of our major corporations have attained their eminence by more than pure chance, predestination, or mystical osmosis. To say that so-and-so was named a director of so-and-so firm because of his "poise" or "perspicacity" defies common sense. No responsible chief executive would accept such meaningless phraseology from any of his subordinates. A candidate's assets (and his liabilities) should be shown in measurable terms. Consequently, every directorate appointment should—and in the future *must*—be supported in balance-sheet fashion. Such a balance-sheet presentation must not be only one man's accounting. Permitting just one person, or even a very intimate group, to decide upon the adequacy of an individual's directorship abilities is an oligarchic procedure too chancy for our times.

A balance-sheet approach to analyzing the adequacy of a given board of directors has the merit of providing an inventory of an individual's top-level decision-making resources. There are, of course, some weighty arguments against the taking of such an inventory; the classic argument that we are dealing with people and imponderables, for example. Yet when corporations hire a secretary or a salesman, they do not hesitate to prepare rigid job descriptions and manpower specifications. To say that board members are beyond such measurement is simply a further manifestation of mystique.

If a candidate for a board of directors is to be subjected to a typical balance-sheet analysis, then more information must be made available about each current director and his specific contribution to the company. There is an obvious obstacle to the application of this scientific management methodology to board members: over the years, through public sufferance, there has developed what might be called a Board Room Seal of the Confessional. What transpires at board meetings is—theoretically at least— "nobody else's business." Whether such secrecy is necessary for competitive reasons is debatable. Much that was secret yesterday is today public knowledge. For example, it was not very long ago that wage patterns prevailing in a given company were also considered to be "nobody else's business." Competitive reasons supposedly made such secrecy mandatory. Today, of course, any union headquarters can provide interested persons with the wage patterns prevailing not only in a specific company but in the entire industry.

Similarly, the cost of borrowing funds from banks was, at one time, a matter of utmost confidence between borrower and lender. Today, a glance at any issue of the *Wall Street Journal* will disclose advertisements, placed by the company, indicating the magnitude of such "secret" transactions, together with interest charges and other very vital terms. Bringing such information into the open has probably engendered a new vitality in our economic system.

If the board of directors is to have a meaningful role in tomorrow's society it seems essential that its Seal of the Confessional be set aside. In a corporate system where logic prevails all the way from the lowest level up to and through the chief executive, secrecy as to how and why certain individuals are selected as directors, together with secrecy as to how and when they contribute to the company's good, must be ruled out.

The first (perhaps sufficient) step would be to put meaning back into the board-room minutes; then, these minutes might be made viewable. Until rather recently, many board-room minutes included verbatim comments and resolutions made by individual directors. There are few if any major boards today, however, which record any but the most terse, almost meaningless, summaries of their regular meetings. A brief generalized record of board action could, of course, reflect a brief generalized meeting and a terse generalized interest and competency on the part of the participants. There is a point, however, where brevity becomes silence—and that is the present trend.

The rationale for brevity in board-room minutes is that a detailed commentary would give government, customers, workers, or competitors undue advantages. A rather summary description of board deliberation and action would be more defensible in cases where the major stockholders participated personally on the board. (This reasoning would not hold, of course, in the case of the large, widely-owned, semi-public corporation, such as American Telephone and Telegraph with its more than 3 million individual stockowners.) It is true that today's owner of corporate stock in this country does periodically receive fairly decent performance summaries. (Most foreign companies feel that disseminating the kind of information found in American companies' reports would be ruinous.) Interim and annual reports, together with proxy statements, give the American stockowner a level of information available in no other nation. But since it has been amply shown that good rather than harm has been the net effect of such company and owner communications in this country, it would seem a logical extension to ask for more information as to what transpires at regular board meetings. At present, the only time stockholders see or hear their directors is at the annual meeting. Unfortunately, it is a distinct rarity at these annual sessions to have any company spokesman except the chairman, president, and one or two key officers address the audience. In quite a few cases, several and sometimes most of the outside directors do not even attend. At the Wilson and Company 1966 annual meeting, "a familiar annual meeting figure, John J. Gilbert, brother of Lewis, asked many questions and was critical that only two of Wilson's nine directors had attended the meeting."[1] It should be pointed out that the missing members are almost invariably outside directors, and that even the largest corporations frequently have rather high director absenteeism at the annual meetings (four directors failed to attend the 1967 United States Steel Corporation annual meeting). At its crucial 1961 annual meeting, the first meeting after the classical electrical industry price-fixing scandal, General Electric Company had less than an 80 percent director attendance. At the 1968 General Electric Company annual meeting only four of the 16 outside directors were present. Yet, in most instances, the annual meeting is the only truly verifiable participation by the directors in board meetings.

Most major corporations claim an approximately 90 to 95 percent attendance rate of directors at regular meetings. This is laudable, if true, but before such claims are accepted they should be subjected to frequent and impartial verification—published minutes distributed to all stockholders, for example, would serve such a purpose. Too, most corporations seem to be trying hard to improve outside director attendance. Quite a few companies pay up to $500 per board meeting and committee meeting attended in addition to retainers in the $5,000 to $12,000 range. Since most special board committees meet on the same day as the board itself, such compensation can be doubled or even trebled. (This could be a major factor in giving some companies, as claimed, a nearly perfect outside-director attendance record at their regular sessions.)

Attendance by itself, however, is no guarantee of performance. Judged on the basis of individual director performance at annual meetings, an observer would have to conclude that members of most boards are inarticulate; also, that practically all boards are unanimous on every decision. (About the only time unanimity is

1/ *Wall Street Journal,* Feb. 16, 1966, p. 4.

lacking is when an insurgent group is making a bold attempt at getting company control.) The very brevity and infrequency of many board meetings militates against effective performance. Delta Air Lines' 1967 annual meeting lasted seventeen minutes; the 1964 annual meeting of Coca-Cola Company was over in seven minutes. Westec Corporation, which figured in a late 1966 stock-manipulation scandal, was even more perfunctory in its regular board meetings. "Here is how one prominent businessman described a pre-August meeting of Westec's board: 'Williams [chairman] gave his spiel, Ernie [President Ernie M. Hall, Jr.] called for a vote and everybody said aye. In five minutes the meeting was over.' "[2] It is interesting to note that Westec's twelve-man board was almost entirely outside director in composition.

About one third of our major companies have board meetings four times a year—or less. It is very difficult to imagine a serious, competent, and dedicated group of directors getting together to discuss major policy matters solely on a quarterly basis. In some instances even though directors might be willing, they are unavailable. The political about-face in Indonesia after Sukarno's regime was ousted provides an example:

> Indeed, the political turnabout has been so rapid that many businessmen were caught unprepared. Goodyear Tire and Rubber Co. was invited to reclaim its tire factory in Bogor April 1, but ceremonies marking the occasion are still pending. The reason? Goodyear's home offices in Akron, Ohio, couldn't round up company directors fast enough to sign the proper powers of attorney for its plant managers.[3]

Under these conditions—outside-director absenteeism, one-hour or even briefer regular sessions, and not-too-frequent meetings—it would be a blind acceptance of the board-room mystique to assume that all is well at the corporate pinnacle. Compounding the problem is the lack of substantial information as to how each director has responded to issues during the board meetings. Because of this secrecy shroud it is impossible to evaluate individual director performance or worth. As a consequence, it almost seems that as soon as a person is designated as a director he becomes

2/ *Wall Street Journal,* Nov. 25, 1966, p. 18.
3/ *Wall Street Journal,* April 18, 1967, p. 30.

omniscient, infallible, and perhaps even omnipotent. Thus, the mystique continues.

One of the surest ways to dispel at least part of this mystique would be to give interested parties, particularly stockholders, employees, customers, and even competitors more information as to what transpires at meetings of the board. Admittedly, immediate and detailed disclosure might give competitors undue advantage. There is, however, minimal force to such reasoning if the information is made public only after a reasonable period of time has elapsed, and in less than verbatim form. For example, the new federal freedom-of-information law provides that agencies such as the Federal Reserve Board must release the records of its policy-shaping Federal Open Market Committee 90 days after each meeting. ("Minutes of the May 23 meeting made public last week, showed a break in the Fed's easy money front, with one member of the committee seeking tighter credit.")[4] Under comparable safeguards, information about private concerns could be made more readily available to the public.

In a parallel instance, even the sacrosanct Secret Cabinet records of Great Britain's government are ultimately available to the public. A recent change in government policy reduced from 45 to 30 the number of years Cabinet papers are restricted. Considering the political character of these documents and their importance to national history and destiny, it is remarkable that they are made publicly available at all. A principal premise, then, is that board-room minutes should be made more meaningful and more viewable. Every stockholder should know which directors attended and which did not attend each meeting of the board and its principal committees. Proposers of significant items should be identified by name. Objectors should be identified and a summary of their objections should be included. Record-keeping of this sort is essential if there is to be any evaluation of the capabilities and contributions of each member of the board. It is time to put an end to blanket and perpetual endorsement of every member of every board.

These suggestions are not so revolutionary as they might initially appear. Our largest publicly-held organization, the United

4/ *Business Week,* Sept. 2, 1967, p. 40.

States government, provides a time-tested and effective pattern. The public's trustees, its duly-elected representatives, conduct most of their business in an open forum. Their dissents and agreements are recorded and made available to all interested parties. And despite a multitude of limitations, including open debate and a recording of votes, our legislative system works rather effectively. (While no doubt back-of-the-scenes maneuvers and cloakroom conniving do play a significant role in the legislative process, it can hardly be said that they play the major role.)

Corporations would probably lose far less than they fear if their strictures on reporting individual director contribution were removed. Actually, there are at present numerous "leaks" in even the most tightly structured security supposedly insulating corporate secrets from the outer world. For example, consider the switch in 1968 by Semon Knudsen, from his executive vice presidency at General Motors to the Presidency at Ford Motor Company. Only the most naive analyst would overlook the "code-cracking" significance of this move. If competing corporations can acquire the innermost secrets of competitors by hiring away top talent, it seems reasonable to assume that board deliberations are not so secret after all.

Then, too, one of the strongest arguments advanced for the inclusion of outside directors on boards is their first-hand acquaintance with the top-level thinking in other corporations on whose boards they serve. While these other corporations may not necessarily or directly be competitors, nevertheless outside directors are viewed as sources of secret information. The point is that if anyone outside a corporate family is given access to confidential information, then such information should logically be made just as readily available to the corporation's stockholders—perhaps to its employees, its customers, and even the general public.

It is obvious that with fuller disclosure of what transpires at meetings of the board there could be some loss, but probably far less than that feared. The only significant loss would be a "loss of face" on the part of honorific but noncontributing directors, inside or outside. With detailed and, one would hope, more meaningful director-performance records available for stockholder scrutiny, voting at annual meetings might become a somewhat more realistic expression of sentiment by the company's owners. Even the proxy system might become more palatable and useful if the voters were given a real choice.

The prospects that this ideal will become a reality in the foreseeable future are slim, however, and without some sort of cataclysmic upheaval to propel our lawmakers into action, corrective measures do not seem imminent. Yet, corrective action could—and preferably, should—be initiated by enlightened management rather than by federal legislation.

In the next chapter there is an implication that perhaps in some vague, nearly imperceptible way there is more than mere chance operating in the structuring of boards of directors. There is an implication that at least our major commercial banks seek representation of certain types of individuals from certain sectors of society on their boards. Their exercise of choice rather than reliance upon pure chance appears to be predicated upon current *need*. If this is so, then there is a distinct possibility that boardroom structuring and the evaluating of directorate performance may not be doomed to eternal mystery. If it can be shown that logic of some sort does indeed condition the board room, even if only in a miniscule way, it becomes possible to study boards and their functions in an empirical fashion. If this is possible, mystique must give way to reason.

# DIRECTORATE PORTFOLIO

In a sense, a company's board of directors is its prime investment, since at least theoretically its board is *the* critical factor in its top-level decision-making process. By analogy, then, it is appropriate to attach the portfolio concept to boards of directors.

In the investment sphere a good portfolio has several basic objectives and characteristics. Perhaps most important, a portfolio should provide a maximum return together with a very high degree of security. To attain these objectives, the prudent investor selects growth prospects and avoids has-been issues. His portfolio then becomes an index of his confidence and good judgment, and his selection criteria are based on logic and the profit motive rather than upon sentimental, or political, or social reasons. Loyalty to a specific stock issue because it once paid well, or because of employment ties or long-time family association with it should play a very minor role in structuring an investment portfolio.

It is also vital that investment risks be spread over an adequate range of items. Overemphasis on any one issue or on any one industry's stock may lead to maximization of profits; but the probabilities generally favor suboptimization through the spreading of risks over a fairly wide investment area. (The rationale of the balanced investment portfolio is accepted as almost an article of faith by most institutional and individual stockholders—the phenomenal growth of mutual funds and investment clubs being one testimony to its effectiveness, the rapid rise in the number of conglomerate industrial firms, another.)

Not too surprisingly, then, there is evidence that adaptations of the portfolio concept are practiced at the board of directors' level, and, seemingly, the men best qualified to advance a particular company's future are named to its board. In portfolio fashion, these selections would be balanced not only for maximization of results but also to avoid a company's "putting all its eggs into one basket." Is this done? For an answer, let us look at several analyses.

Table 1 shows how eight of our top ten commercial banks apply basic directorate portfolio principles to their selection of directors.

TABLE 1. Directorate portfolio changes in eight of the largest U.S. commercial banks 1929 to 1967: Prime Function

| | Number | | Percent | | |
|---|---|---|---|---|---|
| Background | 1929 | 1967 | 1929 | 1967 | Change |
| Industrialists | 149 | 94 | 40.4 | 47.0 | +16.3 |
| Officer directors | 55 | 39 | 14.9 | 19.5 | +30.9 |
| Railroads | 36 | 4 | 9.8 | 2.0 | −79.6 |
| Financiers | 34 | 13 | 9.2 | 6.5 | −29.4 |
| Lawyers | 28 | 7 | 7.6 | 3.5 | −54.0 |
| Insurance | 20 | 12 | 5.4 | 6.0 | +10.0 |
| Merchandising | 12 | 8 | 3.3 | 4.5 | +36.4 |
| Utilities | 12 | 9 | 3.3 | 5.0 | +51.5 |
| Transport (other) | 5 | 2 | 1.4 | 1.0 | −28.6 |
| Real estate | 3 | 0 | 0.8 | 0.0 | − |
| Universities | 1 | 0 | 0.3 | 0.0 | − |
| Publishers | 0 | 3 | 0.0 | 1.5 | + |
| Construction | 0 | 3 | 0.0 | 1.5 | + |
| Entertainment | 0 | 1 | 0.0 | 0.5 | + |
| Government | 0 | 1 | 0.0 | 0.5 | + |
| Unknown | 14 | 2 | 3.8 | 1.0 | − |
| Total | 369 | 198 | 100.2 | 100.0 | |

In 1967 these banks had 198 directors with prime functional backgrounds as shown in Column 2. Industrialists are by far the dominant group among bank directors. Officer directors are the next biggest group.

The first column in Table 1 shows the 1929 representation. The total, 369, is considerably higher than the 1967 total because over the nearly 40-year span there were a number of mergers culminating in the present eight leading banks.

A comparison of 1929 and 1967 data, converted into relative terms in columns 3 and 4, shows some interesting results. There has been an increased preference for industrialists, officer directors, merchants, insurance officials, and utilities executives as bank board members. In marked contrast, the eight leading banks use far fewer financiers, lawyers, and railroad company executives. The latter category, in particular, experienced a very distinct decrease of popularity.

These data are corroborated by a tabulation of *all* the significant business board-room contacts of the bank board members, that is, not only the director's prime capacity but also his memberships on all other major boards. Column 1 of Table 2 shows a total of 901 major business directorships in addition to the bank directorships held by 369 directors comprising the 1929 boards of the

TABLE 2.  Directorate portfolio changes in eight of the largest U.S. commercial banks, 1929 to 1967: Total Contacts

| | Number | | Percent | | |
|---|---|---|---|---|---|
| *Background* | 1929 | 1967 | 1929 | 1967 | Change |
| Industrial firms | 362 | 317 | 40.1 | 52.8 | +31.7 |
| Railroads | 168 | 23 | 18.6 | 3.9 | −79.1 |
| Financial inst. | 104 | 39 | 11.5 | 6.5 | −43.5 |
| Insurance | 86 | 68 | 9.5 | 11.3 | +19.0 |
| Utilities | 73 | 44 | 8.1 | 7.3 | − 9.9 |
| Officer directors | 55 | 39 | 6.3 | 6.5 | + 3.2 |
| Other sectors | 53 | 68 | 5.9 | 11.3 | +91.5 |
| Total | 901 | 598 | 100.0 | 99.6 | |

progenitors of the eight commercial banks. In 1929 the bank directors averaged about two and one-half other directorships. In 1967 the average is slightly higher, three other directorships per director. Table 2 data extends the portfolio concept somewhat by showing the secondary contact values of these directors. These secondary contacts, of course, can have some bearing upon policy-making by the bank board.

Table 2's "total contacts" follow rather closely the patterns shown in Table 1. It can be inferred that railroaders are not in demand as bank directors because they come from a status quo, or even a declining, industry. Similarly, with the tremendous expansion in resources and technical competency within the biggest banks, there is far less need in 1967 as compared with 1929 for outside financial advice. Lawyers, too, although not included in

Table 2, are far less needed on the board since high-caliber legal talent is available for hire.

The portfolio concept is even more evident in the rise and decline in popularity of specific industry representation on bank boards. Table 3 shows how the eight bank boards have shifted preferences during the past four decades. In the earlier period

TABLE 3. Directorate portfolio changes, by industry in eight of the largest U.S. commercial banks, 1929 to 1967

| Background | Prime | | Total | |
|---|---|---|---|---|
| | 1929 | 1967 | 1929 | 1967 |
| Aircraft | 0 | 3 | 5 | 9 |
| Automobile | 3 | 2 | 12 | 16 |
| Cement | 4 | 0 | 10 | 3 |
| Chemicals | 13 | 11 | 29 | 36 |
| Copper | 10 | 4 | 34 | 21 |
| Coal | 3 | 0 | 22 | 4 |
| Elect. equip. | 4 | 7 | 16 | 25 |
| Farm equip. | 7 | 4 | 14 | 8 |
| Food proc. | 13 | 10 | 25 | 27 |
| Machinery | 2 | 4 | 15 | 23 |
| Metals (other) | 6 | 5 | 16 | 10 |
| Meat | 7 | 2 | 11 | 10 |
| Paper (wood) | 5 | 3 | 6 | 17 |
| Petroleum | 10 | 11 | 24 | 22 |
| Rubber | 3 | 1 | 12 | 9 |
| Soap | 3 | 1 | 3 | 8 |
| Steel | 13 | 6 | 23 | 15 |
| Sugar | 7 | 0 | 19 | 1 |
| Textiles | 8 | 6 | 21 | 17 |
| Tobacco | 3 | 2 | 3 | 2 |
| Transp. equip. | 12 | 5 | 23 | 16 |
| Other mfg. | 13 | 7 | 19 | 18 |
| Total mfg. | 149 | 94 | 362 | 317 |

there was a distinct preference for representation from the chemical, cement, coal, copper, farm equipment, food processing, petroleum, steel, sugar, textile, and transportation equipment industries. By 1967, however, all but chemical, food processing, and petroleum had been displaced from this high-preference group. Among the new favorites were the aircraft, automobile, electrical equipment, and machinery industries.

These data seem to support the contention that at least the leading banks change their views over a period of time as to the acceptability of certain individuals on their respective boards. The individual's acceptability seems to be intimately associated with the position he holds and the company he represents, and it appears that the structures of bank boards, at least, are not so much a matter of historical accident, favoritism, or even nepotism, but rather a consequence of logic. The board members tend to include those sectors of our society which are, for large-scale commercial banking purposes, gaining in significance. (Considering that most of these directorates are, for all practical purposes, life-time appointments, change can be almost imperceptible. Consequently, if a comparison is to be made it should extend over a rather long period such as the 1929 to 1967 span.)

An important postulate in this type of analysis is that a directorate portfolio pattern prevailing in the large-scale commercial banking sector need not necessarily be best for other sectors of the economy. In a 35-company sample of large-scale U.S. manufacturing industry in 1967, the directorate portfolio consisted of the components shown in Table 4. From Table 4 it is obvious that large-scale manufacturing industry has quite different directorate portfolio aspirations than does commercial banking. Company officers, former officers, and other industrialists comprise slightly more than 71 percent of the composite board membership in large-scale manufacturing industry, while the major banks have only a 47 percent industrial representation on their boards. Other notable differences are major industries' relative emphasis on the use of educators as directors (2.8 percent) and the lower incidence of insurance executives (0.9 percent), merchandisers (1.3 percent), and utilities executives (2.6 percent).

These data would assume much greater relative proportions if officer directors were not included in the tabulations. The statistics would then measure the relative importance or desirability of various types of outside directors. In such a tabulation, university representation would account for 6.7 percent of major industries' outside directors as contrasted with practically no educational representation on the major bank boards. These statistics reflect a very important difference in the rationale for structuring directorate portfolios for major industrial firms and major commercial banks. Industry relies much more on technological advancement than does banking, and, hence, industry needs educators in its directorate mix. Then, too, industry relies much more, than does banking, on a steady supply of neophyte talent for its junior management ranks. Educators as directors on boards of manufacturing firms supposedly advise on and facilitate the flow of college graduates into the new-employee ranks of industry.

Presumably, then, large-scale industry, in putting together directorate portfolios, realizes that its needs can best be met by boards structured quite differently from those of large-scale commercial

TABLE 4. Sampling of directorate portfolio of 35 of the 50 largest U.S. American manufacturing firms

|  | *Directors* | |
| Background | Number | Percent |
|---|---|---|
| Officer directors | 248 | 46.0 |
| Former officers | 65 | 12.1 |
| Industrialists | 71 | 13.2 |
| Banks | 45 | 8.4 |
| Investment firms | 42 | 7.8 |
| Education | 15 | 2.8 |
| Utilities | 14 | 2.6 |
| Law | 11 | 2.0 |
| Merchandising | 7 | 1.3 |
| Insurance | 5 | 0.9 |
| Government | 4 | 0.7 |
| Railroads | 3 | 0.6 |
| Foundations | 2 | 0.4 |
| Publishing | 2 | 0.4 |
| Other sectors | 5 | 0.9 |
| Total | 539 | 100.1 |

banks. Which poses the big questions: Are directorate portfolios rationally structured? Is some thought given to an analysis of director-candidate attributes and specific board-room needs? The marked differences between the composition of large-scale manufacturing company boards and large-scale commercial bank boards in 1967 provide answers in the affirmative. The rather significant changes which have taken place in board patterns in our largest commercial banks between 1929 to 1967 supports these affirmatives.

Following this line of reasoning, it can be argued that if boards of directors are consciously structured in portfolio fashion, then the portfolio architects must employ selection criteria and measurement techniques of some kind. While intangibly assessed attributes such as judgment, integrity, intuition, acumen, or decisiveness are certainly important, actual selection takes place on the basis of much more prosaic norms. It is need, constantly changing, which dictates a preference for certain types of individuals as directors at certain points in time, and the exclusion of other types of individuals. The dimensions of this need will be the subject of the next chapter.

# DIRECTORATE DIMENSIONS

In spite of John Marshall's classic definition of the corporation as "an artificial being, invisible, intangible, and existing only in the contemplation of the law," there has always been a propensity to associate human qualities with this artificial, invisible, intangible being—to personify it. From personification, the progression has been to reification, the attribution not only of human qualities but also of form and substance, so that 150 years after Chief Justice Marshall's definition, we can seriously question whether to most Americans the corporation is indeed only an "artificial being, invisible, intangible and existing only in the contemplation of the law." Through personification and reification most of us have come to view the corporation as a real being with human qualities and with form and substance.

A somewhat similar circumstance holds for the way we view a corporate board of directors today, though even half a century ago, the board and the owners were virtually synonymous and there was little need to stretch one's imagination to personify and reify the board. Mr. Ford was *the* board at Ford Motor Company, Mr. J. P. Morgan was *the* board of U.S. Steel. But significant changes in ownership and control relationships have occurred in the past fifty years, and in fewer and fewer instances in large-scale enterprise is the board of directors identified with a single person or family name. Today, a great deal of imagination is needed to rationalize both the form and function of the board of directors. And so the processes of personification and reification have come into play.

One of the features of reification, even though much of the

process takes place only within our minds, is a tendency to measure the endowed characteristics. But while there is a great deal of measuring associated with the personification and reification of the corporation, there is far less such measurement of boards of directors' form or function. We can count the number of directors, and we can compute the average age of each—and we now know how much each director is paid for his services—but we fail miserably when we attempt to define and to measure what it is that each director actually does by way of service to the corporation.

One of the difficulties of such an assessment is the belief that directors and boards exist chiefly to provide services such as judgment, prudence, sagacity, intuition, and the like, all rather intangible if taken in their ordinary sense. However, if we look more closely at such supposedly nondimensional attributes as, say, judgment, we can discern at least the outlines of measurable dimensions. Judgment presupposes competency. Pronouncements made by incompetent or unqualified individuals certainly cannot be termed the kind of judgment needed at the top corporate decision-making levels. If this is so, then we come at least a few steps closer to the possibility of quantifying and measuring a supposedly intangible quality. Competency stems from experience and from demonstrated performance, and these attributes can be measured.

The following experiment assumes that many, perhaps most, of the human traits with which we have endowed boards of directors are identifiable, quantifiable, and measurable. They set up what might be termed, *directorate dimensions.* Just as we have individuals varying in height, weight, and other physical and nonphysical aspects, so too corporations and boards of directors differ considerably in their dimensions.

In this particular study, attention is focused upon eight factors or traits presently found in the boards of all large industrial enterprises:

1) Technical expertise (TE)
2) Management experience (ME)
3) Specific economic service (SES)
4) Broad economic sophistication (BES)
5) Image (IM)
6) Asset impact (AI)
7) Interlock (IL)
8) Owners' equity (OE)

The list could easily be lengthened, but these eight traits have been singled out because they are almost always at the top of any list of reasons justifying inclusion of specific individuals on respective boards. And, these traits can be measured.

## Factor definition

It would be quite impossible to set directorate dimensions without first defining each factor. Since subjective appraisal is presently so much a part of directorate analysis and evaluation, no single set of definitions will be universally accepted. The following definitions should, therefore, be viewed only as attempts subject to revision and extension.

1) *Technical expertise* refers to the director's competency requisite to the corporation's endeavors to create utility. Technical expertise is directly proportionate to the educational and the on-the-job experience of the director.

2) *Management experience* is measured by the length and level of service a director has had in positions involving managerial responsibilities related to the major activities of that company.

3) *Special economic service* pertains to extra-company competencies and contacts which are presumed to be helpful, on occasion, to the company's well-being. SES includes government contacts, buyer-vendor preferential status, special legal talent, favorable banking associations, and similar values and attributes. The practice of reciprocity might also be included in this category.

4) *Broad economic sophistication* is the broad-spectrum attribute which is today almost universally assumed to be a most essential directorship ingredient. It can be measured in part by educational background. Of even greater significance is the degree to which the director becomes accepted by business- and economics-oriented groups such as certain governmental, professional, and educational agencies. Publications in this area, even if ghost-written, tend to add considerably to this value. Honorary degrees, even if purchased, are another index. Public addresses, panel participation, and similar public performance are still other pertinent measures of BES.

5) *Image* tends to be identical with press and television coverage. Appointment to honorary and active posts on national and professional committees adds to it. Acceptance in exclusive clubs

and social and political inner circles are also marks of distinction inherent in image.

6) *Asset impact* is one of the more readily quantifiable norms. It is premised upon the belief that membership on the boards of major corporations has more significance than membership on the boards of smaller companies. Membership on the boards of several large corporations generally tends to result in more asset or economic impact than does membership by an individual on a single board. By analogy, adapting the LaPlace criterion of equal likelihood when specific probabilities are unknown, it can be inferred that each director has a proportionate asset impact equal to $\Sigma A/N$ where $\Sigma A$ is the company's asset value, and N is the number of that company's directors on the board. Totaling these respective values for all the boards on which an individual serves sets in quantitative terms his asset impact in our economy.

7) *Interlock* represents the degree to which two or more directors on a board have meaningful association outside that board room. In a more technical sense, interlock refers to interconnected or interrelated corporate managements. This is an increasingly prevalent phenomenon. In some instances the practice has reached such proportions that it can even be termed institutional nepotism, that is, representatives from certain companies or groups tend to perpetuate themselves on the board of a specific company. The concept of interlock can be extended to include mutuality in club, church, political, family, ethnic group, or academic affiliation. The academic establishment's perduring membership on some companies' boards of directors can be viewed as evidence of interlock.

8) *Owners' equity* is a director's personal or family participation in a substantial ownership interest in the company. With the tremendous growth in the size of our major corporations and the expansion in public ownership, this norm should be based on dollar-value of investment rather than percentage-of-ownership.

## Technical expertise

Technical expertise is the most obvious requirement for decision-making at any organizational level. The decision-maker simply must know what it is that he is deciding. He must be acquainted with all the pertinent facts. He must relate these facts to applicable theories and techniques. In the light of given circumstances, he must be able to differentiate alternatives and then select the best course of action.

Despite the strong logic supporting the vital need for technical expertise as a directorate dimension, there has been a distinct downgrading of this factor during the past several decades. This downgrading is the direct consequence of the stress on generalists as top policymakers. In some quarters this vogue has spread to the point where "technical expert" means a person who has plateaued in his promotion potential. While the technician is accepted as a necessary component in the organization, he is often relegated to the lowest portions of the scalar sequence. Reasoning of this sort is based upon the faulty supposition that a technically competent person must invariably be narrow-gauged or myopic in managerial matters.

In many of even our largest corporations this inference is probably correct. Too frequently jobs that require a high degree of technical competency become dead-end jobs. Blame for the resultant overspecialization cannot, however, be placed exclusively upon the individuals who demonstrate the highest level of technical expertise. In many cases top management is equally and perhaps even more culpable. Actually, the company is the real loser because a very qualified segment of its manpower never gets adequate opportunity to develop its potential.

A growing number of progressive firms have approached the dead-end job dilemma by increasing executive mobility. This laudable practice is used extensively by many major companies such as Standard Oil Company (New Jersey). Use of a carefully planned rotational system can be a most effective source of executives combining the best qualities of specialists and generalists. If major corporations are to continue using officers as directors, it is absolutely essential that these officer directors be on an equal plane with the non-officer directors. This makes executive-broadening imperative. While it is true that many key executives can be classified as one-track technicians, too frequently the man who masquerades as a generalist is simply a person with no competency. For example, before a person can be said to have acquired broad economic sophistication, he must have gained experience in the application of specific economic theories and techniques. Many directors, however, pontificate on broad policy matters yet do not even make a pretense of comprehending the more mundane matters.

Within the past decade, counterforces have been generated that have brought the technically qualified director back into prominence. Two of these counterforces are: (1) an increased emphasis on professional stature among directors; (2) the growth of conglomerate corporations.

Among the requisites for professional stature in any area of endeavor is the candidate's competency in all matters that pertain to that area. For example, it was sufficient at one time for a steel company director to be minimally conversant with steel-making technology or competitive patterns in the industry. Technicians took care of the drab details. Technicians still take care of such drab details, but intensified competition, governmental "interference," pressure from unions, and a more business-literate group of stockholders, make it necessary that corporate directors become more technically qualified.

The last item, increased business literacy and interest on the part of stockholders, is extremely important. At the 1965 annual meeting of Countrywide Realty, Inc., for example, there was a proposal to nominate as a director David Kratter, the 24-year-old son of Marvin Kratter, the company's president and chairman. One of the stockholders

> . . . questioned the qualifications of David Kratter, a third-year law student at Yale Law School and Mr. Kratter's son, as one of five director nominees. She asked the younger Mr. Kratter to define the term "cash flow" and to detail Countrywide's most recently reported cash flow position.
>
> After a five-minute delay during which first the Countrywide company counsel and then the elder Mr. Kratter defended the young nominee, David Kratter defined cash flow as "net income plus depreciation and other non-cash charges," and said he had not memorized all the figures from the recent report. . . . Both Kratters defended David's nomination to the board on the ground he was in constant touch with his father and the business, that he was a top student in

his law school class, and that he was his father's "toughest opponent."[1]

There are some very obvious difficulties limiting the testing of director-candidates' technical capabilities, of course, and in technical subjects not all directors should be expected to make perfect scores. But it would seem reasonable to expect a would-be director to rattle off the definition of cash flow without a five-minute delay for exhortation and consultation.

Even more significant with respect to the increased emphasis on technical competency is the remarkable increase in the number of conglomerate firms. Only a short time ago practically every company could be identified as part of a single industry. Within the past ten or twenty years however, the transition from single-industry companies to multi-industry companies has been phenomenal. There is scarcely a major corporation that has not branched out into peripheral endeavor.

Conglomerate corporations, though they have their obvious advantages, are also prone to certain weaknesses. These weaknesses are associated with diversification and decentralization. It becomes humanly impossible for any one director, much less all directors, to be technically conversant in all of the company's lines of endeavor. Yet no board can make meaningful decisions upon matters which it does not comprehend. Consequently, in most cases of conglomerate venture this vital need is taken care of in one of several ways. In a growing number of instances representatives from the more important components are elevated to director rank. These officer directors serve as the technical nexus with the respective component. In a sense, this is simply a modification of the older concept of functional representation on single-product type company boards. Instead of having officer directors representing functional areas such as engineering, production, purchasing, etc., some conglomerates provide technical competency on their boards by inclusion of presidents of affiliate companies or divisions. Lacking this technical competency, the board inevitably becomes simply a ratifying agency.

The logical tendency to add officer directors who head the conglomerate companies' major divisions to the boards of direc-

1/ *Wall Street Journal*, June, 1965.

tors has been strenuously resisted by companies with long-time, outside-director commitments. Quite a few of these outside-director dominated companies are currently experimenting with a substitute technique, the rather radical innovation of having several executives share the company's top post. There are a number of variants of this experiment. At Union Carbide, for example,

> . . . four top executives together constitute the Office of the President. That quadrumvirate runs the huge chemical complex. . . . On Monday mornings the three executive vice presidents meet with Mason (the company's chief executive) to discuss company strategy and thrash out broad corporate decisions. In Mason's view, the Office of the President is a "central point of management authority.". . .
>
> But even this bold venture into joint decision making is a qualified one. For it is worth noting that Union Carbide has not changed the titles of any of the four men. And when they reach a real impasse, the man with the final say is Mason, still the chief executive officer.[2]

General Electric provides another example of a completely outside-director type board which has found its directorate structure inadequate. Prior to 1950, G.E. was run in a rather autocratic fashion. Control was concentrated in a succession of strong-willed and very competent chief executives. In 1950, under the presidency of Ralph Cordiner, a major reorganization took place.

> A total of 110 small companies, grouped into 27 divisions, was given considerable autonomy. In a sense, each of the smaller units was an independent profit center. Over this conglomerate, the Office of the President—consisting at that time of the president, chairman, and five executive vice presidents —exercised control. These key administrators, each vested with the president's authority, limited their activities strictly to planning. . . . It is interesting to note that, in its Office of the President scheme, General Electric was in effect vesting considerable top policy-making in an intermediate group. This was not an executive committee of the board. It was

2/ *Dun's Review,* "More Room at the Top," John Berry, March, 1967, pp. 30 to 31.

much more an adjunct of the president. It would seem, then, that the former centralization of authority was continued in a newer and more palatable form. The outside-dominated board of directors, which formerly served to ratify the decisions of a single president, now simply ratified the decisions of seven "presidents."[3]

Under the Phillipe-Borch regime, the Office of the President ceased to function. At the top of the G.E. organizational pyramid were eight regional vice presidents, 34 vice presidents representing functions or geographical divisions and six vice presidents and group executives. None of these executives was on General Electric's board of directors.

Late in November, 1967, the company announced a major top management realignment, the first since Ralph Cordiner introduced the decentralization of 1951.

General Electric said it was beefing up its top management group to cope with expanding markets and increased volume. The company is adding three executive vice presidents forming, together with the chairman and president, a five-man president's office. . . . This team, G.E. said, will be involved in "companywide commitments and policies that will have both short- and long- term impact on G.E.'s world-wide business. . . . It would not be realistic to envision G.E. facing its projected future with its former, relatively small top-executive team," Mr. Borch said.[4]

This return to the concept of the "president's office" at G.E. underscores the difficulty modern large-scale enterprise encounters in trying to function effectively under the complete control of a single leader. This inference is equally valid for autocratically-run companies with either inside or outside directorates.

Even in cases where no formal steps have been taken to set up the equivalent of a "president's office" quite a few companies with outside boards have permitted a concentration of effective top policymaking in an executive committee consisting of officer

3/ Stanley Vance, *Boards of Directors: Structure and Performance*, University of Oregon, 1964, pp. 70 to 71.
4/ *Wall Street Journal*, Nov. 22, 1967, p. 12.

directors, or in an informal association of three or four top executives. U.S. Steel, for example, for quite a number of years, has had a triumvirate at its head; Chairman Roger Blough, President Leslie Worthington, and chairman of the Finance Committee, Robert Tyson. Each of these individuals represents a different functional area—law, marketing, and accounting. More recently, the newly appointed president, Edwin Gott, replaces marketing with production at the triumvirate level. Despite this division of labor, however, there is still serious question as to the actual division of the chief executive's authority.

Even at this early stage in the experimentation, there are signs that attempts to divide authority in order to get more technical competency into the board room are doomed to failure. Westinghouse Electric, for example, set up a top-level "troika" in 1957, but this attempt to divide the chief executive's authority among three men lasted less than a year. Reflecting on still another unsuccessful attempt to use the "multiple chief executive" concept, Joel Hunter, then president of Crucible Steel, stated, "I still believe in the principle but in our case, at least, the personnel didn't shape up."[5] The story quoting him went on to point out:

> One of the biggest drawbacks of a multiple chief executive, of course, is the information gap that is created the instant responsibility is divided. Unless communications (and understanding) between the dual leaders is well-nigh perfect, trouble is bound to follow. And in its wake come recriminations. In the words of one president disenchanted with his first attempt at making top management a twosome: "When we had two top guys, they just wouldn't cooperate with each other. When there was a slip-up, it was always the other guy's fault."[6]

Perhaps 10 percent of our largest corporations are experimenting with the concept. But to date there has not been a single instance where division of chief executive authority has resulted in complete equality among the dual, troika, quadrumvirate, or quintuplet chief executive. This negative view of hydra-headed corporate structure has considerable bearing on the concept of directo-

5/ *Ibid.*
6/ *Ibid.*

rate dimensions. If stress on comprehension of corporate affairs will ultimately make conventional outside directors obsolete, then some better means must be found to provide the essential technical grooming for all potential directors.

## Management experience

There can be considerable argument over the contention that it is not technical expertise that effective directors need but rather related management experience. Supporting this attitude is the belief that board members do not manage except in the very broadest sense. They review policy matters, referee disputes, select the chief executive, keep a watchful eye on management, regulate salary structures, audit reports, and perform similar services. Contrary to this view, however, is the argument that not one of these services can be performed properly unless the decision-makers are intimately acquainted with pertinent circumstances and situations. Some opponents go so far as to maintain that broad policymaking, per se, is impossible; what would seem to be such policymaking is simply routine ratification. Policy, in every instance, is the attempt at resolution of uncertainty and conflict inherent in every work situation. Those who strive to resolve this conflict must have a fairly decent comprehension of what it is. In this view, policymaking at the very top level must simply be the culmination of the managerial process.

Such a line of reasoning has legal support and historical precedent. Practically every corporation has at the beginning of its by-laws a statement that the basic function of its board of directors is to manage the affairs of the company. This mandate is also set forth in the statutes of every state except Maine. Despite this legal requirement, almost every company hedges on admitting that its board actually manages—because to emphasize this inherent function would necessitate rigid screening of director candidates. There would be little if any justification for including directors who do not have considerable technical expertise pertinent to a given company's pursuits.

Consequently, most companies—without legal sanction—give quite a different interpretation to the requirement that the board manages the affairs of the company. Managing is interpreted as reviewing in very summary fashion selected top policy areas. Undoubtedly if board records were examined it would be apparent that a board seldom modifies the policy matters presented to it by the actual managing group. There are virtually no instances of a board of a major corporation vehemently debating, much less rejecting, a proposal made by its chief executive officer.

Most of our leading executives have accepted as a fact of business life this abdication by the board of its managing function. In order to justify the existence of the board, then, it is assigned a much more restricted role. It is considered as an advisory or ratifying agency—but even here its powers are hypothetical. Pushed to a justification of the typical board, most partisans stress its importance in the selection of the chief executive officer and the management team. It is this duty which, if one stretches his imagination, indirectly fulfills the legal requirement to manage. In a sense, this means that the directors who have a fiduciary obligation to the stockholders delegate this responsibility to other fiduciaries— namely, the company's officers. The legality of such delegation is assumed. There is far less agreement as to the ethical justification.

If all boards of directors actually do select the chief executive officer and all other top corporate executives, then a very necessary function is being fulfilled. However, very few boards do more than make a perfunctory check in most executive appointments. This is understandable. Chief executives in most companies are replaced on an average of once every nine or ten years, and vice-presidential level appointments are even more frequent than this. In our highly dynamic and technical society, the selection and evaluation of executive candidates could easily become an impossible chore. Therefore, this role of the directors has been abridged to one of ratification or rejection, and with the onus of executive placement continuing to expand, even this already much-curtailed function may eventually be removed from the board's jurisdiction and responsibility. The situation, incidentally, is universal in scope, it is not limited to industrial boards, as witness a 1967 episode involving our country's chief executive and the United States Senate. The July 20, 1967, issue of the *Wall Street Journal* carried a story titled "Washingtonian Weds LBJ's Ex-Secretary and Lands Soft Job." The *Journal* reporter, Jerry Landauer, brought out the fact that President Johnson's appointee to a $26,000-a-year position on the Subversive Activities Control Board, Simon F. McHugh, Jr., lacked qualifying attributes. He was only 29 years old and his

> professional preparation for the cushy post consists of a bachelor's degree in business administration earned six years ago at Georgetown University, followed by short stints in four jobs. . . . Mr. McHugh concedes that his employment record doesn't at first glance appear to qualify him for membership on a "quasi-judicial" agency that delves into subversion. But, he observes, "Realistically speaking, there aren't any experts." Also, he adds, "You can get a pretty good idea of the procedures by reading the law and the board's reports."[7]

An interesting aspect of the case is the fact that at the time of the appointment the board had not held a single hearing in 20 months and not one case was pending. The Supreme Court's 1965 ruling that a provision of law requiring registration by Communist party members was unconstitutional had reduced the board's workload to zero.

> [Mr. McHugh's] career seemed to be moving sideways for the most part until he wooed Victoria McCammon, a tall attractive White House secretary who, though now employed elsewhere in the Government, remains a particular Presidential favorite. Marriage to Miss McCammon in August 1966 perceptibly perked up Mr. McHugh's prospects. . . . Mr. McHugh's social life quickened, too. Following a recent weekend visit by the McHughs to the LBJ Ranch, the couple was added, by one Washington society writer, to "list of Great Society insiders—with whom President and Mrs. Johnson most comfortably spend their spare time."[8]

The purpose in recalling this episode is to question the effectiveness of the U.S. Senate as a ratifying board. In theory and by law, the Senate is supposed to confirm such an appointment. Did it? On July 13 a routine notice was inserted in the *Congressional Record*

7/ *Wall Street Journal,* July 20, 1967, p. 1.
8/ *Ibid,*

by Chairman James Eastland of the Senate Judiciary Committee (inviting) interested citizens to submit "any representations or objections" to Mr. McHugh's appointment "on or before Thursday, July 20."... But on the same day the invitation appeared, the committee quietly moved Mr. McHugh's nomination to the Senate floor. It was reported to the Senate moments after the opening buzzer sounded at noon Monday, and at 12:05 p.m. it sailed through the chamber without debate. In the precipitate haste to put Mr. McHugh to work on an agency whose docket is clear, there wasn't even time to list his name on the Senate calendar of Presidential nominees awaiting confirmation.[9]

It can be argued, of course, that the Senate has more pressing problems than the simple confirmation of a Presidential appointment. Nevertheless, in its capacity as the approving or disapproving agent, the Senate was certainly remiss in this instance in getting all the pertinent facts. The very routineness of its action emphasizes a growing imperfection in the role of all trustees. Because of other more pressing commitments, directors or trustees abdicate a supposedly critical function. The logic of the abdication seems sound: the board simply seconds the motion of its chief executive. After all, the board places a supreme confidence in a man designated as chief executive officer, and, theoretically, the chief executive has the organization's good in mind when he selects and nominates individuals for top posts. Therefore, it is reasoned, the actions of the chief executive need only to be ratified by the board.

But ratification, if it implies abdication of rights and responsibilities, reduces the board to an inconsequential group of "yes-men." Yet, there seems to be more rather than less incidence of the "ratifying" board as contrasted with the "questioning" board.

The seriousness of this situation is accentuated by the fact that in the Senate, considered as a board, there is a supposedly effective checks-and-balances control device, the two-party election process. But there are virtually no comparable two-party representations on any of our major corporate boards. Even when several major ownership interests are found within a company, representa-

9/ *Ibid.*

tives of these interests invariably work in consort. It is a distinct rarity for a major corporate board to include an articulate objector.

Since corporate boards do not have the benefit of a built-in, open-and-above-board, two-party system to provide balanced judgment, McHugh-type ratifications are even easier to attain in them than in our Senate. While it might be argued that there is still plenty of give-and-take at some corporate board meetings, the incidence of serious objection cannot be verified because there are virtually no records showing individual members' questions or comments. Few, if any, boards record the minority viewpoints. Although debate is theoretically possible, it is rarely feasible. The technical nature of most issues, together with the brevity of most board meetings, precludes serious objection. The net result is a consensus, unanimous in almost every case, and the consensus is almost always the "management" point of view. Consequently, the corporate board's approval becomes more and more comparable to the Senate's ratification role.

There is one rather important dissimilarity, however. Ratification or rejection of presidential appointees is an extremely incidental role of the United States Senate, but appointment to an executive post in business enterprise is a rather crucial matter. It can be inferred that if McHugh-type ratification of executive appointments is—or should become—the rule in industry, then the functions of the board of directors have eroded perhaps beyond restoration.

Even though the management function of the board of directors has undergone significant evolutionary change, management experience (ME) continues to remain an important directorate dimension. Actually, as shown in the preceding chapter, this factor is probably gaining in recognition. Proven managers, particularly chairmen and presidents of major corporations, are increasingly in demand as directors. In outside-type directorates, ME is particularly necessary since only a very few of the company's experienced managers are on the board and, presumably, outside directors who have outstanding managerial experience will bring this vital ingredient to the board meetings. In predominantly officer-director boards, concerted effort by progressive companies to upgrade their managers results in higher caliber officer directors and greater prominence given the management factor. In all likelihood, management experience will continue to be an important factor in structuring directorate dimensions.

## Special economic service

Historically, the single most commonly observed manifestation of the special economic service factor in directorate dimensions is the inclusion of financiers on corporate boards. In some instances these representatives of the financial community have a heavy investment in the company and, in such cases, their inclusion on the board could be considered as stemming primarily from the owners' equity factor. More frequently, however, the financial representatives are selected for other reasons.

From the company's point of view, these individuals can facilitate financing. Every firm, large or small, needs adequate credit lines. On occasion it must borrow in the bond market. Presumably, the financier director can create adequate credit channels. He can also assist in the selling of large blocks of the company's stock. In addition, the outside-director financier is generally expected to give the company a current and keen insight into the financial field. At times his services expand into merger negotiations, locating director candidates, or attracting influential customers.

There is still, despite the outcries against existing federal regulations, an amazing latitude given financiers who serve as outside directors, a latitude that at times approximates license. The recently terminated career of Mr. Serge Semenenko as vice chairman of First National Bank of Boston, illustrates this point. Mr. Semenenko deserves much praise. As an exile from Bolshevik Russia, he came to the United States via Turkey and eventually earned a masters degree from the Harvard Business School. His rise after joining First National Bank of Boston in 1926 was meteoric. He was an assistant vice president by 1928 and vice president by 1943. At the time of his resignation from the bank he was its vice chairman.

The interesting feature from a special economic service directorate dimensions point of view was the frequency with which Mr. Semenenko intertwined his personal financial dealings with banking transactions he negotiated for corporate clients, a practice generally condemned by banks and bankers. Yet, Mr. Semenenko's career is one continuous sequence of such questionable but legal affairs.

First National of Boston apparently puts no such restriction on Mr. Semenenko, one of the bank's top lending officers. He says, "I make no secrets that I have investments in various companies, and I think it's a good thing, properly handled." He adds: "Whatever investments I've had have always been extremely useful in getting business for the bank, and the bank has never lost money on any loan I made."[10]

This statement clearly shows Mr. Semenenko's and all outside-director financiers' prime loyalty. Any corporation accepting bankers or financiers on its board must recognize that the special economic service factor is a two-way street with the widest and best-paved portion going in the bank's direction.

There seems to be no doubt that Mr. Semenenko brought considerable business to the bank. He arranged, for example, a $35 million loan from six banks to Curtis Publishing Company at a time when that publishing firm was floundering. His own bank, First National of Boston, advanced almost one-third of this sum. As a concomitant, in addition to an interest rate which was one full percentage point above the prime rate, First National Bank of Boston received an additional one-fourth of one percent for acting as agent for the bank.

The bank probably also benefited in ways that weren't announced. One source says Curtis was required to keep hefty compensating balances that earned no interest on deposit at the banks. This meant that Curtis actually had use of only part of the loan but was paying interest on the full $35 million. The source says Curtis also switched some $38 million of company pension funds from another bank to Old Colony Trust Co., a First National of Boston affiliate. Institutions receive substantial fees for managing company trust funds.[11]

10/ *Wall Street Journal,* "How Serge Semenenko Blends His Business and Personal Dealings," William M. Carley, July 17, 1967, p. 1.
11/ *Ibid.,* p. 7.

Mr. Semenenko allegedly profited personally from this association. He bought a considerable block of Curtis' stock at depressed prices. Subsequently, after a significant ore strike on some Curtis Company land, Semenenko sold his holdings at a profit. It is significant that

> ... under the loan agreement, Curtis provided Mr. Semenenko with monthly financial statements, weekly reports on operations and "such other information as [the banks] may from time to time request." When asked about his Curtis trading, and whether use of inside information was involved, Mr. Semenenko dismisses his personal investments in Curtis as "not of any significance."[1][2]

This access to privileged information raises questions about the ethics, if not the legality, of such transactions because the Curtis Publishing Company episode is simply one in a sequence. Other equally tainted Semenenko experiences include an agreement by a group of banks led by First National of Boston to lend Warner Brothers up to $20 million. Just one month before this arrangement, Mr. Semenenko, after a personal purchase of 160,000 shares of Warner Brothers stock at $25 a share, had become a director of that company and a member of its executive committee.

In 1966 Mr. Semenenko was involved in a rather complicated and, perhaps, questionable deal involving the First National Bank and Seven Arts Production Ltd. Several stockholder suits are currently pending challenging this deal. It should be noted that early in 1967 "Jack Warner agreed to pay Mr. Semenenko $1 million over the next 10 years. According to Seven Arts' current proxy statement, the payment is for services 'rendered to Mr. Warner at various times from 1956 including services in connection with the sale' of Mr. Warner's stock to Seven Arts,"[1][3]

The immediate reason for this million-dollar fee seems to be Mr. Semenenko's arrangement of a $19.5 million loan to Seven Arts which needed the money to buy Jack Warner's one-third interest in Warner Brothers. First National of Boston, one of four banks in this deal, advanced $3.8 million. "Documents on file at the Ameri-

12/ *Ibid.*
13/ *Ibid.*

can Stock Exchange show that Mr. Semenenko signed a letter pledging that the original four banks also would give Mr. Warner as much as $5 million if Seven Arts failed to reimburse him, as promised, for any claims he might have to pay as a result of stockholder suits."[14] This provision in itself reflects upon the ethics and legality of the arrangement.

In August, 1967, Serge Semenenko agreed to turn over to the bank the controversial personal fee of one million dollars. "It was learned that the bank has started an investigation into circumstances surrounding the fee. Mr. Semenenko's decision to turn over the money to the bank apparently stems from the investigation."[15]

Mr. Semenenko in explaining his rather generous action stressed that the investigation had nothing to do with his decision. He "agreed to turn the $1 million over to the bank 'because it has become an issue, and because he says he has the bank's best interests at heart.' "[16]

The incidence of payments of huge sums by grateful corporate managements for special economic services rendered by Mr. Semenenko, seems endless. At the December, 1967, annual meeting of the Glen Alden Corporation, the merger of Stanley Warner Corp. and Glen Alden Corp. was approved. The meeting "was marked by several stockholders' vigorous objections to a $3 million finder's fee paid by Glen Alden to David G. Baird and Serge Semenenko. . . . Paul A. Johnston, Glen Alden president, replied that the fee wasn't exorbitant in relation to the value of the services performed. However, he refused to discuss the advantages of the merger in terms of projected earnings."[17] During the preceding five years the company in question, Stanley Warner Corp., had earnings averaging about $5 million annually and paid dividends of about $2½ million annually. These figures are given for comparison with the $3 million finder's fee.

At the 1967 annual meeting of Columbia Pictures Corp., Mr. Semenenko

14/ *Wall Street Journal,* "Semenenko Agrees to Turn Over to Bank $1 Million Personal Fee He Was Promised," August 11, 1967, p. 2.
15/ *Ibid.*
16/ *Ibid.*
17/ *Wall Street Journal,* Dec. 28, 1967.

came under attack from Evelyn Y. Davis, a shareholder, who frequently finds fault with the Columbia management. "What do we need him for?" asked Mrs. Davis. "We invited him on the board," replied Mr. Schneider [the Chairman], "because we think he can perform a great service to the company." "You mean a great service for himself," Mrs. Davis snapped.

Mrs. Davis, quoting from newspaper articles, said that Mr. Semenenko, while a top officer at First National Bank of Boston, often had personal interests in transactions that he arranged for clients of the Boston bank and collected substantial fees for his services.[18]

In this case, Columbia Pictures paid Mr. Semenenko a $400,000 fee for arranging purchase of an 18.7 percent interest in the movie company by J. B. Williams Co., a privately owned New York Pharmaceuticals and toiletries maker. On November 1, 1967, Mr. Semenenko was also "made a vice chairman of Columbia Pictures and a director. He was also elected chairman of a special committee on corporate development. He will receive $44,000 a year, in addition to an annual $6,000 fee as a director. He will also receive $25,000 yearly for secretarial services and office expense because the company isn't providing them."[19]

Special economic services are not restricted to bankers as outside directors. Of comparable vintage are vendor directors. Until recently, the existence of this type of relationship was difficult to prove, but current proxy statement disclosure requirements should bring the practice more into the open and negative reaction on the part of informed and concerned stockholders should then help to diminish this quasi-collusive action. For example, at National Tea Company's 1967 annual meeting, a shareholder asked

... how National could get competitive prices on its milk supply when John F. Cuneo [president of Cuneo Press] who controls 49.7% of Hawthorn Mellody Inc., a Chicago dairy, sits on the board of directors. Last year, National purchased $24,335,000 of dairy products from Hawthorn Mellody. ... Other National Tea suppliers are represented on the board,

18/ *Wall Street Journal,* Dec. 21, 1967, p. 4.
19/ *Ibid.*

including W. Garfield Weston, chairman of George Weston Ltd., Toronto, who controls 53.3% of National's outstanding stock. A George Weston subsidiary, Weston Biscuit Co., supplied National stores with $2,800,000 of bakery products last year.[20]

In addition to the vendor-director form of special economic service, this factor includes a great variety of difficult-to-label associations. For example, Great American Industries Inc., a firm in which trading was suspended on the American Stock Exchange for several lengthy periods during 1966, seems to foster this type of contact. Mr. George Shiarella, a Great American Industries director elected in 1967, was a party to a proposed acquisition of Worth Exploration Company. "Monitor Petroleum Company, a partnership in which Mr. Shiarella owns a 50% interest . . . will receive a brokerage fee of 11,000 shares of the common stock of the company for its service in bringing the parties together."[21]

Another director, Bernard D. Marren, the company's financial vice president purchased jointly with his wife, Great American's "controlling interests in United States Baking Company, Inc., consisting of 1,135,631 shares of common stock and 1,097½ shares of Series A Preferred Stock. . . . Management is satisfied that the terms of the sale to Mr. and Mrs. Marren compare favorably with the terms the company could have received from a non-affiliated person."[22]

Whether or not the company could have done equally well or better in a sale to some other party, Mr. Marren's role in this transaction highlights another form of "insider" deal. Fortunately, most such occurrences are rather infrequent and in relatively small companies.

Great American Industries also serves to illustrate still another and much more common variety of special economic service. "Messrs. Levy, Murphy and Stolz, of which firm Irving H. Stolz, the Secretary and a director of the company, is a member, were paid $17,500 for legal services rendered to the company during the fiscal year ended December 31, 1965 and $23,950 for legal

20/ *Wall Street Journal,* March 22, 1967.
21/ Great American Industries Inc., *Proxy Statement,* Jan. 25, 1967, p. 5.
22/ *Ibid.*

services rendered to the company during the fiscal year ended December 31, 1966."[23]

The question is not the equity of payment for services rendered, but rather the negative special economic service implications. When a company tolerates business dealings with legal, insurance, public relations, or advertising firms whose partners are also directors of the company, then suspicions should be aroused. A perusal of the proxy statements of our 500 largest corporations will show that about one in four engage in this practice, the fees involved being generally in the $75,000 to $150,000 range but, on occasion, exceeding $1 million.

Probably the most reprehensible form of the SES factor is the use by a director of his power and private information for personal gain. Early in 1967 the United States District Court in Chicago approved an $825,000 payment by 13 directors of Hilton Hotel Corporation in settlement of a stockholder's suit. This was one of two similar suits charging Hilton's directors, four officers and nine outside directors, with illegal profits on sale of stock to the corporation. The complaints state "that the 13 directors sold 101,650 shares of Hilton Credit Corporation to Hilton Hotels in 1963 at a price above the market price. The directors received $4.8 million . . . in the deal."[24]

At times, stress on the special economic service factor approaches the ludicrous. "A Coca-Cola director says it's 'accepted practice now that all members of the organization are to do all they can for bottlers and to get coke into every outlet possible'; he proudly reports that he was recently responsible for having a Pepsi-Cola dispenser replaced with a Coca-Cola dispenser at a hospital on whose board he serves."[25]

The 1965 Texas Gulf Sulphur Company case is a classic illustration of reverse SES. A total of 13 officers, officer directors and outside directors, were accused of using inside information relative to a rich Canadian copper ore discovery for personal gain. Texas Gulf Sulphur stock spurted from a low of $17 to $71 soon after the public announcement of the rich copper ore strike.

One of the accused was Thomas S. Lamont, retired vice chair-

23/ *Ibid.*, p. 4.
24/ *The Oregonian,* Portland, Ore., Jan. 2, 1967.
25/ *Wall Street Journal,* Sept. 20, 1965, p. 13.

man of Morgan Guaranty Trust Company. "Shortly before 10:45 a.m. on April 16, 1964 Thomas S. Lamont stepped away from the Manhattan board room of the Texas Gulf Sulphur Co. and phoned an officer of Morgan Guaranty Trust Co. of which Lamont, 66, is retired vice chairman. The Texas Gulf board meeting had broken up, and Director Lamont advised the banker to watch the Dow-Jones ticker for good news about the company . . . between 10:45 and 10:59 a.m. Morgan Guaranty bought 8,000 shares of Texas Gulf for its accounts. Morgan Guaranty paid between 32 5/8 and 34 for the stock."[26] In a few days the stock had risen to $71.

Although there were a number of technicalities involved in this case, including the fact that Mr. Lamont did not personally benefit in the transaction, there is a negative SES implication. If outside directors are assumed to function as pipelines for information flow between two or more companies which share their loyalty and services, then questions must be raised as to the value of such directors.

It should be evident from these illustrations that the special economic service factor is often abused. What ostensibly appears to be a potential service to the corporation, turns out to be a device for individual or syndicate gain. The Metro-Goldwyn-Mayer 1966 proxy battle (discussed below in the *Owners' Equity* section) is a good example.

In February, 1967, a stockholder suit was filed against both the chairman and the president of U.S. Smelting, Refining and Mining Company, dissident nominees for MGM board membership. In the stockholder complaint, U.S. Smelting officials Martin Horwitz and Jack Wilder "were accused of serving as part-time employees to the detriment of the company while trying to win control of Metro-Goldwyn-Mayer Inc. for their own personal benefit."[27]

On the victorious side there were similarly suspect actions. In July, 1967, the MGM board considered the purchase of John Blair and Company. Several of the directors voiced the objection that the proposed purchase price of slightly less than one MGM share for each John Blair share was much too generous—on the day of the announcement, MGM stock was selling at $58 while Blair

26/ *Time*, "When Private News Is Public," July 16, 1965.
27/ *Wall Street Journal*, Feb. 16, 1967, p. 28.

stock was priced at $32.50, and the premium, thus, would be equal to almost $25 million.

A key figure in the current discussions has been Allen Klein, who heads a New York entertainment and investment concern in his name. A supporter of the MGM management in its successful proxy fight against dissident Philip J. Levin early this year, Mr. Klein is believed to have been active in bringing MGM and Blair together. He spoke for the purchase of Blair at MGM's meeting last week. Mr. Klein is believed to hold about 150,000 MGM shares.[28]

The special economic service factor is prominently mentioned in the Analysis Examples in Part II. The Wheeling Steel Company, prior to 1966, provides a classic example of vendor-directors, the General Aniline illustration shows the consequences of political patronage as a special economic service factor, and in the General Dynamics Corporation analysis a somewhat different aspect of the role of government as a customer and the SES factor are related.

Most of our major corporations seem to have downgraded SES as a factor in selection of directors. Tremendously expanding markets, ever more complex technologies, much more readily available financing, and similar changes on the economic front have diminished the role of the individual who can provide a "special service." Even in the political sphere, instead of the too obvious juncture of politicians and a company's board, far more subtle associations have developed.

## Broad economic sophistication

For all practical purposes economics is synonymous with business enterprise. At one time it was enough for a businessman to know how to make his own product and how to sell it. While the basic principles still apply, the economics that the enlightened businessman must grasp today far transcend that of a generation ago. It is a distinct rarity today, even in smaller scale business, for a firm to make a single product, and expanding product mix means economic complications. Technological change, intensified

28/ *Wall Street Journal,* July 31, 1967, p. 6.

competition, organized labor, governmental controls, imports from abroad, and a host of other variables make it impossible for the businessman to remain in economic isolation.

As a consequence, there has been a very noticeable transformation in the economic makeup of the successful enterpriser, a transformation that has been effected both in a better comprehension of economics and in its application. The best evidence that a businessman must know more about the broader aspects of business is the continuing climb in the educational level of directors. In 1900 approximately 29 percent of the chief executives of major corporations had earned college degrees; in this executive group, only 9 percent had advanced or graduate degrees. At present, of the 876 directors in the 52 largest U.S. companies, 735 (83 percent) have earned a first degree and 163 have advanced degrees. Only 141 directors have either not attended an institution of higher learning or failed to graduate.[29]

The remarkable feature about this acquisition of higher education at the board-room level is the growth in graduate degrees. Almost one-fifth of this group of directors had earned a graduate degree and among officer directors in industry the figure was somewhat in excess of 25 percent as compared with 19 percent for outside directors. At DuPont, for example, six of the ten officer directors have earned doctorates.

It might be argued that the increase in the number of executives with degrees is simply a manifestation of escalating educational standards throughout our society. But it can also be shown that the demand for better-schooled executives has been partially responsible for elevating our national education norms. This counterargument gains force from the continued vogue of management development programs.

Practically every major university has recognized the need to provide the advancing executive with opportunities for management development, with Harvard Graduate School of Business the distinct leader in this field. To date more than 6,000 business executives have participated in Harvard's programs. In addition, Harvard has taken the lead in giving academic strength and respectability to graduate work in business. It has been in the forefront in

29/ *California Management Review,* "Higher Education for the Executive Elite," Stanley Vance, Summer 1966, Vol. VIII, No. 4, p. 22.

using the words "business administration" in degree titles. Its MBA's (Master of Business Administration) are found in the ranks of virtually all of our better-run organizations. Harvard, almost singlehandedly, pioneered in doctoral programs specifically designated as business administration. Its first venture in this area was called Doctor of Commercial Science. Subsequently, this degree was retitled, Doctor of Business Administration. Today, more than one third of the doctorates pertinent to business administration granted annually are DBA's. Other leading universities, such as Indiana, Washington, Oregon, Colorado, Michigan State, Illinois, Southern California, and at least a dozen others, now grant a degree bearing the designation, Doctor of Business Administration. Within another generation an MBA will almost be a prerequisite for membership on our major corporate boards and, ultimately, it is not beyond the realm of possibility that the DBA will be a requirement for entrance into the board room.

It is false, of course, to assume that an academic degree qualifies an individual for top organization posts. Nevertheless, the individual with the DBA or MBA has demonstrated that he has an interest and a competency in business matters. This is more than can be said for some outside directors who reach the board room by nonbusiness routes.

There is other academic evidence that the BES factor has become very important. Practically every major university has a number of businessmen serving as trustees or in other advisory capacities, and in a number of instances the majority of the trustees of a given university are industry leaders. (It can of course be argued that many of these appointments follow an executive's promotion to a company's board of directors and that therefore the BES factor would have less significance in the director-selection process.) In addition, the number of business leaders who are recipients of honorary degrees continues to grow. Gestures of this sort by universities are sometimes viewed with cynicism. In some cases the granting of the honorary degree is a not-too-subtle approach for gift or grant purposes. But it should be pointed out that honorary degrees are almost always subject to the approval of university faculty committees. The likelihood that such committees will routinely approve an honorary degree to an undeserving person seems to be minimal.

A seemingly laudable broad economic sophistication move

which is still barely perceptible is the endowing of chairs of learning at universities. At present there are approximately 65 endowed professorships for faculty in business administration in a population of more than 20,000 university teachers of business. About two new chairs are being established annually. For example, "a $500,000 professorship has been set up by the University of Minnesota to explore what it calls the dense thicket of relationships between business and government and the middle ground of non-profit and community organizations. The new chair of business and government relations is named after Frederick R. Kappel, Minnesota '24 and former chairman of AT&T."[30] While most such gestures are of an ex post facto character, they do support the contention that academic association and broad economic sophistication have something in common.

The University of Michigan's Businessman's Hall of Fame, planned to open in 1969, illustrates this reciprocal recognition. The Hall of Fame honoring American business leaders will be housed in the University of Michigan's new $5.2 million advanced management center which will be part of the Graduate School of Business Administration. "A panel of 200 electors made up of businessmen, educators, public officials and business reporters will do the nominating and electing. Although there will be room for 100 Business-Men of Fame, it is expected that no more than 50 or 75 will be picked within the next half century."[31]

Other manifestations of the BES factor include publications by industry spokesmen. Within the past decade or two, there has been a remarkable flow of literature from corporate headquarters, with articles by eminent executives appearing in the leading business periodicals. For example, Donald P. Kircher, Singer Company's chief executive, had an article, "Now the Transnational Enterprise," appearing in the *Harvard Business Review*.[32] Harold S. Geneen, International Telephone and Telegraph's chief executive, wrote on "The IIuman Element in Communications" for the *California Management Review*.[33] Michael L. Haider, chairman of Standard Oil Company (New Jersey), contributed "Tomorrow's

30/ *Business Week,* Nov. 4, 1967.
31/ *Wall Street Journal,* Jan. 14, 1967.
32/ *Harvard Business Review,* "Now the Transnational Enterprise," Donald P. Kircher, March to April 1964, Vol. 42, No. 2.
33/ *California Management Review,* "The Human Element in Communications," Harold S. Geneen, Winter 1966, Vol. IX, No. 2.

Executive: A Man For All Countries" to the first issue of the *Columbia Journal of World Business.*[3][4]

This is only a random sampling. The list would become exceedingly long if papers presented to meetings of technical groups were included. As a rule these contributions are published in the "Proceedings" of that group's meeting. For example, Monroe J. Rathbone, former chairman of Standard Oil Company (New Jersey), had his address, "A Businessman's View of Some Antitrust Problems—Particularly Mergers, Acquisitions and Corporate Size," published in the Proceedings of the American Bar Association's 1965 Spring Meeting.[3][5]

Leading executives are increasingly in demand as speakers at meetings of all sorts of organizations. This "podium" visibility is very definitely related to broad economic sophistication. While exposure of this sort is generally tinged with a soft-sell of the speaker's company and its products, the real selling job is that of broad economic ideas. As a rule, industry spokesmen have proven to be quite eloquent and convincing. They tend to do an equally good job when discussing trade, technical, or theoretical topics.

Critics allege that many of these speeches and papers are ghost written. This may be so. If it is, however, then it seems to be simply the emulation of a practice that has become widely accepted in many other areas. Politicians deliver talks written by someone else, and quite a few celebrities attach their names to books actually written by a ghostwriter. Voices are dubbed in for stage performers who lack musical talent, and it is the rare comic who writes all of his own skits or concocts all of his jokes. To say this is not intended to justify ghostwriting. If it occurs, it simply supports the thesis that top executives recognize the importance of the communications media.

Broad economic sophistication is also manifest in the increasing number of top businessmen who take an active official role in technical and professional societies. In some cases the demands arising out of an excessive number of conferences which an execu-

34/ *Columbia Journal of World Business,* "Tomorrow's Executive: A Man For All Countries," Michael L. Haider, Winter 1966, Vol. 1, No. 1.

35/ *Proceedings of the Section of Antitrust Law,* "A Businessman's View of Some Antitrust Problems—Particularly Mergers, Acquisitions and Corporate Size," Monroe J. Rathbone, American Bar Association, Spring Meeting, Washington, D.C., April 8 to 9, 1965.

tive attends might be viewed as a hindrance to his corporate duties. As a rule, however, participation in professional and technical group meetings can be considered as an attempt at self-development.

Considering all of the foregoing, it is apparent that a certain competency and sophistication in broad economic matters is a positive factor in the selection of both top executives and of board members. From available evidence it seems that this factor, broad economic sophistication, will become one, if not the most important consideration in future structuring of corporations' directorate dimensions. This is not necessarily an argument for the inclusion of outside directors who already have attained recognition in this factor. The stress should rather be toward a concerted attempt by corporations at expanding horizons for their own aspiring executives. Major corporations in particular must provide the means and motivation for their own higher caliber personnel to acquire these necessary attributes. Reliance upon outside sources can result in the neglect and waste of local corporate resources.

## Image

One of the most significant changes in the status of industrial leaders is their acceptance into practically all of the upper strata of our society. A comparison of *Who's Who in America,* Volume 1 (1899 to 1900) with Volume 34 (1966 to 1967) highlights this transformation. Roughly estimated, of the first *Who's Who* listing of 8602 persons, only between 1 and 2 percent were from the business community. A random sampling of the most recent compilation (which has 61,967 listings) reveals that almost one third of those listed are business leaders. This remarkable expansion—from less than 200 to approximately 20,000 listings—is about twice the total growth rate of *Who's Who in America.* Just a generation ago, only the top one or two executives of our very largest corporations were selected for *Who's Who* inclusion. Today this selection process extends deeper into the ranks of the bigger corporations and also covers a widely expanded number of companies.

Recognition by *Who's Who in America* and similar compilations is certainly not the best or only image criterion. Business leaders are much in demand as trustees and advisors for our most prestigious universities. Eleemosynary organizations, such as the Red Cross and Salvation Army, actively seek out businessmen for their top councils. There is scarcely any area of community or public endeavor where business leaders are not prominent in the highest advisory and policy-making levels.

A cursory count of American Telephone and Telegraph's board shows approximately 120 directorships in nonprofit organizations. These include a score of university trusteeships, six Business Council representatives, four National Safety Council memberships, etc. Admittedly, AT&T's board is somewhat distinctive in its high-image composition. Still, there are quite a few major corporations which approximate this outside recognition of their board members. Some of this recognition can be attributed to factors such as broad economic sophistication or financial eminence. Most significant, however, is the image factor resulting from the public recognition and acceptance given these individuals.

There are many examples of high-image directors who presumably get bountiful returns for the indirect services they give the corporation. In October, 1964, Colonel John H. Glenn, Jr., was elected to the board of Royal Crown Cola Company. As inducement "the West's first man in space got an option on 60,000 of the company's shares at $19.81 each. Since R.C. shares are now orbiting above $24, Glenn's paper profits have already soared over the $250,000 mark. If the company's earnings keep climbing, Cola should land the astronaut safely on millionaire's row."[36]

In a somewhat comparable situation, Prince Bernhard of the Netherlands was a relatively poor person in 1937 when he married Queen Wilhelmina. As the Queen's consort, however, he was much in demand for image purposes as a director of Dutch corporations, and over the years he has been placed on the boards of the ten largest companies in the Netherlands. Direct compensation for such services plus indirect payments eventually made him one of the Netherlands most wealthy men.

Stress on image can have the worst of aristocratic overtones. For example,

36/ *Time,* April 16, 1965. In 1968, Royal Crown Cola reached a high of 40½. At this level, Glenn's paper profits could be estimated at $1,250,000.

In Britain, where a company's list of directors often reads like a tear sheet from *Burke's Peerage,* many a titled tycoon sits on more boards than he can count. Lord Boothby, 62, a longtime Tory backbencher who is one of this happy breed himself (he has "eight or nine" directorships), explained last week just what directors do in return for adding prestige to corporate letterheads. "No effort of any kind is called for, " he told an audience of Yorkshire clubwomen. "You go to a meeting once a month in a car supplied by the company. You look both grave and sage, and on two occasions say 'I agree,' say 'I don't think so' once, and if all goes well, you get $1,440 a year. If you have five of them, it is total heaven, like having a permanent hot bath."[37]

In quite a few instances the image factor is intimately linked to special economic service considerations. "Hamilton Life Insurance Company of New York named Jackie Robinson, former Brooklyn Dodger baseball player co-chairman and director and named two other Negroes to the board in an announced move to expand in the Negro market. Mr. Robinson said he has bought a substantial share of Hamilton Life stock and the other new directors will be stockholders."[38] As a consequence, owners' equity is also a factor in these board room appointments.

As a final example of this mixture of image plus special economic services plus owners's equity, it is interesting to review the meteoric career of Mortimer M. Caplin at Prentice-Hall. Shortly after he left government service, the former Commissioner of the Internal Revenue Service joined Prentice-Hall as a director and chairman of the executive committee, at the same time acquiring stock in the publisher of books and business services. His responsibilities at Prentice-Hall include helping that firm to expand its tax and business service activities, but he has stated that his primary interest will be his duties as senior partner of his law firm, Caplin, Battle and Harris, of Washington, D.C.

In some respects the factor of image has always been a significant reason for selecting and utilizing certain individuals as board

37/ *Time,* Oct. 5, 1962.
38/ *Wall Street Journal,* June 23, 1966.

members. However, the trend has accentuated and will probably continue to become more important as the ownership base in publicly held corporations expands. There seems to be a sentiment in many quarters that a high image factor provides integrity, stability, and a safeguarding of the public interest. This could be so. A person of good repute and national prominence would very likely be a most reluctant party to any corporate actions which might reflect negatively upon his reputation. On the other hand, if the man-of-prominence has minimal technical competency matched with an equally low degree of interest in corporate affairs, then the public has a very poor guardian protecting its interests. Even with competency and dedication, nationally prominent figures rarely have surplus time for extraneous activities. In this event, the image factor adds little to the board's value either.

Currently in the industrial sector of our society, for directorate dimension purposes, the image factor is significant in only about one fourth of our leading corporations. In another one fourth of our leading corporations, the image factor has little or no impact, but the likelihood is high that in the near future there will be some increase in the importance of this factor. Yet it is highly unlikely that image will, in the foreseeable future, ever assume the proportions in industrial boards that it presently has in other sectors of our society. In the banking sphere, for example, the image factor is two or perhaps even three times as significant as it is in manufacturing industry.

It is in the field of education, that Image is a most vital factor at the trusteeship level. One of the best examples is Harvard's 32-man Board of Overseers. Membership on this board and similar education posts has reciprocal image-value. When, as at Harvard, the board's image factor is exceedingly high, that particular board rarely serves in any operating or decision-making capacity. "Generally, the Board of Overseers routinely approves all decisions of the Harvard Corporation, made up of the president and treasurer of the university and five outsiders. In fact, George Bennett, treasurer of Harvard, calls the board a 'consenting body.' "[39] Harvard's Board of Overseers has almost a perfect record of approving actions of the Harvard Corporation.

39/ *Wall Street Journal,* June 15, 1967, p. 1.

Harvard's "board of directors" is not alone in its inactivity. Its academic peer, Yale University, has a comparably passive but prestigious ruling body known as the Yale Corporation. This group consists of six "fellows" elected by alumni balloting plus ten "successor trustees." This latter group who, once appointed, serve until mandatory retirement at age 68, jointly pick their own replacements. The Yale Corporation, in theory at least, "manages all finance and investment, must give recorded approval to each course of study, faculty appointment and degree. In practice, said [member] Dean Acheson, 'we don't interfere with the running of the college. This would be the quickest way to louse things up.' Instead, the Corporation applies itself seriously to its key job, which is to pick the president of the university and usually ratifies his decisions."[40]

At both Harvard and Yale, the respective ruling bodies very obviously provide more than just image. Nevertheless this is a very prominent attribute diligently sought for in promising candidates to either the Board of Overseers or the Corporation.

The image factor is equally significant in most nonprofit organizations. Hospital boards, government-sponsored commissions, boards of community ventures, and similar organizations view image as a most essential attribute in the top policy-making agency. The motives are varied. The most obvious reason is to facilitate the flow of funds. An equally important but less frequently admitted purpose is to exert influence and pressure when necessary.

The rather recent turmoil over the attempts by the Internal Revenue Service to plug some glaring loopholes in respect to tax-exempt organizations provides an excellent example. One specific tax loophole allowed educational and other nonprofit groups to escape any government levy on their publishing income. Tax-paying publishers had for many years been protesting such a free status, and early in 1967 this exemption of 700 tax-free periodicals was ended by a ruling of the IRS.

"Except for pressure brought to bear on the Treasury Department and Congress by the lobbyists for the tax-free publications, the IRS would probably have issued its ruling years ago."[41] Among the lobbyists, in an extended sense of the term, are quite a

40/ *Time,* June 28, 1964, p. 59.
41/ *Time,* October 7, 1966.

number of image-type directors. For example, the 23-man National Geographic board of trustees includes some of our nation's most influential citizens. In this group are William McChesney Martin, Jr., Crawford H. Greenewalt, Earl Warren, Curtis E. LeMay, Juan T. Trippe, Laurance S. Rockefeller, and many other equally well-known individuals. Not one of these individuals provides technical, managerial or financial services for National Geographic. Their chief function is to set a lofty image level. With an exceedingly high image factor such as that attained by the *National Geographic,* even the most rambunctious rebel would hesitate before launching an institutional attack.

As was stated earlier, image is intimately associated with public recognition and acceptance. As our larger corporations become more and more public in character, it will become imperative to provide even the smallest stockholder with the equivalent of the public defender. Men of image, despite their limitations, seem to be eminently qualified to serve in this capacity. But a pertinent problem is how such public figures can acquire adequate competency to perform in more than a perfunctory fashion. Also, it is essential to involve these individuals intimately in corporate affairs so that they will perform with enthusiasm. Despite the relative attractiveness of high-image individuals as directors, image does not of itself guarantee competency, diligence, or even integrity. Taken alone, image is inadequate as a directorate dimension.

## Asset impact

The economic establishment, if such an elite group exists, is simply a manifestation of centripetal forces. "Like attracts like," "birds of a feather flock together," and similar adages tell us that there are inclinations among individuals to seek out associates from among peers. The magazine *Business Week* has stated that "when you join a corporate board the odds are increasing that you will be tabbed for a job as director of another corporation." This peerage need not, of course, be perfectly equal in all facets of endeavor.

Asset impact in one sense implies a measure of peerage. It points to individuals who have been accepted into the directorate group and hence partake of peerage. However, within this group of "equals" there is considerable diversity and inequality. It would be presumptuous, for example, to equate board members of General Motors Corporation and Curtis Publishing Company. Yet in 1967, both companies appear in *Fortune*'s listing of our largest industrial firms. General Motors is at the top of the list; Curtis Publishing is at the bottom.

To date no attempt has been made to measure the degree of difference in membership on two different boards. The lack of such measuring units attests to the inherent difficulties. Projection of the asset impact norm is, consequently, a very tenuous and experimental venture.

Asset impact, as viewed here, refers to a specific individual's proportionate influence in our economy. The measure premises that:

1) Membership on a major corporation's board has more "impact" than membership on a small company's board.

2) Each director ultimately has one vote and hence a theoretical equality on the board. (This assumption obviously does not hold in all cases.)

3) On the basis of this assumed equality, each director's "weight" can be viewed as one proportionate share of the company's assets. Thus, a firm with 15 directors and $150 million in assets has an equivalent of $10 million per director asset impact.

Applying this norm to the top and bottom firms on *Fortune*'s 1967 list shows each General Motors' director with an AI of $12,916 million divided by 25, or $517 million per director. By comparison, Curtis Publishing Company's $95 million assets are "shared" by 13 directors for an average of slightly more than $7 million per director.

There are, of course, some rather serious objections to equating directors on this basis. Nevertheless, all other things being equal, General Motors' directors, each with an average asset figure of $517 million, should be considered as having more *impact* in our society than a Curtis Publishing director, who has only a $7 million average. While it would be difficult to prove that the prestigious General Motors' director wields more power in the absolute sense, he very likely is, on the total scene, more accepted and more listened to than the typical Curtis Publishing director.

If this inference is accepted, then it is possible to determine each individual director's asset impact. The arithmetic involved is simple: The proportionate asset shares represented by each directorate held by an individual are totaled to give that director's relative asset impact. For example, Frederick R. Kappel, retired chairman of American Telephone and Telegraph, is a member of six major boards of directors. His asset impact would be computed as follows:

| Directorship | Assets (in millions) | Directors | Relative AI (in millions) |
|---|---|---|---|
| American Tel. & Tel. | $35,218 | 19 | $1,853 |
| Standard Oil (N.J.) | 13,853 | 16 | 866 |
| Metropolitan Life | 23,512 | 28 | 840 |
| Chase Manhattan | 15,776 | 24 | 657 |
| International Paper | 1,305 | 18 | 73 |
| General Foods | 857 | 14 | 61 |
| | | | $4,350 |

Kappel, with $4,350 million has the highest ranking asset impact in American industry. A close runner-up, just prior to his retirement as chairman (and as a director) of Standard Oil Company (N.J.), was Monroe J. Rathbone. His total asset impact at the time (1966) was slightly in excess of $4 billion. At present, even though he has relinquished his Standard Oil (N.J.) board seat, he is still second-ranked in the country, with an AI from seven directorships of roughly $3,470 million.

A serious limitation of this evaluation technique is the disproportionate weighting that results from membership on the boards of a few of our leading firms. For example, an American Telephone and Telegraph directorship, with an average asset impact of $1,853 million, is a guarantee that the recipient will rank near the top among asset impact leaders. The next highest proportionate individual asset impact values are $1,026 million for Prudential Insurance, $866 million for Standard Oil Company (N.J.) and $840 million for Metropolitan Life Insurance. Obviously, a combination of directorships from among the companies with the greatest asset valuations will result in a high individual asset impact ranking. In the following listing (Table 5) of 30 of our leading directors on the asset impact norm, every one of AT&T's board members is included. And practically every other individual on

TABLE 5. Thirty top-ranked directors, asset impact basis

| Number of firms | Director | Asset impact (in millions) |
|---|---|---|
| 6 | Frederick R. Kappel | $4,350 |
| 7 | Monroe J. Rathbone | 3,470 |
| 3 | Thomas F. Patton | 2,743 |
| 13 | J. Victor Herd | 2,727 |
| 6 | Lloyd D. Brace | 2,723 |
| 7 | John J. McCloy | 2,696 |
| 5 | Henry T. Heald | 2,643 |
| 4 | C. Douglas Dillon | 2,585 |
| 5 | Eugene J. McNeely | 2,595 |
| 3 | William M. Batten | 2,516 |
| 4 | J. Irwin Miller | 2,507 |
| 5 | James R. Killian | 2,470 |
| 5 | Edward B. Hanify | 2,465 |
| 4 | H. I. Romnes | 2,376 |
| 5 | William A. Hewitt | 2,320 |
| 7 | Ben S. Gilmer | 2,204 |
| 4 | John D. deButts | 2,077 |
| 3 | William White | 1,928 |
| 9 | Stuart T. Saunders | 1,920 |
| 4 | William B. Murphy | 1,918 |
| 5 | Howard J. Morgens | 1,817 |
| 4 | Gilbert W. Fitzhugh | 1,815 |
| 6 | Richard K. Mellon | 1,587 |
| 5 | Charles G. Mortimer | 1,577 |
| 4 | Birny Mason, Jr. | 1,466 |
| 2 | Michael Haider | 1,469 |
| 4 | Roger Blough | 1,357 |
| 6 | Donald P. Kircher | 1,301 |
| 13 | Harold H. Helm | 1,279 |
| 7 | William K. Whiteford | 1,174 |

this list is a director on one or more boards of our top 10 companies.

In Table 5, the first figure designates the number of major directorships held, the second figure the individual's aggregate asset impact. The combined asset impact of these 30 directors is approximately $66 billion. On an average, each of these 30 directors represents an asset impact of $2.202 billion.

For comparison purposes it is interesting to note that the combined assets of our 186 leading corporations were, in 1967, equal to more than $545 billion. This group of corporations had 2,288 directors. On the average, this means that each of their directors represents an asset impact of about $240 million.

It must be stressed that statistics of this sort should be handled with caution. Higher or lower ranking on an asset impact basis does not in itself imply excellence, competency, judgment, or any other attribute presumably requisite for membership on a major board of directors. The only inference being made from this analysis is that, *in general, the greater a director's aggregate asset impact, the greater will be his impact on the socioeconomic scene.*

This inference is necessarily conditioned by other facts of economic life. In practically all of our major enterprises, the chief executive officer invariably has a far greater impact than does any other single member of his board. Yet, statistically, the chief executive's asset impact is recorded as a single unweighted average. Then, too, a person's character, acceptance, competency, participation, and similar factors certainly condition his asset impact. There does, however, seem to be some cogency in the assumption that being a member of a high asset impact board enhances a director's chances for being preferred as a candidate for other boards. And it very likely adds to the weight accorded a director's opinions in the deliberations of his respective boards.

### Interlock

On October 13, 1965, Congressman Emanuel Celler, chairman of the House of Representatives Committee on the Judiciary, introduced H.R. 11572. The purpose of this bill was to amend section 8 of the Clayton Act to prohibit certain corporate management interlocking relationships. The model bill would virtually put an end to most major bank and insurance company boards as presently constituted. There are some limitations on the application of this proposed law. One of them is that the firms must be in interstate commerce. Another is that at least one of the interlocking companies must have a net worth of $1 million or more. But it can readily be seen that despite these limitations at least 80 percent of all industrial and financial activity would be subject to severe restrictions on board structuring if this bill became law.

In essence, Congressman Celler's bill would make it unlawful for any board to include directors from companies which are judged to be competitive. For example, several recent additions to Sears, Roebuck and Company's board would very likely be judged illegal if Congressman Celler's bill were made law. Prior to 1966, Sears, Roebuck had two members of its board who had steel industry associations—John D. deButts and Homer J. Livingston, both of whom were on Inland Steel's board. This inclusion of two Inland Steel directors on Sears, Roebuck's board seems natural—both companies are Chicago-based. However, in 1966, Bethlehem Steel invited Crowdus Baker, president of Sears, Roebuck, to its board. And in 1967, United States Steel added Gordon M. Metcalf, chairman of Sears, Roebuck to its board. This interlock, through Sears, Roebuck, of three leading steel companies would certainly be questioned under the proposed legislation. As a conservative estimate, probably 80 percent of our 500 leading corporations have comparable indirect interlocks.

The more direct form of interlock, where directors of competing firms serve on one another's boards, is illegal and, consequently, avoided assiduously by most firms. On occasion, legal action must be taken to prevent such direct interlock. In 1953 the United States District Court ruled that Mr. Sidney Weinberg could not hold interlocking directorships concurrently in Sears, Roebuck and B. F. Goodrich. (Mr. Weinberg resigned his directorship in Sears but retained his B. F. Goodrich position.)

In 1958, Sidney Weinberg sought to be named a trustee of Sears, Roebuck Savings and Profit Sharing Pension Fund. The trustees, three or four company officers plus two "outside" trustees, vote the Fund's holdings in Sears stock; at that time, these holdings amounted to approximately 20 million shares. Mr. Weinberg was forbidden by the Court to become a Sears Pension Fund trustee. It was evident to the Court that such participation by Mr. Weinberg would have been an indirect reinstitution of the interlock forbidden in 1953.

The increasing incidence of interlocking boards, particularly in large-scale banks, insurance companies, and manufacturing industry, is a demonstrated fact. Congressman Celler's bill H.R. 11572 is firmly supported by a 270-page report from the House Committee on the Judiciary Antitrust Subcommittee (Subcommittee No. 5). This report, "Interlocks in Corporate Management," documents the existence and extent of the practice. For example, the four leading New York commercial banks had a total of 109 interlocks with insurance companies alone (see Table 6).

TABLE 6. Direct interlocks between the four largest New York commercial banks and insurance companies

| Bank | Total insurance cos. interlocks | Interlocked with | | | |
|---|---|---|---|---|---|
| | | Metro-politan | Pru-dential | Equi-table | New York Life |
| Chase Manhattan | 22 | 4 | 0 | 3 | 1 |
| First National City | 25 | 2 | 1 | 0 | 1 |
| Manufacturers Hanover | 31 | 0 | 1 | 1 | 1 |
| Chemical Bank | 31 | 1 | 1 | 3 | 3 |

Source: U.S. House of Representatives, Committee on the Judiciary Staff Report, "Interlocks in Corporate Management," U.S. Government Printing Office, Washington, D.C., March 12, 1965, p. 183.

On p. 192 the Report states: "Although insurance companies and banks are in direct competition, the staff study disclosed that the 10 largest life insurance companies had more than 195 interlocks with banks and that the 10 largest fire and casualty companies had more than 160 direct interlocks with banks."

The interlocking maze is not confined to banking and insurance. The staff report shows, as one example, six corporations with nearly 400 interlocks (see Table 7). Note that all six companies have ample opportunities for cross-communications through the medium of the five banks.

The Celler Committee report provides strong logic supporting the need for additional restrictive legislation:

Perhaps the most significant aspect of the common director problem is the concern that, by means of this device, inordinate control over the major part of U.S. commerce would be concentrated in the hands of so few individuals that the normal social and political forces relied upon to maintain a free economy would be ineffective to correct abuses. Ingrown relations, closely knit corporate identities and the ability to wield economic power on a wide front, were feared because they carry the seeds of a "business aristocracy" that would not be compatible with basic tenets of the political and economic democracy embodied in the antitrust laws.[42]

The Report summarizes the objections to corporate management interlocks into three broad categories: (1) matters of anti-

42/ U.S. House of Representatives, Committee on the Judiciary Staff Report, "Interlocks in Corporate Management," U.S. Government Printing Office, Washington, D.C., March 12, 1965, p. 5.

TABLE 7. Some typical industrial and commercial corporation interlocks

| | | Interlocked with | | | | |
|---|---|---|---|---|---|---|
| Company | Total interlocks | Chase Man- hattan | First National | Manufac- turers Hanover | Chemi- cal | Morgan Guaranty |
| General Motors | 63 | 1 | | | | 1 |
| Ford | 56 | | 1 | | 1 | 1 |
| Chrysler | 55 | 1 | | 2 | | 1 |
| AT&T | 104 | 2 | | 1 | 1 | 2 |
| B. F. Goodrich | 52 | 1 | 1 | 2 | | 2 |
| Phelps Dodge | 64 | | 1 | 2 | 1 | 1 |

Source: U.S. House of Representatives, Committee on the Judiciary Staff Report, "Interlocks in Corporate Management," U.S. Government Printing Office, Washington, D.C., March 12, 1965, p. 185.

trust significance, (2) conflicts of interest, and (3) debasement of the quality of available business leadership.

The first two objections have long been the subjects of vehement debate; the third objection has gotten far less attention—but despite this, the third objection probably provides the strongest reasons for a reexamination of the practice whereby an individual can serve two competing masters. "A debasement of management occurs from the fact that restriction in the number of opportunities for management experience by reason of interlocks may result in deterioration in the quality of service available for policymaking and decisionmaking functions."[43]

There can be little argument that interlocks do inhibit maximum development of corporate executive talent. In theory, at least, the board of directors is the summit in the corporate hierarchy. In a democratic organization, channels for promotion are presumably open to anyone—assuming he has talents which he uses effectively. Movement up the executive ladder up to and into the board room should, in a competitive society, be the strongest motivational force. Unfortunately, excessive interlock results in relatively fewer channels for promotion for dynamic executives. In some companies, such as General Electric or AT&T, there is virtually no opportunity for a competent executive to reach the company board room. A simple arithmetical computation allocating the number of board seats available to company personnel among

43/ *Ibid.*, p. 8.

TABLE 8. Probability of directorship attainment in selected companies

| Company | Probability |
|---------|-------------|
| AT&T | 1 : 217,000 |
| General Electric | 1 : 175,000 |
| General Motors | 1 :  62,000 |
| United States Steel | 1 :  51,000 |
| Ford Motor | 1 :  40,000 |
| Chrysler | 1 :  27,000 |
| Texaco | 1 :  27,000 |
| Standard Oil (N.J.) | 1 :  12,000 |
| Mobil Oil | 1 :   9,000 |
| DuPont | 1 :   4,500 |

that company's work force shows tremendous variance among companies. Table 8 gives the probabilities for directorship attainment by company personnel in ten of our largest corporations.

From Table 8 it can be seen that in some of our major companies the chance for elevation to the board room holds virtually no motivational meaning for that company's employees. And it should be noted that the biggest odds against advancement for company personnel are in those corporations with extremely high incidences of interlocks.

There is a frequently heard argument, particularly in heavily-interlocked companies, that many new opportunities are being opened up for dynamic executives in freshly-created senior, executive, group or administrative vice presidencies. In a growing number of instances, industrial corporations are emulating the banks and insurance companies in their multiplication of vice presidencies. The ten largest commercial banks in 1964 had a total of 1268 vice presidents, or an average of 127 per bank. By contrast, our industrial firms with the most liberal vice-presidency policies had:[44]

| Company | Vice presidents |
|---------|-----------------|
| United States Steel | 54 |
| Westinghouse Electric | 43 |
| General Electric | 36 |
| General Motors | 32 |
| Radio Corporation | 27 |

44/ *Bankers Magazine,* "The Bank Vice Presidency: Last Stop on the Line," Stanley Vance, Vol. 147, No. 4, Autumn 1964.

But by far the greatest portion of industrial firms still restrict the number of vice presidencies to a more meaningful 8 to 12 in number.

An emphasis on the vice presidency as the terminus for a successful career is inadequate, however. Every sensible career executive knows that there is limited room at the top, but the odds should not be so greatly against him without good reason. In the large commercial banks, the probability that a vice president will ever be designated a director is a discouragingly low two chances in one hundred (0.02). In large-scale industries, these probabilities range from about one chance in five (0.20) in outside-type directorates to about three chances in four (0.75) in companies with predominantly inside-type boards.[45] When interlocks reduce the probabilities for a capable top executive to attain the ultimate—a seat on his company's board of directors—then there is need for reappraisal.

Interlocks result from a variety of reasons, of which financial aggrandizement is the most obvious. However, social factors, political considerations, nepotism, and even good-neighborliness can be initiating forces. Laurel Valley Golf Club, opened in 1960 in the western Pennsylvania community of Ligonier, is one good example of a locale most favorable for the development of interlocking associations. With initiation fees of $6,000 and dues of $600 a year, Laurel Valley can be termed an exclusive club. Its 200 members include the elite of the Pittsburgh-area business leaders. This reference is certainly not a condemnation of this type of association. Nevertheless, contacts of this type lead to a form of industrial inbreeding and social stratification.

Another form of interlock is the excessive favoritism for family members or intimate friends as directors. Nepotism, in the strict dictionary sense of the term, is on the decline in large-scale industrial enterprise. Once familiar names such as Goodrich, Seiberling, Wilson, Manville, Owens, Reynolds (tobacco), Eastman, Studebaker, Armstrong, Carrier, Chrysler, Cudahy, Westinghouse, to name a few, no longer appear on the boards of companies bearing these family names. In 1925 there were six Armours on the board of Armour and Company; at present there are none. Swift and

45/ *Ibid.*

Company in 1925 had five members of the family serving as directors; it has only one today. The Procters and Gambles numbered four directors on the board of P&G in 1925; one Gamble represents the families today. Even as recently as 1950 there were ten family representatives on the board of Hoover Company; today this family representation has declined to a mere two. (There are, of course, some notable exceptions to this trend, such as Ford, Firestone, Dow, and DuPont.)

While founder-family names are relatively less prevalent today in large-scale industry, nepotism and interlock are still common in other sectors. In May, 1967, *U.S. News and World Report* commented,

> Coming up fast in Texas—and in the burgeoning financial empire of Lyndon Baines Johnson—is his 23 year old son-in-law, Patrick Nugent.
>
> Mr. Nugent, who settled down with his bride, the former Luci Baines Johnson, in Austin after their marriage last August, has become an established figure in Texas banking circles.
>
> Along with Jake Jacobsen, a former White House aide who recently returned to his law practice in Austin, Mr. Nugent was elevated to the board of directors of the Citizens National Bank of Austin in early May.
>
> J. W. Munson, the bank's president—described Mr. Nugent as "quite a capable young man."[46]

Maxine Cheshire of the *Los Angeles Times-Washington Post* Service quoted from Pat Nugent (when a friend here asked if he would return to school in the fall), "I don't see how I can find the time. I'm on so many boards of directors now that I stay pretty busy."[47]

It is situations of this sort which raise serious questions about the selection process and functions of most boards of directors. The action by the nation's chief executive has ample precedent in our larger corporations, as the following reference to Owens-Corning Fiberglas—definitely not an isolated illustration—shows.

46/ *U.S. News and World Report,* "Pat Nugent—Growing Figure in the Expanding Johnson Empire," May 22, 1967, p. 19.
47/ *The Oregonian,* Nov. 9, 1967.

Boeschenstein, who will be 71 in July, is also devoting considerable attention to the question of executive succession. . . . The elder Boeschenstein says Owens-Corning has no bias against relatives coming into the business. "You have to guard against nepotism in the worst form, however," he says. "Relatives have got to have the guts to measure up to the job, and I think I have demanded more of Bill [his son] around here than others in comparable positions." This is an observation that other company officials heartily confirm.

The chairman continues: "I'll say that Bill has a chance at the job [the presidency], but then I can think of three or four others around here who will also have a chance." That may be. But the comment is generally greeted with jovial skepticism by knowledgeable people in Toledo.[48]

In April, 1967, Owens-Corning Fiberglas' board of directors had an addition: William W. Boeschenstein, the 41-year-old son of the company chairman. In October, 1967, he was named executive vice president.

A new version of the nepotistic tendency seems to be emerging, one that we might call "institutional nepotism." In this practice, a retiring director bequeaths, or so it seems, his board seat to another member of his firm. Of course, the heir is officially designated by a vote of the board and by ultimate approval of the stockholders. In some instances this succession process seems to have a proprietary or quasi-proprietary justification, for example when the naming firm has a sizable investment in the second company. Or sometimes the quasi-proprietary connection follows long-time legal or investment counseling. For example, in 1929 Waddill Catchings, then a partner in the firm of Goldman Sachs, was on the boards of National Dairy Products, B. F. Goodrich, Continental Can, and Cluett Peabody. Subsequently, these directorships were awarded to Sidney Weinberg, a partner in Goldman Sachs. Mr. Weinberg served as director in these companies for the next 30 to 35 years. By 1964, John L. Weinberg, then aged 39, had assumed the board-room seats once held by his father, Sidney Weinberg, and previously by Waddill Catchings, at National Dairy Products, B. F. Goodrich, and Cluett Peabody. Charles E. Saltz-

48/ *Business Week*, "Owens-Corning Molds an Industry," March 4, 1967, p. 124.

man, another Goldman Sachs partner, assumed the seat held by his predecessors, Sidney Weinberg and Waddill Catchings, at Continental Can.

The following is a partial list of 1966 appointments which appear to have been influenced by institutional nepotism. The host company, shown in the first column, seems to have provided a quasi-permanent seat on its board for a member from the corresponding firm in the parent company column. For example, when Cleo Craig (AT&T) retired from the board of United States Steel, he was succeeded by H. I. Romnes, also from AT&T.

| Host company | Recent appointee | Former director | Parent company |
|---|---|---|---|
| U.S. Steel | H. I. Romnes | Cleo Craig | AT&T |
| Anaconda | R. Houquet | J. S. Rockefeller | First Nat. City Bank |
| Atlantic Richfield | E. O. Patterson | C. D. Dickey | Morgan Guaranty |
| National Distillers | W. K. Sanders | W. G. Maguire | Panhandle Eastern Pipe |
| Kaiser Cement | J. B. Bonny | H. W. Morrison | Morrison Knudson |
| Air Reduction | C. P. Rather | C. T. Chenery | Southern Nat. Gas |
| Phelps Dodge | E. L. Palmer | R. S. Perkins | First Nat. City Bank |
| Armstrong Cork | W. J. Kyle | Mr. Ingersoll | Buchanan & Ingersoll |
| Crocker-Citizens National Bank | P. E. Haas | W. A. Haas | Levi Strauss |
| Cleveland Cliffs | G. S. Devine | W. J. Tuohy | C&O-B&O RRs. |
| Harris Intertype | R. W. Morse | T. K. Glennan | Case Institute of Technology |

The pacesetters in this fairly recent phenomenon seem to be the largest banks. For example, a tabulation of the nepotistic tendencies, both familial and institutional, apparent in the board rooms of our ten largest commercial banks reveals the following:

| Type of nepotism | Number of nepotistic directorates | Percent of Total |
|---|---|---|
| Direct Family | 21 | 7 |
| Indirect Family | 10 | 3 |
| Institutional | 57 | 19 |

This tabulation is based on a total of 453 directors in 1929 and 299 directors in 1966.[49] The latter figure is smaller because of mergers, resulting in fewer directors.

49/ Stanley Vance, "Institutional Nepotism," University of Oregon, 1966, pp. 9 to 12 (unpublished).

It is evident that the prevalence of institutional nepotism, estimated at about 19 percent in the ten largest banks, is significantly
higher than the 7 percent familial-type nepotism.

The surest way for any publicly-held corporation's board to lose
sight of its basic purpose is to endow board-room seats to families
or to other companies. The practice invites suspicion of collusion
and favoritism. It diminishes competition for board seats. Non-
favored companies are virtually excluded from consideration. If
the practice continues, it will undoubtedly invite therapeutic treat-
ment from reformers and trustbusters.

Nepotism, familial or institutional, is only one manifestation
of interlock. A more common type of interlock is the seemingly
harmless association on a "neutral" board of two or more directors who are also on the boards of competing companies. This
form of interlock, as mentioned, is particularly noticeable in banks
and insurance companies.

In addition to Congressman Celler's proposed legislation, there
is action in other legislative quarters. In one of its studies the
House Banking Committee, chaired by Representative Patman of
Texas, has

> charged that laws intended to maintain bank competition are
> being thwarted by "interlocking relationships" among many
> financial institutions. . . . "For example," Mr. William
> McChesney Martin, Federal Reserve Board chairman, was
> quoted as stating, "the same person may serve banks that are
> in direct competition with one another and interlocking rela-
> tionships are permitted between commercial banks and mu-
> tual savings banks, despite the fact that the former have come
> to compete actively in fields formerly served principally by
> the latter."[50]

In the House Banking Committee's report,

> The staff said its data showed "an extensive web, of stock-
> holdings and corporate interlocks" among 48 financial insti-
> tutions in a number of cities. The data "strongly" suggests
> that links among financial institutions "result in the en-

---

50/ *Wall Street Journal,* "Interlocking Ties Thwart Laws to Maintain Bank Competition, House Study Charges," July 31, 1967, p. 3.

trenchment of management and lessening of competition."
... In a number of areas, insurance companies have significant stock holdings in banks. This is unhealthy, the staff
alleged, because insurance companies and banks have a "very
lucrative" joint interest in selling credit life insurance on
loans made by banks.[51]

Interlock, per se, seems to be objectionable because of its aristocratic connotations and because it can lead to collusive action.
In too many instances it can also result in unethical and illegal
endeavor. This is particularly the case where interlock is inextricably meshed with special economic service or owners' equity. The
classic Westec Corporation financial fiasco illustrates this point.
Westec's directors were predominantly outsiders, but with intimate personal or financial interlocks with Westec's president or
chairman. The stock manipulations by Westec's corporate leaders
resulted in the company's suspension from stock trading on the
American Stock Exchange August 25, 1966, and its eventual recourse for protection under Chapter 10 of the Federal Bankruptcy
Act. In the subsequent litigation, certain of Westec's outside directors were indirectly accused of dereliction of duty.

A New York City stockbroker, who is a director of ill-
fated Westec Corp. testified in New York Federal district
court that he didn't make any effort to check the financial
standing of individuals who bought large blocs of Westec
stock through him in the Summer of 1966. . . . The broker-
director, Robert W. Bull, a partner in the New York Stock
Exchange member firm of Ross, Law, Bull and Co. testified
in bankruptcy hearings that he placed orders totaling over $6
million with G. C. Haas & Co. for Westec stock without ever
doing a credit check on individuals placing the orders and in
many cases without even seeking authorization for the individuals to buy the stock.
Mr. Bull said he channeled the Westec orders through Haas
on a commission-splitting arrangement. . . . A Haas partner,
Richard W. Ince, another Westec director, also testified that

51/ *Ibid.*

he did little or no research into the financial standing of individuals placing the orders.

The two are the first directors of Westec to testify. . . . Both Mr. Bull and Mr. Ince have been directors of Westec since the 1950's when the company, before a series of mergers and acquisitions was called Western Gold and Uranium Corp.[52]

The interlock factor is almost certain to decline in importance as a directorate dimension: it connotes conflict of interest, as the illustrations testify. Interlock and its collusive and questionable connotations are not solely an industrial directorate phenomenon, however, as recent reaction to interlock and multi-directorate members of Michigan's universities' boards of trustees emphasizes.

Late in 1967 the Michigan Attorney General interpreted a new state conflict of interest law "to mean that officers and directors of banks and companies that do business with state colleges cannot sit on the school boards."[53] In subsequent developments, "six trustees who were on boards of banks that did business with the state schools resigned their college board posts. Eight other officials and trustees including the presidents of Eastern Michigan, Central Michigan, University of Michigan and Michigan State resigned bank board posts."[54]

One of the trustees involved was Eugene B. Power, chairman of University Microfilms Inc., a Xerox subsidiary, who was elected in 1956 to the University of Michigan board of regents. Mr. Power allegedly was responsible for moving considerable microfilming business to Xerox. Another individual involved was Michigan State's long-time president, John N. Hannah, and his Vice President for Business and Finance and Treasurer, Philip Jesse May, who were alleged to have been parties to a series of questionable dealings involving their interlocked directorships and jobs.

Whatever the facts of the Michigan episode, it remains true that if men of eminence are to retain the respect of the public it is imperative that they keep themselves above suspicion. Since by its

52/ *Wall Street Journal*, Nov. 13, 1967, p. 5.
53/ *Wall Street Journal*, "Michigan: Campus Conflict of Interest" by Roger Rapoport, Dec. 5, 1967, p. 16.
54/ *Ibid.*

very nature, interlock implies preferential association, men of integrity will have to learn how to avoid it while at the same time discharging their obligations to society as men of eminence.

## Owners' equity

Almost four decades ago Adolf A. Berle, Jr., and Gardiner C. Means put forth the thesis that ownership of major United States corporations had become so diffused that the individual shareholder was virtually powerless. There were a number of important implications in their study, foremost among which was the conclusion that corporate control had slipped out of the hands of entrepreneurs and the families of company founders. Statistically, the study had considerable substance. In our major corporations the trend is distinctly toward steadily smaller percentages of individual stock ownership. A half century ago Henry Ford owned most of the stock in his company; today, the members of the Ford family have a total ownership interest of about 11 percent in the Ford Motor Company.

There is, however, another aspect to the Berle and Means' thesis. In a recent article, *Fortune* pointed out that "In approximately 150 companies on the current *Fortune* 500 list, controlling ownership rests in the hands of an individual or of the members of a single family."[55] This conclusion is based upon the supposition that a 10 percent stock ownership is adequate for control purposes in most large enterprises, and there is logic in this supposition. Nowhere near the hypothetical 51 percent majority vote is needed for effective control. Actually, *Fortune*'s 10 percent figure is somewhat high for our larger companies. Prior to Douglas Aircraft's 1966 and 1967 difficulties, Donald Douglas, Sr., and his son owned only one eighth of 1 percent of the company's stock, yet exercised undisputed control. Although the Rockwells own only 3 percent of Rockwell-Standard stock, they continue to run the company. Richard K. Mellon has been head man at both Alcoa and Gulf Oil and he personally owns only about 3 percent and 2 percent respectively of these companies' stock. J. C. Penney continued to run the enterprise he founded, even though since the

55/ *Fortune,* "Proprietors in the World of Big Business," Robert Sheehan, June 15, 1967, p. 179.

early 1930's he had only about a 1 percent ownership interest, having lost financial dominance in the 1929 crash. The Verity family, instrumental in founding Armco Steel, owns less than one tenth of 1 percent of Armco's shares; nevertheless, late in 1965 Calvin William Verity, Jr., was appointed chief executive of the company.

In smaller companies, by contrast, there is still need for a larger percentage of ownership for continued control. Within the past decade quite a few complacent individuals or groups in control of a company have realized too late the inadequacy of a less than 51 percent voting control. The deposition of Herbert W. Hoover, Jr., from the top post at Hoover and Company is a good illustration. Despite his heritage and inheritance, including 37.3 percent of the voting stock and 7.2 percent of the nonvoting stock, Mr. Hoover was unable to get enough votes to retain control of the company which first his father and then he had run from its inception in 1909.

Early in August, 1967, U.S. Smelting and Refining Company took over control of Cudahy Company. The control maneuver was effected through an option to acquire 272,000 shares, equivalent to 18 percent of the company's common shares. The meat-packing company, long a family-held firm, had experienced considerable difficulty during the preceding decade, and during that period there were several top-level shifts involving family members. The last such change was the appointment of Edward Cudahy as chairman, president, and chief executive officer. After a short time, Mr. Cudahy relinquished the president's role. In another year he withdrew from his chairmanship, directorship, and the chief executive's position. In the most recent control shift, U.S. Smelting, with only an 18 percent interest, has been permitted to name five persons to the nine-man board. In addition, one holdover director is said to have made the moves resulting in the takeover. There are a growing number of parallel cases.

Although Berle and Means' thesis has not been borne out completely, there have been some significant changes in American Industry's ownership structure. Figure 3 is an attempt at approximating graphically these ownership shifts. At the turn of the century founder-entrepreneurs were distincly the dominant force in both ownership and control of our largest companies. At least half

FIGURE 3.  Estimated owners' equity allocation, major companies, 1900 to 1970

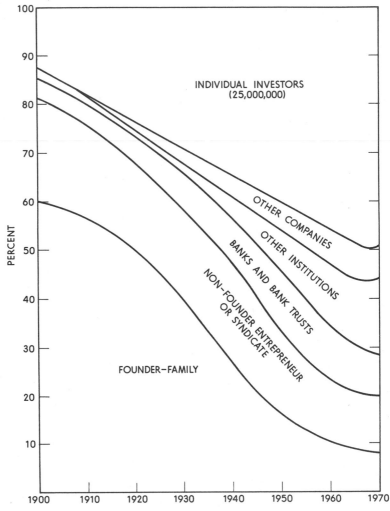

and perhaps even more of owners' equity was concentrated in the firm's founder and his family. The sum of typical individual investor ownership, by contrast, then acccounted for only 12 to 15 percent of total corporate common stock.

Since 1900, founder-family ownership has dwindled to about 8 or 10 percent, and individual stockholders, primarily because of the phenomenal increase in their number, now hold about half of all major company ownership. In 1900, individual stockowners numbered several hundred thousand. At present, the 24 million individual owners of stock are increasing at the rate of one million annually. Despite this rapid increase, however, the individual-ownership relative ratio will, undoubtedly, soon begin to show a decline.

The single greatest increase in stock ownership in the past twenty years has been among institutional investors—pension

TABLE 9. Institutional investors in selected companies

| | Holdings | | Number of investors |
|---|---|---|---|
| Company | (Percent) | (000) | |
| DuPont | 31.9 | 14,747 | 805 |
| United Aircraft | 20.5 | 2,402 | 146 |
| Anaconda | 19.6 | 2,139 | 102 |
| Deere | 18.8 | 2,750 | 188 |
| Armco | 18.3 | 2,706 | 235 |
| Burlington Ind. | 17.7 | 3,430 | 115 |
| Boeing | 17.1 | 3,331 | 104 |
| ITT | 17.0 | 3,442 | 166 |
| Continental Can | 17.0 | 2,081 | 294 |
| Inland Steel | 16.9 | 3,092 | 234 |
| General Motors | 3.7 | 10,683 | 1,276 |
| Standard Oil (N.J.) | 5.8 | 12,662 | 1,177 |
| AT&T | 1.9 | 9,782 | 1,091 |
| IBM | 10.1 | 5,468 | 1,063 |
| Texaco | 8.7 | 11,646 | 948 |

Source: Compiled from Harris, Upham & Co. *Stock Guide,* Standard and Poor's Corporation publishers, 1966.

funds, mutual funds, insurance companies, nonprofit institutions, and bank trust funds. These institutional investors "already own more than 20% of the shares listed on the New York Stock Exchange, up from 12.7% in 1949—the first year the exchange published institutional holdings."[5][6]

Table 9 provides a summary view of the ownership positions institutional investors hold in 15 of our leading corporations. The upper portion of the table lists ten companies in which institutional investors have more than one sixth of the total voting

56/ *Business Week,* Nov. 26, 1966, p. 139.

power. The lower portion shows the five companies with the largest numbers of institutional investors. This table considers only large-scale manufacturing enterprises. In this category, institutional investors own about 11 to 12 percent of the equity in our 100 largest firms, a ratio that varies considerably among industries. In the rubber industry, the median figure is 12.6 percent; in the automobile industry, it is only 5.9 percent. However, in the airline sector of the transportation industry the median figure exceeds 25 percent. Similarly, our largest banks are about 25 percent owned by institutional investors.

Tremendous growth in this new category of stockholders has generated new forces pertinent to directorate dimension factors. Up to rather recently it was the practice of most institutional investors not to take an active role in the management of any company in which they had an interest. Instead, when the institutional investor was dissatisfied with policies or performance on the part of any given company, he simply sold his holdings. There is increasing evidence that passivity of this sort may give way to more active intervention.

In the spring of 1967, Metro-Goldwyn-Mayer was the scene of a vigorous proxy battle for control of the board and company management. The insurgent group was led by Philip J. Levin. Fourteen mutual funds and two closed-end investment companies held a total of 1,423,000 shares of MGM stock—more than one fourth of the 5,043,000 shares outstanding. "One of Levin's associates had observed earlier that his campaign was directed largely at a 'single man sitting up in Boston': Edward C. Johnson II, Puritan Fund's president. Puritan's holdings in MGM were more than twice the size of any other investment company's; furthermore, Johnson controlled the 52,000 shares owned by the Fidelity Trend Fund, which is part of the same mutual fund complex."[57]

In the final voting, the dissidents, even though they had the votes of six of the fourteen mutual funds, lost the battle. Puritan Fund sided with management. The management slate won by a margin of 691,000 shares. Obviously, a switch of Puritan's 404,000 votes could have turned defeat into victory for the dissident group.

57/ *Fortune*, "The Mutual Funds Have the Votes," Arthur M. Louis, May, 1967, p. 150.

This and similar episodes raise a serious question: Should mutual funds be permitted to vote their shares? This theme under the title, "The New Power in Top Management Decisions," was the subject of a mid-November, 1966, American Management Association Conference in New York. At this meeting some experts argued that fund managers are not themselves the owners of the shares they vote. Consequently, permitting mutual fund managers to vote such stock results in giving them unwarranted power. On the other hand, the manager is assumed to have a fiduciary responsibility. This line of reasoning supports the contention that mutual funds should look after their investors' interests.

The outcome of this debate can have major impact upon the shaping of directorate dimensions. Followed to one extreme, it can turn mutual funds into more stable corporate investors. If the major mutual funds take an active role in company management, even to the extent of designating directors, then the funds' flexibility in selling a given company's stock is drastically reduced. Losing directorate representation would be a powerful inducement for a mutual fund to hold on to its stock even when that company's profit prospects were not the best.

This more intimate association at the directorate level between mutual funds and host company has other implications. A juncture through one or more company directors would give the mutual fund an "insider's" advantage. There is very strong objection in some quarters, particularly the government, to giving mutual funds access to information generally confined to a company's board room. Yet, such practice has been condoned and, in fact, has been practiced perhaps since the inception of the stock market more than 175 years ago. As one simple illustration: "Lehman Brothers is the investment advisor for One William Street, a mutual fund, and Lehman Corp., a closed-end investment company; and Lehman Brothers partners sit on the boards of about a score of companies represented in the two portfolios."[58]

Although mutual funds are currently under scrutiny, the largest of all institutional investors, bank trust departments, have long practiced interlocking with companies in which they had sizable holdings. There is a strong possibility that focusing attention upon

58/ *Ibid.*, p. 206.

the new board-room role of mutual funds will help clarify the issue. There is even a slight chance that voting privileges on "indirect" ownership may be curtailed. The procedure by which fiduciaries elect other fiduciaries needs closer policing. Ultimately, only holders "in fee" may possess the right to vote and elect their own trustees. Extending this privilege so that trustees select another level of trustees could be interpreted as an unwarranted extension of the trusteeship principle.

Although not quite parallel, the federal government's curtailment of voting rights of the two major owners of Owens-Corning Fiberglas could conceivably be used as a precedent. Owens-Illinois and Corning Glass helped form Owens-Corning Fiberglas in 1938. Each firm still holds a 31 percent ownership interest. "Under a 1949 Federal district court ruling, both Owens-Illinois and Corning Glass can't vote for an Owens-Corning director unless the court approves and the companies must have approval from the U.S. Attorney General to vote on other Owens-Corning matters."[59] This ruling was made despite the fact that the next biggest shareowner, Harold Boeschenstein, O-C F's chairman, thus gets undisputed control. His actual 5 percent interest in the company is equal to about 14 percent effective voting power.

The curtailment of all institutional investor voting privileges is a distinct possibility. With an increased incidence of MGM-type episodes, the imposition of restraints probably will even become a necessity.

One further consideration of major change in the owners' equity factor needs attention. Because of progressive income tax rates, executive salaries sometimes lose their motivational impact. As spiraling inflation decreases real dollar values by approximately 2 percent each year, salaries tend to rise astronomically as a partial offset. This pushes salaries into progressively higher tax brackets. Consequently, most executive pay increases do not add proportionately to the executive's real income. Except for the ego-satisfying aspects of high salaries, there is a diminished value in direct compensation. Thus, indirect compensation seems to have much in its favor.

Among the most popular indirect compensation techniques is

59/ *Wall Street Journal*, March 22, 1967, p. 28.

the stock-option plan. Approximately two thirds of the 1,300 companies listed on the Big Board have option plans. The logic for stock options is very sound. Participation by managers and even rank-and-file workers in ownership should develop mutuality of interests, leading to more effective individual and corporate performance.

The early and very favorable response to stock options led, in 1964, to the imposition of significant restraints. The typical 15 percent discount was abolished. Prices are now set at levels prevailing on the open market on the day the option is granted, and the executive must exercise his option within five years (previously, a ten-year limitation applied). In order to qualify for capital gains, the stock must be held a minimum of three years rather than the conventional six months. An even more stringent requirement is that the option holder must exercise higher-priced options which might have been granted earlier for the same class of stock.

Despite these constraints, stock options continue to be popular. Even after the 1964 rulings, the annual survey by Arch Patton, a director of McKinsey and Co., shows no decrease in the options' popularity. The most serious limitation stems from the vagaries of the stock market. With a five-year time limit for exercising options, it is imperative that the stock market climb significantly during the tender period. Otherwise, stock options are valueless.

From a directorate dimension point of view, stock options provide an avenue by which a company can get a new breed of interested owners. It will never approximate the original owner-entrepreneur, but if the original entrepreneurial dynamism was really generated because of ownership interest, then it would be to our economy's benefit to find at least a substitute force. Sizable stock ownership by key executives seems to be the best alternative. Opponents argue that such plans are give-aways, diluting legitimate owners' equity. (Yet it can be contended that a more highly motivated management will result in better performance and an enhanced value of the investor's interest.)

Opponents also contend that in our major corporations latecomer executives cannot possibly ever acquire a dominant stock ownership comparable to the original entrepreneurs' interest. This is obviously correct. "Chairman Frederic G. Donner, for example, owns only 0.017 percent of G.M.'s outstanding stock, but it was worth about $3,917,000 recently. Chairman Lynn A. Townsend owns 0.017 percent of Chrysler, worth about $2,380,000. Their interest in the earnings of these investments is hardly an impersonal one."[60]

As a rule, even a fraction of 1 percent ownership in a major corporation is evidently a strong goad to more effective performance. However, in the directorate dimension context, much of this inducement comes *after* an executive is designated a director. Consequently, some questions can be raised as to the significance of this type of owners' equity in the designing of a company's directorate dimensions.

60/ "Proprietors in the World of Big Business," *op. cit.,* June, 1967, p. 242.

# BOARD ANALYSIS

The first step in analysis is to structure a simple matrix. Each director's "worth" to the corporation is expressed numerically for each of the eight dimension factors, with values for each factor ranging from 0 to 10. For example, factor 8, owners' equity (OE), is categorized on the basis of the current market value of each director's common stock holdings in that company, the eleven grades for this factor being arbitrarily set as:

| Grade | Extent of ownership |
|-------|---------------------|
| 0 | No financial interest |
| 1 | $ 50,000 to $ 99,999 |
| 2 | $ 100,000 to $ 199,999 |
| 3 | $ 200,000 to $ 499,999 |
| 4 | $ 500,000 to $ 999,999 |
| 5 | $ 1,000,000 to $ 2,499,999 |
| 6 | $ 2,500,000 to $ 4,999,999 |
| 7 | $ 5,000,000 to $ 9,999,999 |
| 8 | $10,000,000 to $19,999,999 |
| 9 | $20,000,000 to $49,999,999 |
| 10 | Family has controlling interest |

In this way, each director on a given board is assigned a point value for each of the eight factors. Points are then counted both vertically and horizontally. The vertical tabulation shows, in quantitative terms, the significance of each factor. Summing the point values for all eight factors provides a base for computing the relative significance of each of the eight factors. If this summed value is divided into each of the factor totals, the resultant percentages show the greater or lesser importance of each factor in specific

93

boards of directors. This permits comparison. If the tabulations are not converted into relative terms by this division, faulty inferences are likely to result because the size of the board would then appear as the strategic factor. Increasing the number of directors would, obviously, have much bearing upon the size of the absolute values associated with the pertinent factors, and it would be very difficult to compare directorate dimensions of one company with those of another.

Totaled horizontally, the point summations provide an index of individual director worth to the corporation. This total, however, provides no weighting of relative factor importance. Doubling or even trebling the weight for a specific factor could change the evaluation drastically. Then, too, an individual director might be considered essential to a given board for some factor not included in our selected eight.

## Graphic representation

Both vertical and horizontal summations can readily be converted into relative or percentage values by simple division. The resultant percentage values facilitate comparison and eliminate the bias of directorate size. These relative values can also be used to portray directorate dimensions graphically. Such graphs, of course, are only approximations; they are not precise measurements.

In structuring the respective graphs, each factor can be viewed as one side of an octagon. The length of each side is proportionate to the relative value of that factor. Fixing the junctures of factors 1 and 8, and factors 4 and 5 at permanent points on the graph will produce octagons of fairly equal size, which should facilitate comparison. Each factor is measured off counterclockwise. For example, assuming values of 18, 12, 9, and 15 percent respectively for the first four factors, and setting the vertical axis at 6 inches, results in the graph shown on the following page.

## Sector analysis

The eight factors instrumental in this experiment are unique in that they lend themselves to a pairing procedure. For example, technical expertise (TE) and management experience (ME) are both intimately associated with getting the best possible product to the greatest possible market. These two factors can be said to be vital to product acceptance.

The next two factors, special economic service (SES) and broad economic sophistication (BES), are significant for peer acceptance. A quarter of a century ago the SES factor seemed to be extremely important in this regard. More recently, SES, viewed as vendor, buyer, banker, or legal service value, has become somewhat sus-

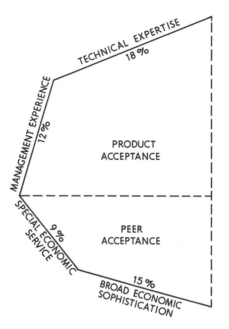

pect. Broad economic sophistication (BES), on the contrary, is "in" at the present time. Stress on this sector is manifest in the tremendous growth of management development programs, the importance of master of business administration degrees, increased readership of professional-technical journals, the amazing proliferation of professional meetings, and in all the many other activities associated with professional management.

The third couplet factors, image (IM) and asset impact (AI), are associated with public acceptance. While these norms might seem intangible, they are reflected in identifiable and measurable phenomena. The increasing stress on shareholder, community, governmental, and public relations attests to the growing recognition of this sector's importance.

Finally, interlock (IL) and owners' equity (OE) constitute the fourth couplet, personal acceptance. Obviously, attributes such as personal charm are important in this regard. However, the prime personal acceptance ingredients are quite dependent upon social, financial, hereditary, and political considerations.

The factor-coupling process yields still additional relationships. Product acceptance and personal acceptance measure management orientation. Both sectors and the pertinent four factors associated with them are primarily and intimately associated with actively running the affairs of the company.

Conversely, peer acceptance and public acceptance have minimal impact upon corporate management and organization. These two sectors and the four factors associated with them are prestige oriented. The relative proportions of these two "hemispheres" will indicate whether a particular board of directors is more concerned with the management and control of the company or with providing image and prestige.

The four sectors can also be viewed latitudinally. The two left-hand sectors, product acceptance and peer acceptance, are part of the broad and very important economic function. The right-hand sectors, public acceptance and personal acceptance, are intimately part of the legal-social function.

Figure 4 shows graphically how the eight factors (designated by abbreviations) structure the four acceptance sectors, which four in turn indicate the relative extent of management orientation and prestige orientation, together with the relative significance of economic function and legal-social function.

The directorate dimensions obtained from the eight-factor point values assigned individual board members are the results of the corporate personification and reification processes. In the illustrations beginning below, it will become clear that no two companies have identical directorate dimensions. Even more significantly, board of directors' dimensions tend, over time, to change within a given company. This is particularly true when directors are added or replaced.

The ability to modify the pertinent dimensions is very important. It permits a company, through its board, to adapt to chang-

FIGURE 4. Graphic presentation of directorate dimensions

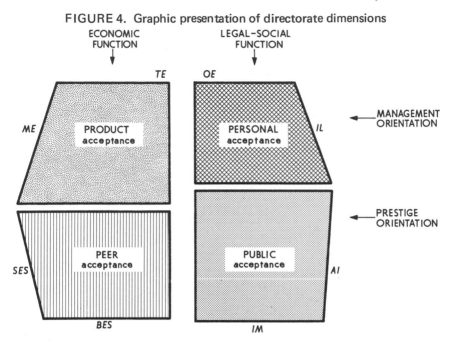

ing circumstances. Without such flexibility it is almost a certainty that bureaucratic stratification, and perhaps stultification, would drastically impede our economic system's dynamism. In other words, modification in corporate dimensions is, so to speak, a manifestation of the Darwinian thesis of "adapt or perish." It should be stressed, however, that some of this adaptive process might be more a matter of emulation than of real need-satisfaction. There is a propensity in corporations (as well as in human beings) to follow in the footsteps of the leaders. While this may not always be a bad practice, it can on occasion result in misfit directorate dimensions.

As stated previously, the personification and reification processes result in a great variety of directorate dimension patterns. Without additional corroborating data, however, no inferences should be made as to the superiority of one pattern over another.

For example, an exaggerated product acceptance sector does not necessarily mean that the board of directors is optimally structured. Similarly, expansion or contraction of any given factor or sector is good or bad only in the context of present and future board-room functions. By analogy, no man should be indicted because he is tall or short, plump or skinny, brachycephalic or dolichocephalic. Neither should a corporation be condemned if it stresses one or more factors or sectors—if in so doing it optimizes performance.

### Illustration 1: Ford Motor Company, 1942

To test the model, a specific corporation's board of directors must be selected for analysis purposes, with each director measured in terms of the eight factors and their eleven gradations. As a first example, we will use the Ford Motor Company's 1942 board of five directors (see Table 10). The small size of this board and the past preeminence of its members permits easy analysis. Henry Ford, for example, is ascribed the maximum allowable points for management expertise, image, interlock, and owners' equity. (There may be some objection to his 9-point allocation for technical experience, particularly since by 1942 Mr. Ford had removed himself from most immediate operations' problems. Similarly, there may be considerable disagreement on the factor-point assignment for the other members of the board.)

It is interesting to note that the vertical tabulations seem to indicate only five factors as having significance in the structuring of the 1942 Ford Motor Company board of directors. Of these five, technical expertise, management experience, interlock and owners' equity are vital factors, while image, although important in both absolute and relative terms, can be attributed almost entirely to the world-wide renown of the company's founder. (Other members of the board are assigned points in the image category for what might be called "reflected" glory.) No points are assigned to any member of Ford's 1942 board for special economic service or asset impact factors. There should be minimal disagreement on this score.

In analyzing the vertical tabulation, the seemingly low summation of 145 points is not significant since the 1942 board consisted of only five members. The meaningful values are the resultant percentages obtained by dividing the sum total of points (145) into each factor's total.

These relative values measure the importance of the eight factors in the structuring and functioning of *this* particular board. There is an assumption in this inference; namely, that rational individuals make the decisions involved in selecting and utilizing the respective boards. Assuming rationality, greater or lesser stress will be placed upon these eight factors, or some unlisted factor, depending upon what attributes the ultimate decision-makers deem essential for their corporation's well-being. These top decision-maker sentiments, convictions, or even biases determine that company's directorate dimensions.

TABLE 10. Directorate dimension measurement, Ford Motor Company directors, 1942

| Director | TE | ME | SES | BES | IM | AI | IL | OE | $\Sigma$ Pts. | % |
|----------|----|----|-----|-----|----|----|----|----|------|---|
| Henry Ford | 9 | 10 | 0 | 6 | 10 | 0 | 10 | 10 | 55 | 37 |
| Edsel Ford | 4 | 6 | 0 | 3 | 3 | 0 | 10 | 10 | 36 | 25 |
| Mrs. H. Ford | 0 | 0 | 0 | 0 | 3 | 0 | 10 | 10 | 23 | 16 |
| Sorenson | 9 | 7 | 0 | 0 | 2 | 0 | 0 | 0 | 18 | 12 |
| Craig | 7 | 6 | 0 | 0 | 0 | 0 | 0 | 0 | 13 | 10 |
| $\Sigma$ Factor Pts. | 29 | 29 | 0 | 9 | 18 | 0 | 30 | 30 | 145 | – |
| Factor % | 20 | 20 | 0 | 6 | 12 | 0 | 21 | 21 | – | 100 |

There is also meaning in the horizontal summations, but as previously stressed, caution must be exerted in drawing inferences in this area. On a strictly numerical basis, it could be deduced from Table 10 that even in the early 1940's the Ford Motor Company's founder still had the most influential role in board-room decision-making. But the 55, 36, 23, 18, 13 point values assigned respectively to the five members of the 1942 board are on the basis of only the eight pertinent and unweighted factors; injecting a weighting system or adding factors could affect the point allocation.

The vertical or eight-factor point values for the 1942 Ford Motor Company's board of directors listed in Table 10 are shown graphically in Figure 5. It can be readily seen from Figure 5 that a quarter of a century ago the two top sectors, product acceptance and personal acceptance, were of prime importance. The board at that time distinctly had a management orientation, a logical consequence of preoccupation with technical expertise, management experience, and founder-ownership of the firm. Reference to practically any reliable history text will substantiate that the 1942 Ford board was management-oriented.

The prestige orientation portion of the graph, consisting of the peer acceptance and public acceptance sectors, was quite incidental in 1942. Once again, the literature of that period bears out the inference that the Ford Motor Company a quarter of a century ago was not overly concerned with the several facets associated with prestige or image building. The disproportionate stress on

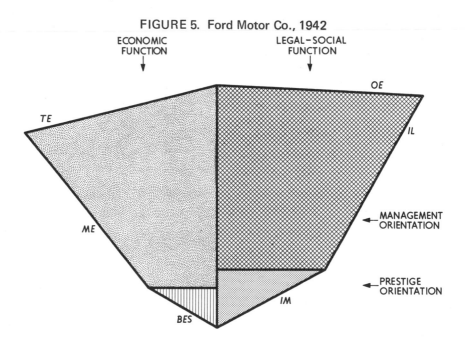

FIGURE 5. Ford Motor Co., 1942

management orientation is vividly portrayed in the relative size of the combined product and personnel acceptance sectors. The bottom two portions of Figure 5, which represent the prestige orientation components, are very definitely subordinate.

The eight factors and four sectors shown in Figure 5 can be viewed in still another context. The left-hand sectors, product acceptance and peer acceptance, are basically associated with business aspects or the economic function. The right-hand sectors, personnel acceptance and public acceptance, while still having meaning in the economic sphere, are far more a part of the legal-social function. While the contrast in size between the left and right hemispheres is not extreme, keep in mind that much of the 1942 legal-social function size is the concomitant of the company's founder-owner's views and stature.

## Illustration 2: Ford Motor Company, 1968

The next, and more difficult, task is to measure the present Ford Motor Company board's directorate dimensions using the same evaluation norms. Table 11 is such an attempt. The top portion of Table 11 measures the officer directors of the board and the bottom portion measures the outside directors. (The eight-factor summation of 484 points—the 1942 figure was only 145 points—in no way implies that the present board is superior to the company's board of 25 years ago. Today's board is simply bigger.)

Using the summed value of 484 points as a divisor yields the respective values for each of the eight pertinent factors. A com-

TABLE 11. Directorate dimension measurement Ford Motor Company board of directors 1968

| Officer Director | TE | ME | SES | BES | IM | AI | IL | OE | Σ Pts. | % |
|---|---|---|---|---|---|---|---|---|---|---|
| Henry Ford II | 8 | 9 | 0 | 9 | 10 | 1 | 10 | 10 | 57 | 12 |
| A. R. Miller | 7 | 8 | 0 | 5 | 5 | 0 | 0 | 5 | 30 | 6 |
| Benson Ford | 7 | 6 | 0 | 4 | 6 | 0 | 10 | 10 | 43 | 9 |
| C. H. Patterson | 7 | 7 | 0 | 4 | 3 | 0 | 0 | 5 | 26 | 5 |
| W. C. Ford | 6 | 5 | 0 | 4 | 5 | 0 | 10 | 10 | 40 | 8 |
| J. S. Bugas | 6 | 7 | 2 | 6 | 5 | 1 | 0 | 6 | 33 | 7 |
| L. A. Iacocca | 7 | 8 | 0 | 5 | 3 | 0 | 0 | 4 | 27 | 5 |
| J. E. Lundy | 6 | 6 | 0 | 4 | 2 | 0 | 0 | 4 | 22 | 5 |
| R. Stevenson | 6 | 6 | 0 | 4 | 2 | 0 | 0 | 3 | 21 | 4 |
| S. E. Knudsen | 9 | 9 | 7 | 6 | 6 | 0 | 0 | 0 | 37 | 8 |
| *Outside Director* | | | | | | | | | | |
| P. C. Cabot | 0 | 2 | 6 | 6 | 5 | 6 | 5 | 1 | 31 | 6 |
| C. L. Burgess | 0 | 4 | 4 | 2 | 2 | 4 | 3 | 0 | 19 | 4 |
| A. T. Taylor | 0 | 3 | 1 | 2 | 1 | 3 | 0 | 0 | 10 | 2 |
| C. G. Mortimer | 0 | 2 | 4 | 5 | 4 | 6 | 5 | 1 | 27 | 6 |
| F. D. Murphy | 0 | 2 | 1 | 2 | 5 | 1 | 0 | 0 | 11 | 2 |
| R. S. Oelman | 0 | 5 | 2 | 4 | 3 | 5 | 3 | 0 | 22 | 5 |
| S. Weinberg | 0 | 1 | 6 | 7 | 6 | 3 | 3 | 2 | 28 | 5 |
| Σ *Factor Pts.* | 69 | 90 | 33 | 79 | 73 | 30 | 49 | 61 | 484 | |
| *Factor %* | 14 | 19 | 7 | 16 | 15 | 6 | 10 | 13 | | 100 |
| Officers % | 14 | 15 | 2 | 10 | 9 | 0 | 7 | 12 | | 69 |
| Outside % | 0 | 4 | 5 | 6 | 6 | 6 | 3 | 1 | | 31 |

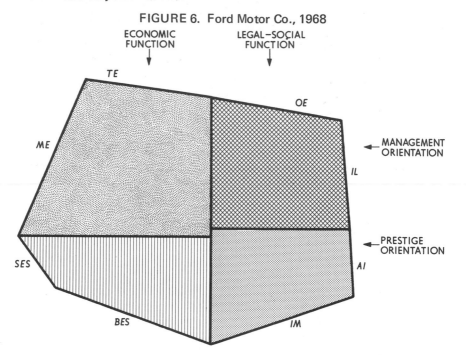

FIGURE 6. Ford Motor Co., 1968

parison of these relative values with those obtained for the 1942 board shows that there have been some rather obvious changes in Ford Motor Company's directorate dimensions during the past quarter century. Technical expertise, interlock, and owners' equity, while still very prominent, have all been somewhat downgraded, though image and management experience have retained their high rankings. The weight given to image, however, is no longer attributable to a single individual. The remaining factors, and particularly broad economic sophistication, have gained in prominence.

Figure 6 shows graphically the contrast between the present Ford Motor Company directorate dimensions and those prevailing a quarter century ago (Figure 5). In particular, there is a noticeable shrinkage in the factors which structure the two top sectors, product acceptance and personal acceptance, the sectors associated with management orientation. This is the control function, primarily concerned with getting the job done effectively and profitably.

The two bottom sectors, peer acceptance and public acceptance, have expanded proportionately. These two components are associated with the prestige orientation hemisphere. It would appear from Figure 6 that those vested with the responsibility for structuring Ford Motor Company's board of directors are today much more concerned with the degree to which each director can improve the company's peer and public acceptance.

The left half of Figure 6 includes product acceptance and peer acceptance. These sectors and their four factors have economic implications, and this half of the graph could be labeled the economic function hemisphere. The right-hand portion of Figure 6, consisting of the personal acceptance and public acceptance sectors, constitutes the social-legal orientation hemisphere.

Directorate dimensions, once set, tend to endure, at least in the short run, though, as the comparison of Figures 5 and 6 shows, drastic changes can occur in these dimensions over a long period. The effects are only partially, or perhaps only quasi-measurable, and the causes are probably even less evident. At Ford Motor Company, the immediate cause for much of the directorate dimension change would seem to be the addition of outside directors to what had been an officer-director-type board. Actually, the Ford board in its earlier years might be viewed as a one-man board. Note in the bottom two lines of Table 11 that technical expertise continues to be supplied entirely by officer directors. The next factor, however, related management experience, is today contributed in part by outside directors; a quarter of a century ago, the company filled this need exclusively from its own talent. The obvious implication is that today's directorate decisions require a type of management experience which Ford's executives alone cannot readily supply. Consequently, this need is met by recruiting directors from outside the company. The third factor, special economic service, has gained in prominence, with the entire increase due to outside directors. Similarly, outside directors have contributed to all the other factors except owners' equity (and, of course, technical expertise). In the owners' equity factor, the adoption of a rather liberal stock-option plan has transformed all of the officer director group into fairly substantial stockholders. However, this move has been nowhere near adequate to compensate for the relative decrease in Ford family stock ownership.

The conversion of horizontal point summations into relative

figures also sheds some light upon the current prominence of out-side directors on the Ford board. Most obviously, expansion of the board from five to seventeen members has resulted in a relative fragmentation of director contribution. In the 1942 board, Henry Ford had *the* dominant position. In the 1968 board, Henry Ford II has the major role but a number of other directors also have a

TABLE 12. Directorate dimension comparison 1942 to 1967: Ford Motor Company

|  | *Percentage* | |
| --- | --- | --- |
|  | 1942 | 1967 |
| *Factor* | | |
| Technical Expertise | 20 | 14 |
| Management Experience | 20 | 19 |
| Special Economic Service | 0 | 7 |
| Broad Economic Sophistication | 6 | 16 |
| Image | 12 | 15 |
| Asset Impact | 0 | 6 |
| Interlock | 21 | 10 |
| Owners' Equity | 21 | 13 |
| *Acceptance* | | |
| Product | 40 | 33 |
| Peer | 6 | 23 |
| Public | 12 | 21 |
| Personal | 42 | 23 |
| *Orientation* | | |
| Management | 82 | 56 |
| Prestige | 18 | 44 |
| *Function* | | |
| Economic | 46 | 56 |
| Legal-Social | 54 | 44 |

significant influence. The horizontal point tabulation, of course, can be debated. For example, it might be contended that Ford's chief executive should be assigned more than 57 points. Or a simple switch in weighting technique from Laplace's criterion of equality in weights to a system of unequal weights could produce a major change. For example, a trebling of the owners' equity and technical expertise factor weights would reduce the composite top-level decision-making and advising impact of the outside-director group from (a theoretical) 31 percent to about 20 percent.

In addition to the obvious changes in the eight corporate dimension factors at Ford during the past quarter century, there have been some accompanying modifications in the resultant sectors (see Table 12). There is, presumably, less preoccupation with product acceptance, although this is still a dominant consideration. Peer acceptance has expanded most noticeably. In this, and in the growth in public acceptance, the Ford Motor Company is simply emulating patterns pioneered and prescribed by other firms. Both of these prestige orientation components have been emphasized by the inclusion on the board of seven well-known outside directors. This shift toward prestige orientation is quite vividly shown in the significant increase (from 18 to 44 percentage points) in the respective sectors during the past quarter century. Keep in mind that this is a relative situation; consequently, a gain in the prestige component must be accompanied by a comparable loss in the management component. Note also that the economic and legal-social functions have been reversed in priority. This is chiefly the consequence of the de-emphasis of interlock and owners' equity.

## Summary

The concept of directorate dimensions rests upon several premises, namely:
1) That there are individual differences among directors in both ability and performance.
2) That these differences can be identified, categorized, and measured. (Point allocation values are given in the Appendix.)
3) That the sums of the factor values, weighted when feasible, are a reasonable index of relative factor significance.
4) That these relative factor values can be so structured that they give a visual presentation of a board's purpose, policies, and philosphy.

## Horizontal tabulation or peerage

These premises are associated with the columnar, or vertical, tabulations. The row, or horizontal, summations of allocated points can be used for a somewhat different purpose. Presumably, the more points an individual receives, the more purposeful is his presence on that board. That is, given a specific corporation's value system, each director's worth to the company is evidenced by his relative ranking. It has been emphasized that in this presentation the Laplacean hypothesis of "equal likelihood" suggests use of equal weights. Consequently, by adjusting factor weights to conform more nearly to prevailing corporate value systems, more representative rankings can be obtained. (Injection of corporate value systems into the analysis would most likely necessitate use of additional factors.)

In theory, including corporate value systems in an analysis of this kind would yield very meaningful and possibly useful information about a company's philosophy and its prime set of values. What little pertinent information is available, however, is generally tainted with public relations propaganda. In most instances there seems to be no authoritative, detailed, and publicly expressed corporate value system which could provide the basis for a legitimate weighting scheme. Therefore, the best that can be ventured under the circumstances is to proceed using the equal weighting technique.

# PEERAGE

In the earlier evolutionary phases of corporate development, one-man control was the rule rather than the exception, and this was a logical concomitant of the transition from individual proprietorship to the corporate form of enterprise. As a consequence, a half century ago almost all boards of directors, even in the larger corporations, tended to be legal fictions rather than purposive, decision-making entities.

When top-level control is centered in one or a very few board members, it is reasonable to assume that the less-than-effective other members of the board will, usually, have minimal directorship stature. This feature, in a limited sort of way, is evident in the horizontal point tabulations in the directorship dimension tableaux of Ford Motor Company (Tables 10 and 11 in the previous chapter). The horizontal figures are summations for each director of the eight factor values, and once again the cautions on interpretation of these figures should be mentioned: the resultant ranking of individual director "importance" on a particular board is for illustration purposes, not for precise measurement.

Part (A) of Figure 7 shows graphically the hypothetical ranking of the five members of the 1942 Ford board (Table 10 provides the basic data). A quarter of a century ago, the Ford directors had 13, 18, 23, 36, and 55 points respectively. Inspection of either the raw data or the graph shows a very obvious skewness. A logical inference can be made from this fact: Henry Ford, the company's founder, was distinctly set apart from the rest of his board, at least on the basis of the eight factors studied.

The particular pattern shown for 1942 is quite typical for

boards which are generally termed "authoritarian." A strong man, sometimes alone and on occasion in consort with a few other highly visible, highly articulate directors, runs the show. The gap between the mean or median point value and the top one or two values is always pronounced. This might be interpreted as indicating that the board consists of at least two levels of importance —a one-man or an oligarchic elite, and a group of "little" men.

There are numerous instances of this authoritarian pattern in modern organizations. If the data in Table 13 in the next chapter, which show Wheeling Steel Corporation's 1966 director-point values, were plotted on a graph, the result would be almost identical with the graphic presentation in Figure 7A. The respective Wheeling Steel values for 1966 were 7, 10, 12, 14, 18, and 39. In this instance, Norton Simon, in typical entrepreneurship fashion, dominated his six-man board. As an interesting sidelight, immediately after Mr. Simon left the Wheeling board early in 1967, the new directors, with "values" of 8, 9, 15, 18, 21, and 27, formed a far less dispersed pattern.

Skewness then, can be viewed as graphic portrayal of preeminence on the part of one or a very few directors. It might also be

FIGURE 7. Ford Motor Co., peerage

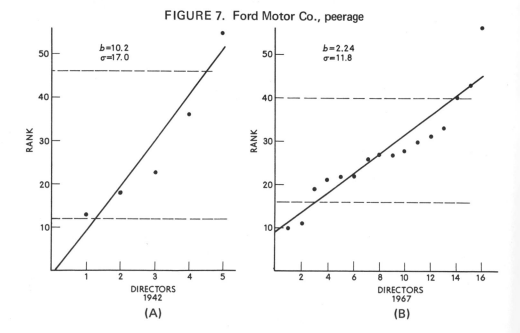

(A)    (B)

considered as a characteristic of a board manifesting strong-leader and authoritarian traits.

In contrast, equalitarian boards are marked by a central tendency of director valuations. While the chief executive will, obviously, be assigned more points because of his position and because he has far more opportunity to develop his stature, this executive gap is far less pronounced than that in authoritarian examples.

In equalitarian boards, even the chief executive tends to deal with peers. This is extremely important for industrial democracy, participative management, and related concepts. If one board member or a few of the board members are so preeminent that they appear to be several social, economic, political, educational, or even technical levels above the rest of the board, joint decision-making is nearly impossible. In meaningful group decision-making, peerage is vital. If it is lacking, the danger of unilateral or authoritarian decision-making is very real, despite surface indications of democratic action.

The preceding comments do not, as might be inferred, apply strictly to the inside-director, outside-director controversy. Most founder-owner-type corporations initially, and for the biblical three-generation span, tend to be authoritarian. At the same time, very many outside directorates are equally authoritarian when the outside directors are of minimal directorate-dimension stature. Even when outside directors are peers of the company's chief executive officer, they can still impart the authoritarian skewness to the graphic portrayal through lackadaisical and ineffective board-room performance. This leads to the obvious suggestion that a ninth analysis factor be added to the present eight, a factor that might be termed "Effective Participation." Unfortunately, under the present scheme of things, it is impossible to gauge such a critical factor.

Central tendency and, by inference, equalitarian and authoritarian manifestations can be measured statistically. The best known index of dispersion around a central point is the standard deviation, $\sigma$. It purports to show to what degree the items in the sample cluster about a midpoint. For our purposes, however, it has more than the usual limitations since the distribution patterns are not normal; the skewness factor complicates precise measurement. Nevertheless, even with this limitation in mind, a calculation of pertinent standard deviations can provide one index of equalitarian-authoritarian trends in boards of directors.

As evidence, contrast the Ford's 1942 board of directors' standard deviation $\sigma = 17.0$ with the comparable 1968 $\sigma = 11.8$. The second value implies a relatively greater clustering and, hence, more semblance of point-equality among directors—an approach to peerage and a greater stress on the democratic process.

Standard Oil Company (N.J.) prior to its recent addition of four nonemployee directors had $\sigma = 5.0$. This value is perhaps the epitome of a democratic-type directorship. It signifies that the probabilities are very high that the members of Standard Oil's board will be approximately equal. There will, of course, be variance due to the fact that the chairman and the president are generally given additional points—at least for image and equity ownership. Then, too, neophyte directors will invariably be a few points shy of average, simply because they are new. There is also another inference in instances of relatively low standard deviations such as the Standard Oil Company (N.J.) 1965 value of $\sigma = 5.0$. As a rule in modern large-scale enterprise, such a low peerage value can be attained only when virtually all board members are assigned high point values. Consequently, if peerage is to prevail, then the company must select men of demonstrated competence and eminence either from its own ranks or from outside the company. Standard Oil Company's addition of four nonemployee directors has modified the pertinent standard deviation so that the current figure is $\sigma = 7.7$. In this respect the company's board now becomes more like Ford Motor Company's board in its authoritarian-equalitarian characteristics. On the basis of this single criterion, it appears that peerage at Standard Oil is still very important but somewhat less so than it was during the period of the entirely employee-director board. In the 1967 top-management reshuffle of Wheeling Steel Corporation, an opposite manifestation is obvious. With Norton Simon holding the dominant position, the 1966 board had a $\sigma = 12.3$. However, the 1967 board structure change resulted in a $\sigma = 7.3$, the consequence of replacing Simon and his nontechnician associates with several men who are technically and managerially conversant with the steel-making business.

Forty years ago (1927), United States Steel Corporation had a board whose members, "point-wise," were quite widely spread.

The 1927 board's standard deviation was about 13.2 but, beginning early in the 1950's, this was narrowed to approximately 9.4. (In this respect, U.S. Steel's board is not too far different from the boards of Ford Motor Company or Standard Oil Company [N.J.].)

Peerage can also be shown by the slope (b) of the hypothetical trend line. In any instance where the slope of this trend line is pronounced, it can be inferred that there is considerable variance among individual directors' rankings. Conversely, when the slope is minimal, near-equality in directors' rankings can be assumed. As an illustration, the Ford Motor Company's 1942 board of directors had a trend line slope of about 10.2. The comparable trend line slope for the 1967 Ford Board (Part B of Figure 7) is only 2.24. Standard Oil Company (N.J.) had a $b = 1.0$ value in 1965 but changed to a $b = 1.4$ value in 1967. The addition of nonemployee directors presumably accounted for this accentuating of the trend-line slope.

Over the past 40 years, U.S. Steel has reduced its trend line slope from $b = 2.8$ (1927) to approximately $b = 1.9$ (1967). While an inspection of Wheeling Steel Corporation's trend-line slope for individual directors' dimensions indicates the same direction of change, the very small sample reduces validity. Wheeling Steel's board under Norton Simon in 1966 had a slope of $b = 5.3$. The spring 1967 change in directors reduced the slope to $b = 3.8$.

The conceptual appropriateness of the statistical measures of standard deviation and trend-line slope to peerage in boards of directors is shown graphically in Figures 8 and 9. It can be inferred that boards whose directors are equal or nearly equal on the basis of the eight supposedly significant directorate dimensions will have:

1) A fairly small standard deviation ($\sigma$), or
2) A fairly low trend-line slope (b) value.

Conversely, boards characterized by a one-man or by an oligarchic control have:

1) A relatively larger standard deviation ($\sigma$), or
2) A relatively bigger trend-line slope (b) value.

In theory, the more vertical the trend line, the greater the degree of authoritarianism. A completely vertical line would mean one-man control. On the other hand, as the trend line levels off horizontally, equalitarian tendencies become more manifest. A strictly horizontal trend line would mean absolute equality of all board members. These extremes are, of course, hypothetical. Neither a horizontal or vertical slope would be practical in our present economic system.

On the basis of available evidence, it appears that during the past 20 to 30 years the slopes of the trend lines of boards of our larger corporations have moved somewhat toward the horizontal.

FIGURE 8. Hypothetical authoritarian board

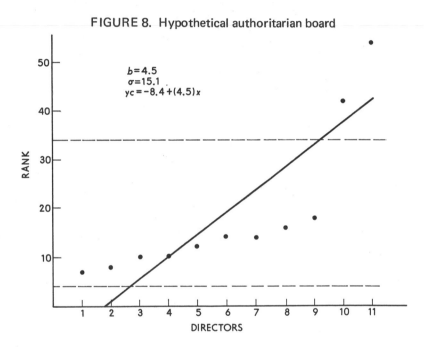

This implies a recognition of the need for peerage and a greater degree of board member equality. In a similar manner, the respective standard deviations have narrowed, but not to as noticeable a degree. One of the reasons for this lag is the increased emphasis on the use of our leading industrialists as outside directors; their managerial expertise, broad economic sophistication, image, asset impact, and interlock ratings tend to be rather high. This means that many of these outsiders rank rather high in the eight factor evaluations. From one point of view, this can be a democratizing force. The chairman or the president of a specific company will be less inclined to be arbitrary in his decisions if his board includes outsiders of eminence who take an active role in corporate affairs. There are, however, some serious questions as to the extent of participation by and involvement of such eminent outside directors.

Another reason for a fairly large standard deviation in some distributions is the lag in the development of first-rate officer directors. Despite what too frequently passes for systematic top-management development in our major corporations, too many of

FIGURE 9. Hypothetical equalitarian board

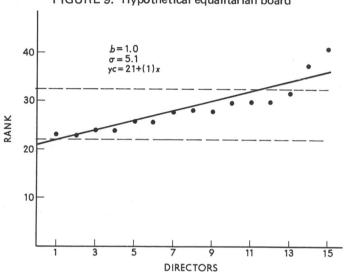

them subscribe to the osmosis theory of executive promotion. There is much substance in the popular belief that certain individuals will move upward no matter what their individual performance. There is, of course, entirely too much reliance on chance in such a fatalistic approach. If our major corporations continue to use high caliber nonemployee directors, then it is imperative that the officer directors on their boards be of equal stature. Lacking this stature, officer directors will degenerate to the level of super-technicians, their function devolving into that of serving solely as technical advisors to the effective corporate control center. In quite a few instances, the corporate control center consists of one person—the chief executive officer. More frequently, control is shared—to an extent—by two or three key officers; and in a number of cases, influential, capable and dedicated nonemployee directors have a meaningful voice. However, the significant point relative to peerage is that in most boards where the control center does not include all or nearly all the members of the board, both the $\sigma$ and slope (b) values tend to be high. To repeat, in order to minimize the dispersion among board members, a concerted effort must be made to increase the directorate dimension values of the officer directors.

There is a practical purpose in this suggestion. Indications show that serious limitations are otherwise imposed upon the availability of high-caliber nonemployee directors. Among the more evident of these limitations are:

1) A feeling on the part of better-informed stockholders that their top officers have a big-enough job to do in running their own company. Participation as outside directors of other companies implies that top officers are not fully occupied in their principal capacities.

2) Outside directorships were at one time honorific, unpaid posts—but this is definitely not the case today. Virtually all outside directors in major corporations currently receive between $5,000 and $10,000 annually as retainer fees. In addition, they are paid from $100 to $500 per meeting of the board or of its special committees. Some outside directors could, depending upon their committee assignments, attend up to 50 or more such board and committee meetings each year. Their total income from these meetings—retainer plus meeting allowances—could thus be between $15,000 and $25,000 per year. Three or four such lucrative appointments could equal an executive's salary. In all fairness, should not such outside earnings be paid to the executive's company and not to the executive serving as an outside director? Is he not otherwise "moonlighting" to the detriment of his own firm?

The increasingly higher pay for outside director services is almost certain to attract negative stockholder and government attention. It would be intriguing to discover the eagerness with which outside directorships would be vied for if there were no cash compensation, and if all indirect payments for special economic services were declared illegal. In all likelihood, much of what we are told is dedication, public-spiritedness, and other, similar altruistic traits would diminish drastically, perhaps to the point of invisibility.

3) Director liability, despite current attempts at providing insurance coverage, will discourage many well-meaning executives from accepting outside directorships. There is a marked increase in "derivative suits," so called because the plaintiff's right to sue is not based upon any alleged wrong done personally to him, but derives from the fact that he is a stockholder in the company he claims has been damaged. By the end of 1965, Westinghouse Electric Corporation had paid out $52,351,000 to settle suits in which customers complained they had been overcharged as a result of the classic electrical industry conspiracy. (It has been estimated that Westinghouse may eventually pay as much as $126 million to settle all of the suits.) As a result of these customer suits, a stockholder suit initiated in 1961 and still unresolved

> charges that top Westinghouse executives either mismanaged the company, if they participated in the price-fixing, or were negligent if they didn't participate but failed to find out about the price-fixing and stop it. In either case, the suit demands that the executives repay to Westinghouse every cent paid out to settle the customers' damage claims.[1]

Even if adequate insurance coverage is provided by a company, many high-caliber executives will be discouraged by the attendant publicity or even notoriety when derivative suits are initiated. Even more ominous is the possibility that the courts will eventually decide that directors as trustees are liable for losses attributable to lack of diligence, lack of interest, or lack of competency on the part of the board or its individual members.

4) The merger movement resulting in the conversion of most surviving major firms into conglomerates will definitely decrease the availability of outside directors. It was difficult enough to avoid allegations of conflict of interest even when companies tended to concentrate activity in one or a very limited number of product lines. It becomes virtually impossible for executives of

1/ *Wall Street Journal,* "Executives in Court," Wayne E. Green, June 29, 1966, p. 1.

conglomerate firms to serve on each other's boards since the odds are that they will compete in one or more areas.

If circumstances militate against the long-run reliance on eminent outside directors to give a board an equalitarian balance, then steps must be taken to insure equally eminent directors from among the company's executive ranks. This is imperative. Otherwise, the trends toward decreasing trend-line slopes (b) and standard deviations ($\sigma$) as expressed graphically, will be reversed. This would be an incongruous development in the current social context where practically every sector of world society is moving in the direction of greater democratization.

The concept of directorate dimensions has its limitations and imperfections. Nevertheless, it is a first attempt at breaching the mystique that hinders our better acquaintance with corporate boards and their directors. Part of this first attempt must be the removal of the halos we usually place above corporate heads. Directors are people, not deities. We cannot assume that elevation to a directorship is accompanied by an instantaneous infusion of knowledge, dedication, and virtue. The act of election to a board in no way changes the new director's competency, personality, or morality, and as a consequence, we must agree that if the board members perform as normal, competent, and diligent human beings, then their group deliberations are subject to all the imperfections of *everyman's* experience in group action. Unanimity in board decisions must be a deliberate hoax, or at least a concerted farce. Our own daily associations with our fellow men show how difficult it is to get unanimous expression. Unanimity, for all practical purposes, can only be the product of oppressive authoritarianism.

The basic principles underlying the directorate dimensions analytical approach are not really new. The use of factors, factor definition, point allocation, and point summation are, for example, fundamental to all merit-rating and job-evaluation techniques. Both merit rating and job evaluation continue to be used in appraising organizational line and staff performance, and here we are appraising people and attributes, imponderables and nonmeasurables. By the same token, directors are proper subjects of study and evaluation. Their individual and group performance can and should be analyzed, measured, and evaluated.

The next section of this book will attempt to show how the concept of directorate dimensions applies in a number of diverse, actual situations, documented cases based upon reporting from such publications as the *Wall Street Journal, Business Week, Fortune, Dun's Review, Forbes,* and *Time.* In particular, the *Wall Street Journal* deserves special mention as being a distinct leader in providing the public with factual and pertinent information on corporate affairs.

The following individual company appraisals, then, are the product of the author's opinion, based upon the best available information. When comparable appraisals are attempted by better-informed individuals closer to the scene of action, then even more valid results will be obtained.

# Part II
ANALYSIS EXAMPLES

# WHEELING STEEL CORPORATION

The tendency is for a corporation to continue a given set of directorate dimensions. This constancy in structure is achieved through fairly rigid board-member selection policies. For the most part, like succeeds like. On occasion, however, this pattern is broken. Wheeling Steel Corporation's experience in the mid-1960's is an example of such a change. Within a three-year period, Wheeling Steel's board had two drastic changes in its dimensions.

Norton Simon, through Hunt Foods and Industries, began acquiring Wheeling Steel stock in 1962. By the end of 1964, Hunt Foods owned 254,706 shares, or 11.8 percent, of Wheeling's outstanding stock. Mr. Simon then assumed the chairmanship of the company. Within a year, he had whittled the sixteen-man board down to a mere seven members, all but two of whom were Hunt Foods' associates. This transformation left Wheeling without a single director with steel-making experience. In addition to ousting the technicians, Simon also deposed a group of directors who had had significant vendor relationships with the company. Foremost among these were the chief officers of Hanna Mining Company and Cleveland-Cliffs Iron Company, both of which are Wheeling Steel's major suppliers. Cleveland-Cliffs also owned 102,432 common shares of Wheeling stock. In addition to deposing the vendor directors, Simon instituted legal proceedings.

Hanna Mining, M. A. Hanna, and Cleveland-Cliffs were accused of conspiring for more than twenty years to monopolize the Great Lakes iron-ore trade and of victimizing Wheeling by artificially maintaining high prices. These were only the most important of the suits Simon filed. Lee C. Paull, Jr., a former Wheeling director and head of a family firm that for over thirty-one years wrote substantially all of the insurance policies for the company, was sued for allegedly overinsuring Wheeling for his own agency's benefit. Also a suit against Blaw-Knox, builder of the troublesome eighty-inch mill that was the central component in the modernization program.[1]

In April, 1965, Simon appointed Robert M. Morris as President and chief executive officer of Wheeling. Mr. Morris was previously vice president and general manager of Monsanto's organic chemical division. At the 1965 annual meeting "when a stockholder asked Mr. Simon if Mr. Morris had any steel experience, the chairman responded, 'He will, very rapidly.' 'Wheeling Steel,' said Mr. Simon, 'is fortunate to have a man with broad business experience and management competence like Mr. Morris to take over the reins at this time, when challenges of new technology and new markets face the steel industry.' "[2]

Obviously, the new board was dominated by Norton Simon. Unfortunately, the new board's performance was, from a profit point of view, quite miserable. Losses in 1965 totaled nearly $5 million on sales of $270 million, and losses in 1966 were even greater, more than $12 million for the two-year period despite record sales.

The first sign of Simon's weakening control at Wheeling Steel was his late 1966 resignation as board chairman and director of the company. Presumably, this was to facilitate a rumored merger with Crucible Steel. Simon had, early in 1966, acquired a substantial position in Crucible Steel, estimated at about 535,000 of the 4,200,000 common shares outstanding. As a consequence, he was invited by Crucible Steel's management to help halt a raid by an insurgent group. Mr. Simon and three of his Hunt Foods' staff were subsequently put on Crucible's twelve-man board of directors.

One of the Simon team named to Crucible's board was Robert M. Morris, president of Wheeling Steel. The other two Simon ap-

1/ *Fortune*, "Antidisestablishmentarianism at Wheeling Steel," Dan Cordtz, July, 1967, p. 133.
2/ *Wall Street Journal*, April 29, 1965, p. 12.

pointees were Jack R. Clumeck, vice chairman of Hunt's finance committee and also a Wheeling director, and Raymond Rich, chairman of McCall's Corporation, in which Hunt Foods has about a 36 percent ownership interest. The interlock of Hunt Foods, Wheeling Steel, and Crucible Steel did not initially give any concern to the participants, the public, or government trust-busters. Early in 1966, "Both Mr. Hunter [Crucible's chief executive] and Mr. Simon stressed there was no conflict in Hunt Foods' stock interest in two major steelmakers. Wheeling produces basic carbon steels, while Crucible specializes in stainless, alloy and tool steels."[3] Meanwhile, Simon received a $100,000 annual salary as Wheeling's chairman plus a $50,000 salary from Crucible Steel. Asked by stockholders at both Crucible's and Wheeling's annual meetings how much time Simon dedicated to these companies, spokesmen for both firms stated "Mr. Simon can do more in 10 minutes than some men can do in 10 years."[4]

One of the strongest reasons for a merger was that "Wheeling, at least according to some steel analysts, might profit from a merger because it would make available to the company management talent at Crucible."[5] At this point, Wheeling Steel's lack of steelmaking expertise and related management experience was very evident by the conspicuous absence of officer representation on its board. Even its chief executive had had no prior association with the steel industry. "Only five of the top fourteen executives had any background in the business."[6]

Less than a year later some doubts seem to have arisen as to the legal feasibility of the merger. "Wheeling [had] already made preliminary inquiries with the Justice Department as to whether interlocking directors would be a hazard to approval of the merger. The answer, obviously, was enough to cause Simon . . . to cut himself out of the board of Wheeling."[7]

In mid-April, 1967, the *Wall Street Journal* reported that Hunt Foods had sold 77,353 shares, or 3.6 percent, of Wheeling's outstanding common stock to Pittsburgh Steel. An equal number of shares was also sold to several Kettering family members. In these

3/ *Wall Street Journal,* Jan. 13, 1966, p. 23.
4/ *Wall Street Journal,* April 29, 1966.
5/ *Wall Street Journal,* Jan. 24, 1966, p. 2.
6/ "Antidisestablishmentarianism at Wheeling Steel," *op. cit.,* p. 133.
7/ *Time,* Dec. 2, 1966, p. 90.

transactions, Hunt Foods lost about $654,000. Hunt's position in Wheeling was thus reduced to 100,000 shares, or about 4.6 percent, of the outstanding stock. Even this block was, in a sense, pledged to Pittsburgh Steel, which received a proxy to vote this stock for five years. Hunt agreed not to acquire any additional Wheeling stock before 1972 and gave Pittsburgh Steel the right of first refusal on Hunt's remaining 100,000 shares. In late December 1967 Hunt Foods sold this block to Pittsburgh Steel for $21.50 a share.

The change in ownership was accompanied by a major change in Wheeling management and directors. Allison R. Maxwell, Jr., president of Pittsburgh Steel was named chairman and chief executive officer and Donald C. Duvall, executive vice president of Pittsburgh Steel, was named president. Both were also put on Wheeling's board. Concurrently, these newly designated Wheeling officials also served in their management and directorate positions at Pittsburgh Steel. Two additional new members included an investment banker representing the Kettering family interests and Paul L. Miller, president of First Boston Corporation, a leading investment banker. Miller's investment firm had taken an active role in financing Wheeling's modernization program. He was also instrumental in interesting the Kettering group in structuring a new management for Wheeling. The four Hunt Foods' representatives vacated their Wheeling Steel board seats. "One Wheeling Steel director called the Hunt Foods' decision 'a constructive thing.' He asked: 'what does a pickle and peach man know about running a steel company'?

"A steel financial analyst added, 'once you dilute Simon's role, things can skate easier.' "[8]

The propelling factor in this sudden switch out of Wheeling Steel seems to have been a mounting pressure from financial interests which were underwriting Wheeling Steel's capital-improvement program totaling $150 million over a three-year period. Surprisingly enough, despite the apprehension of difficulties stemming from the previous interlock, the control situation was practically duplicated. It was conceded that Pittsburgh Steel was

8/ *Wall Street Journal,* April 20, 1967, p. 2.

invited into Wheeling Steel's board room "to provide steel operating knowhow which Wheeling Steel sadly lacks despite Mr. Simon's efforts to woo knowledgeable steel men to the company. . . . The financial interests are said to feel that Mr. Simon has been out of his element in the steel business.

" 'Pittsburgh Steel will definitely bring something to the ball game,' a Wheeling director avers. He says, 'they're not too hot on performance, but they've got good facilities and management.' An analyst remarks, 'Simon hasn't been able to hire a good operating man but Pittsburgh is five or six deep in operating people in some positions.' "[9]

As an interesting sidelight of this illustration, Norton Simon's move out of Wheeling Steel was soon counterbalanced by his deeper involvement in Crucible Steel. By late April, 1967, he had, through Hunt Foods, acquired about 22 percent of Crucible Steel's common stock. This control was evidenced by his appointment of John C. Lobb as president of Crucible Steel. Like his counterpart, Robert Morris, whom Simon had designated president at Wheeling Steel, Lobb had no steelmaking experience. He was formerly executive vice president for the technical industrial products group of International Telephone and Telegraph. The significance of this move is that Mr. Simon still seems convinced that the operating heads of major corporations need have no technical experience prior to appointment to their executive and directorate posts. In theory, of course, it was not Mr. Simon but rather Crucible's board which designated Lobb as the new president and chief executive officer. However, Mr. Hunter, the outgoing chief executive who was now elevated to the board chairmanship, "said the initial talks about getting a new executive officer were 'initially discussed between Hunt and Hunter' and that it wasn't until later that the rest of the Crucible board was brought in. Mr. Hunter added though, that Mr. Lobb 'was essentially my choice' "[10] Mr. Hunter's sentiments and actions are, however, being tested legally. A dissident group of stockholders initiated litigation charging that "Hunt Foods, led by Norton Simon, chairman of Hunt's finance committee, 'only bought its Crucible stock after

9/ *Ibid.*
10/ *Wall Street Journal,* April 27, 1967.

TABLE 13.  Change in Wheeling Steel's directorate dimensions, 1966 to 1967

| Directors | TE | ME | SES | BES | IM | AI | IL | OE | ΣPts. | % |
|---|---|---|---|---|---|---|---|---|---|---|
| *1966* | | | | | | | | | | |
| Norton Simon | 0 | 6 | 5 | 5 | 7 | 3 | 7 | 6 | 39 | 39 |
| R. M. Morris | 0 | 6 | 0 | 3 | 0 | 0 | 5 | 0 | 14 | 14 |
| J. R. Clumeck | 0 | 0 | 0 | 1 | 0 | 1 | 5 | 0 | 7 | 7 |
| Stella Russell | 0 | 2 | 0 | 2 | 0 | 1 | 7 | 0 | 12 | 12 |
| G. L. Levy | 0 | 2 | 6 | 2 | 1 | 2 | 5 | 0 | 18 | 18 |
| M. Chappelear | 0 | 3 | 4 | 2 | 1 | 0 | 0 | 0 | 10 | 10 |
| Σ Factor Pts. | 0 | 19 | 15 | 15 | 9 | 7 | 29 | 6 | 100 | – |
| Factor % | 0 | 19 | 15 | 15 | 9 | 7 | 29 | 6 | – | 100 |
| *1967* | | | | | | | | | | |
| A. R. Maxwell | 7 | 8 | 2 | 3 | 1 | 1 | 5 | 5 | 32 | 27 |
| D. C. Duvall | 7 | 7 | 1 | 2 | 0 | 1 | 5 | 3 | 26 | 21 |
| L. C. McKenna | 0 | 1 | 4 | 1 | 0 | 0 | 0 | 5 | 11 | 9 |
| P. L. Miller | 0 | 6 | 5 | 4 | 3 | 4 | 0 | 0 | 22 | 18 |
| G. L. Levy | 0 | 2 | 6 | 2 | 1 | 2 | 5 | 0 | 18 | 15 |
| M. Chappelear | 0 | 3 | 4 | 2 | 1 | 0 | 0 | 0 | 10 | 8 |
| Σ Factor Pts. | 14 | 27 | 22 | 14 | 6 | 8 | 15 | 13 | 119 | – |
| Factor % | 12 | 23 | 18 | 12 | 5 | 7 | 13 | 11 | – | 100 |

obtaining Crucible President Joel Hunter's illegal agreement to turn over control of Crucible to Hunt Foods.' "[1] The dissidents' suit was first won in Cook County Circuit Court, overruled by the Appellate Court, and late in June, 1967, ruled in favor by the Illinois Supreme Court. Since it seeks to enjoin Hunt Foods and Wheeling Steel from voting any stock owned or controlled by Hunt Foods for the election of directors or the inclusion of Hunt Foods' representatives on Crucible's board, this legal action can be precedent setting.

The changes in directorate dimensions at Wheeling Steel are shown numerically in Table 13. The most significant changes between 1966 and 1967 are the sizable decrease in the interlock factor and the relative stress on the technical expertise factor. Noticeable increases are also posted for owners' equity and management experience. The product acceptance sector has been the prime recipient in this shift in emphasis. The personal acceptance sector, for obvious reasons, has diminished somewhat.

The net effect of the replacement of Hunt Foods by Pittsburgh Steel and other financial interests in the control center on Wheeling Steel's board of directors has been twofold:

11/ *Wall Street Journal,* June 26, 1967.

1) A noticeable shift in the management orientation hemisphere from the personal acceptance to the product acceptance sector.

2) A reemphasis on the economic function hemisphere. Where previously legal-social functions were paramount, now the economic function is.

The structural changes are even more apparent in Figures 10 and 11. In the 1966 presentation, the personal acceptance sector

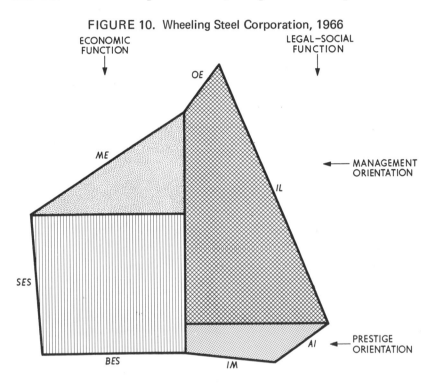

FIGURE 10. Wheeling Steel Corporation, 1966

seems disproportionate. This is not the result of Norton Simon's ownership interest, which, through his Hunt Foods' connection, never exceeded 12 percent, but rather the predilection of the Hunt Foods' group for the interlock factor. In the 1967 graph, Figure 11, both these factors are still important but somewhat less so as compared with 1966.

Technical expertise, virtually nonexistent in the 1966 board, helps reduce the size of that board's product acceptance sector. Adding just two technicians, perhaps even in a part-time capacity, helps expand the 1967 product acceptance sector into dominant size. (Obviously, the graphing of Figure 11 would have to be modified drastically if the Pittsburgh Steel team of Maxwell-Duvall actually performs only in an absentee, figurehead, or part-time capacity at Wheeling Steel.)

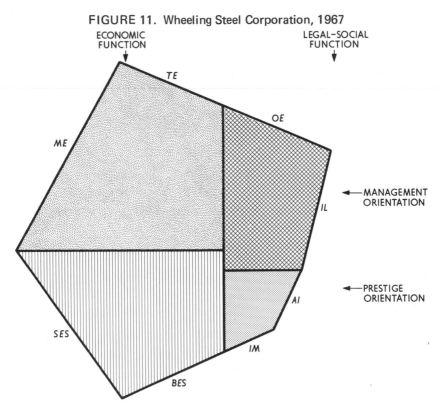

FIGURE 11. Wheeling Steel Corporation, 1967

The most important inference to be drawn from the Wheeling Steel illustration is that the technical expertise and management experience factors are vital directorate dimensions, with their significance particularly evident in times of stress. In a period of relative stability or prosperity, the momentum generated by the corporate body itself is usually sufficient to compensate for a sluggish board of directors. Second-rate leadership is much more noticeable when times are tough. It might be concluded that if an economic enterprise is to remain resilient, it *must* include among its directors a sufficient number of its top personnel to guarantee proper proportions to the vital dimensions of technical expertise and related management experience.

FIGURE 12.  Wheeling Steel Corporation, peerage

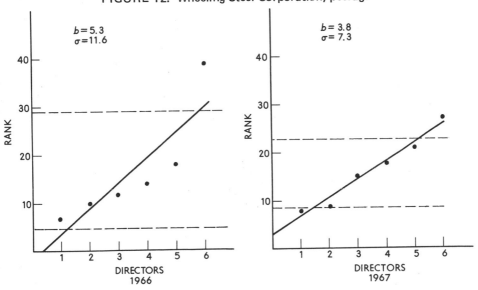

# E. I. DuPONT de NEMOURS AND COMPANY

Almost every excellence rating of major American corporations has E. I. DuPont de Nemours and Company at or near its top. Various reasons are set forth to explain this almost universal recognition of outstanding corporate performance: DuPont's willingness to accept risk, its stress on advanced technology, its superb management development process, its effective use of committees, its remarkable balancing and meshing of authority and responsibility, and particularly its control-chart appraisal technique—all have been singled out as causal factors.

In all likelihood, DuPont influence has been at least partially responsible for the initial momentum at General Motors. Since the two firms' financial and personnel association goes back to 1915, GM's classic concept of decentralization of operations and centralization of staff activities was no doubt at least partly inspired by DuPont's example. In 1921, Mr. Donaldson Brown, then DuPont's treasurer, a director, and a member of its Executive Committee and the Finance Committee, became vice president in charge of finance for, and a director of, General Motors Corporation. Mr. Brown continued to serve on GM's board until 1959, on DuPont's board until his death in 1965. It is not mere coincidence, then, that somewhat similar top-level corporate policies have prevailed in both companies—that both companies have been remarkably successful.

The DuPont control-chart system deserves more attention than it has received. Donaldson Brown "originated the company's chart system of financial control, which is based on the concept of return on investment."[1] The chart system is based on the realistic premise that "a manufacturing enterprise can best measure and judge the effectiveness of its efforts in terms of *return on investment*. The charts are, therefore, designed to place primary emphasis upon this ratio and to permit critical examination of all factors that produce the end result."[2] It is important to note that these "charts are prepared for and are used by the Executive Committee in reviewing with each general manager the results of his department's operations."[3] While a detailed analysis of the chart system's merits and mechanisms is beyond the scope of this presentation, the significant point is that this vital control device is integral to the directorate dimensions which have prevailed at DuPont for perhaps the last half-century.

DuPont's Executive Committee consists entirely of officer directors. It is this group of "technicians" which puts the chart system to such effective use. In DuPont's case, the term "technicians" means that practically every member of its Executive Committee has had university training in chemistry (at least six of its officer directors hold doctoral degrees in chemistry or related areas). This stress on the technical competency of its board's executive committee is extremely important..

The Executive Committee has over-all responsibility for the operating affairs of the company. In addition to formulating policy as a committee, its members act individually as advisers in various fields, such as sales, research, personnel, etc. They have no administrative duties in connection with departmental operations, however, and thus are free to give their time and effort to the business of the company as a corporate unit. The chairman of the Executive Committee is the president of the company and the other members are vice presidents; its regular meetings are held each Wednesday.[4]

1/ *DuPont Annual Report,* 1965, p. 31.
2/ *Executive Committee Control Charts,* E. I. DuPont de Nemours and Company, Wilmington, Del., Fourth Printing, p. 7.
3/ *Ibid.,* p. 5.
4/ *Ibid.,* p. 3.

Careful consideration of DuPont's Executive Committee's functions indicates that it is this group of nine officer directors which actually manages the company.

While the Executive Committee, its chart system, and similar controls are important, other very significant forces should not be overlooked. At DuPont there is a fairly active Finance Committee which meets twice monthly. This group "exercises jurisdiction over the company's financial affairs, including final approval of major expenditures and commitments for new facilities and other purposes."[5] This Finance Committee consists of seven DuPont family members, a banker, and one company vice president. This committee's work seems to be fundamental to the remarkably successful checks-and-balances system which has helped elevate DuPont to the pinnacle of excellence. This delicate checks-and-balances-system results in what seems to be an inordinately large board of directors. Currently there are 28 members on DuPont's board. These directors can be placed, with some overlapping, into three categories. There are 10 officer directors, of whom 2 are DuPont family members. There are 12 former officers, of whom 4 are DuPont family members. In addition, there are five other directors who are DuPont family members. The board includes only one person who might, by stretching the imagination, be classified as an outsider.

This tripartite division of officers, former officers, and family members gives DuPont a most effective top policy-making level. For example, the dominance of the Finance Committee by the DuPont family provides an invaluable overseeing by interested owners, while the heavy concentration of top-caliber technicians in the Executive Committee gives the company the necessary technical expertise and managerial acumen. The third major component of the board, the 12 former officers, constitutes an informal advisory board.

This structuring manifests itself in terms of directorate dimensions in the relatively large product acceptance and personal acceptance sectors. The stress on technical competency—and, hence, on product acceptance—is evident in the educational backgrounds of the directors. A majority of DuPont's directors have under-

5/ *Ibid.,* p. 3.

graduate degrees in technical areas, with Massachusetts Institute of Technology by far the leading single academic contributor of technical talent to the board.

The personal acceptance sector is exceptionally visible at Du-Pont because both the owners' equity and interlock factors are prominent there. The company has for some time stressed executive participation in ownership through a very acceptable stock-option program. This program, coupled with the large DuPont

FIGURE 13. E. I. DuPont de Nemours, 1968

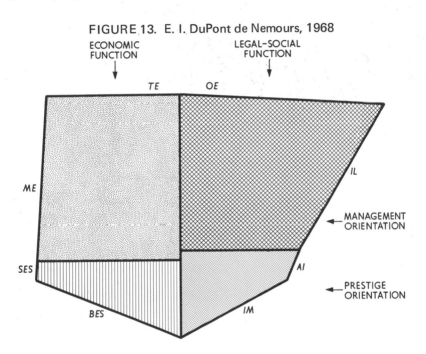

family holdings, results in a very noticeable extension of the owners' equity line in Figure 13. The aggregate direct ownership by board members is nearly 600,000 common stock shares plus 1,500,000 shares of Christiana Securities. In addition, eleven members of the board with DuPont family affiliation are stock-owner "associates," as defined by regulations of the Securities and Exchange Commission. Together with other individual and corporate "associates" this group owns an additional 550,000 shares of Christiana Securities Company common stock. Conservatively estimated, considering stock market fluctuations, DuPont's directors, as a group, have in the neighborhood of about $1 billion invested in their company. Even the Ford Motor Company's director holdings do not match this pattern. The three Ford family member-directors personally hold about 5 million shares of Ford common stock, together with another 3 million shares held by their immediate families. The other Ford directors own about 400,000 shares. The market value of the combined Ford director holdings could be estimated at about $450 to $500 million.

The interlock factor is quite prominent at DuPont, but almost all of this effect is a consequence of the family interlock. Actually, there is very little interlock in the sense that two or more DuPont directors have directorate contact on other company boards. Congressman Celler's subcommittee report on "Interlocks in Corporate Management" notes that "the management of DuPont was interlocked with managements of relatively few other corporations. . . . Multiple interlocks included six with the Wilmington Trust Company and six with Christiana Securities Co., the holding company for the DuPont interests."[6]

The expanded product acceptance and personal acceptance sectors shown in Figure 13 result in a very noticeable emphasis on management orientation. If any one factor is to be singled out as being most responsible for DuPont's remarkable performance record, it probably should be its stress on management orientation. Most of its directors seem to be completely, wholly, and entirely dedicated to the affairs of the company. This is particularly true of the Executive Committee which, for all practical purposes, runs the company.

The relative insignificance of the peer acceptance and public acceptance sectors at DuPont is obvious both in Figure 13's graph and in the low associated numerical values. This should not be interpreted as lack of awareness on the part of the DuPont board of the importance of these sectors. These two areas do not figure prominently in the graph because of the almost incidental impact of special economic service and asset impact as factors in director selection. The other two factors, broad economic sophistication and image, are not much smaller, in graphic presentation, than comparable values in other major organizations. On the surface,

6/ *Interlock in Corporate Management.* A staff report, Antitrust Subcommittee, Committee of the Judiciary House of Representatives, March 12, 1965, p. 134.

however, it appears that DuPont is far more inclined toward management orientation than toward prestige orientation.

Neither should the almost equal size of the economic function and legal-social function hemispheres be misinterpreted. The significant stress placed upon the components of the product acceptance and the personal acceptance sectors results in these heavy proportions. Incidentally, this is a concomitant of the tripartite structuring of the board. It reinforces the contention that control

FIGURE 14. DuPont, peerage

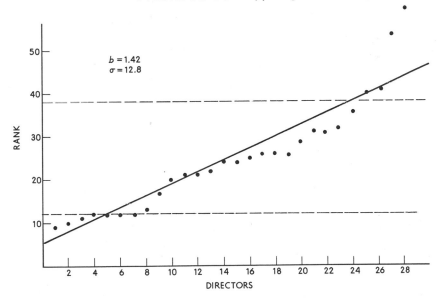

at DuPont is shared by (1) a group of very competent and active managers who keep the company technologically and competitively alert; (2) a group of major owners who keep an eye on not only their own financial stake but on that of every investor in the company; (3) a group of retired "senior citizens" who through long service have demonstrated their competency and loyalty.

As is evident in Figure 14, on an authoritarian-equalitarian basis, DuPont cannot be classified at either extreme. While the slope of the trend line (b = 1.42) would seem to indicate a recognition of peerage, the rather large standard deviation ($\sigma = 12.8$) nullifies such an inference. The reason once again can be found in the tripartite structuring of DuPont's board. The nine lowest-ranked members of the board are nonfamily former officers. Their present "worth" to the board, on the basis of the 8-factor evaluation, is minimal, which tends to increase the standard deviation. The point allocations given to DuPont family members for interlock and owners' equity tend to exaggerate these members' roles. It is partially for this reason that two members of the board have been assigned the disproportionately high point values of 54 and 60. (This also extends the standard deviation and accentuates the slope of the trend line.)

In summary, it might be inferred that DuPont's formula for success is at least partially discernible in the directorate dimensions graph of Figure 13. However, there is probably less authoritarian control than the heavy incidence of DuPont family participation would imply. The strong emphasis on product acceptance in Figure 13 indicates that the board is intimately concerned with running the affairs of the company, and the expanded personal acceptance sector means that interested owners are keeping a constant vigilance over management. The minimal stress on special economic service and asset impact would seem to indicate that DuPont's board considers prestige matters almost incidental.

While in a number of respects DuPont's directorate dimensions resemble those that typify the entrepreneur-owner-family form of top-level decision making, there are in its dimensions a number of significant differences. For instance, there is no single dominant owner, despite the incidence of DuPonts. Ownership on a large scale has been extended to nonfamily top officers through stock-option plans. Only one DuPont participates in the vitally important Executive Committee. Most of the officer-directors rank fairly high on the 8-factor evaluation. These and other forces give some semblance of equalitarian structure to DuPont and a reasonable degree of peerage which was (and is) almost never found in the old-style entrepreneur-owner type of board. All things considered, DuPont seems to provide a directorate model worthy of emulation.

# UNION CARBIDE CORPORATION

The second largest chemical company in the country, Union Carbide, provides an illustration of a company that might be termed an antithesis to DuPont. In its origin, the present Union Carbide was an amalgamation of five small companies. In 1917, a group of midwest utility men, led by the wealthy Cornelius Billings, put the company together and in the process gave both it and its board of directors some long-enduring characteristics. In its earliest structuring, board membership was preponderantly from the financial community. At one time the board included seven bankers, two lawyers, one industrialist and three company officers. The company continues to have considerable outside representation on its board. At present, there are four officers, one retired officer and six outsiders serving as directors. At times, the inside-outside director balance has swerved to as much as a 2 to 11 ratio.

Since World War II, Union Carbide's performance has been significantly outdistanced not only by DuPont but also by quite a number of other major companies in its industrial area—Monsanto and Dow, for example. In the past 11 years, DuPont—despite the court-ordered divestiture of its significant General Motors' holdings—has managed to stay in the number 12 spot among American corporations in terms of sales volume dropping to number 13 only in 1968, but Union Carbide during this same period has dropped from number 22 to number 25 in ranking. (Monsanto moved from 87 to 41 and Dow improved from 77 to 53.) There are, undoubtedly, many explanations for Union Carbide's relatively poor performance not only in sales volume but also in earnings. The focus in this analysis is on the role of the board of directors in its capacity as the prime decision maker.

137

As one consequence of its origin, Union Carbide's operating components have had considerable autonomy, resulting in very little central direction, with consequent diversity in objectives and practices.

> There was a corporate operating committee, but it did little except review proposed capital outlays; and it consisted mainly of division presidents, who, although they spent much of their time competing for capital funds, rarely criticized one another's programs in a relevant way. So the operating committee didn't really operate at all; it was essentially a group that reported what was going on. The parent company was as obscure as if it had been headquartered in London, and even in Wall Street nobody knew much about it.[1]

The process of integrating divisional interests and coordinating endeavors proceeded rather slowly. Much of the credit for change belongs to Birny Mason, Jr., current chairman of the company, although the corrective moves were initiated under Morse Dial's chairmanship.

Union Carbide's General Operating Committee, formerly known as the Capital Projects Committee, now has prime responsibility for operational matters. The group consists of four group vice presidents, two executive vice presidents, and two vice presidents serving as treasurer and secretary. A Financial Operating Committee consisting of the treasurer, controller, and two other vice presidents controls financial matters.

As in so many companies with predominantly outside director representation, Union Carbide's Executive Committee is a vestigial remnant. Its five members, including the president, former chairman, and three outside directors, have practically no meetings, and no meaningful impact on the company's operation. The inability of outside directors to meet frequently and to discuss semi-technical issues in depth makes such an executive-committee structure an anomaly. Perhaps in recognition of this serious imperfection, Union Carbide has quite recently embarked upon an important top-level restructuring. The chairman, president, and two executive vice presidents have been designated as the "President's Of-

---

1/ *Fortune,* "Union Carbide's Patient Schemers," Gilbert Burck, Dec., 1965, p. 148.

fice." The functions of the four men are substantially the same. They constitute a quadrumvirate in which Mason is first among his peers.

> This collective top-management arrangement, which is being adopted by other corporations here and abroad, is in part a recognition of the fact that the boss of any worldwide and diversified organization, in an era of change-by-technology, needs more and more help. But at Union Carbide the concept of the President's Office is more than an attempt to make life easier for its top executive. The corporation has adopted the principle, to a degree practically unique in U.S. business, that management decisions can usually be made better by working groups with diverse views and experience than by individuals.[2]

Without disparaging the concept of the President's Office, it must be stressed that this gesture might be "too little and too late." Union Carbide, like its counterparts experimenting with the "President's Office," has for a very long time had an equally effective mechanism available for use—this is the Executive Committee. Unfortunately, in too many outside-type directorates, the function of the Executive Committee has been reduced to nothingness by the inclusion of outside directors. Structuring the Executive Committee as a miniature board of directors rigidly constricts its utility. There is a vivid contrast between Union Carbide's and DuPont's Executive Committees. At DuPont, the nine-man, all-officer director Executive Committee meets frequently, makes the meaningful decisions, and runs the show. Only at this fairly late date does Union Carbide seem to have recognized the vital need for just this sort of top-level decision-making group.

The contrast between Union Carbide and DuPont is even more vividly seen in their respective directorate-dimension graphs (cf. Figures 13 and 15). Table 14 shows the approximate extent to which the board of directors of these two companies differ in their pertinent dimensions.

The prime differences between these two leading chemical companies seem to lie in just four of the eight factors. DuPont stresses

2/ *Ibid.*, p. 147.

technical expertise and owners' equity, while Union Carbide looks for special economic service and asset impact in its directors. While DuPont directors include ten officers and twelve former officers, Union Carbide has only four officer directors and one former officer serving as a director. While DuPont directors have a financial stake of about $1 billion in the company, Union Carbide directors as a group own less than 150,000 shares with a market

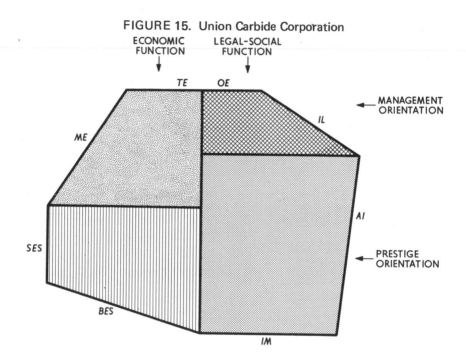

FIGURE 15. Union Carbide Corporation

value of less than $10 million. DuPont puts practically no emphasis on either special economic service or asset impact, while Union Carbide rates these factors as being quite important.

A number of other features deserve comment. Note from Table 14 that DuPont attains practically the same level of broad economic sophistication as Union Carbide, and DuPont relies entirely upon its own executives, former officers, and owners. As a consequence of this limitation, the DuPont board's image factor tends to be somewhat, but not seriously, minimized. Although both companies put a fairly equal stress on interlock, there is a very significant difference in the impact of this factor. At DuPont, interlock rates high because of the very large representation of family members on the board and because of Wilmington Trust and Christiana Securities tie-ins. There are no interlocks in the more conventional sense. At Union Carbide there are at least eight obvious interlocks involving every one of the six outside directors, including a member of the legal firm which acts as Union Carbide's

TABLE 14. Comparison: Union Carbide and Du-Pont

| | Union Carbide | DuPont |
|---|---|---|
| *Factor* | | |
| Technical Expertise | 8 | 14 |
| Management Experience | 15 | 17 |
| Special Economic Service | 9 | 2 |
| Broad Economic Sophistication | 17 | 16 |
| Image | 14 | 11 |
| Asset Impact | 18 | 2 |
| Interlock | 12 | 15 |
| Owners' Equity | 6 | 23 |
| | | |
| *Acceptance* | | |
| Product | 23 | 31 |
| Peer | 26 | 18 |
| Public | 32 | 13 |
| Personal | 18 | 38 |
| | | |
| *Orientation* | | |
| Management | 41 | 69 |
| Prestige | 58 | 31 |
| | | |
| *Function* | | |
| Economic | 49 | 49 |
| Legal-Social | 50 | 51 |

legal counsel. This last relationship results in substantial annual payments by the company to that director's firm; in 1967, this payment was $172,500.

The difference in factor emphasis is, of course, reflected in the acceptance sectors. DuPont is concerned with product and personal acceptance, while Union Carbide concentrates on peer and public acceptance. These differences in boards of directors' dimensions have, undoubtedly, affected corporate philosophy and performance.

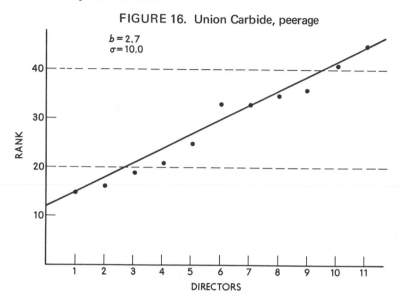

FIGURE 16.  Union Carbide, peerage

The contrast is equally evident in the orientations of both companies. DuPont is control- and management-oriented, while Union Carbide is far more directed toward image and prestige in its directorate structuring. In the interpretation of the functions, it is important to note that despite equal numerical values there are major differences between the companies. At DuPont the major stress within the economic function comes from technical expertise. In contrast, Union Carbide attains the same level of economic function as DuPont by emphasizing peer acceptance. There is an even greater disparity in the legal-social function, with DuPont placing greater reliance upon personal acceptance, Union Carbide on public acceptance.

Compared on an authoritarian-equalitarian basis, there is not much difference between the two boards. Union Carbide has a much greater trend-line slope ($b$ = 2.7 as contrasted with DuPont's $b$ = 1.4). However, Union Carbide's standard deviation, $\sigma$ = 10.0, indicates a greater degree of clustering when compared with DuPont's standard deviation of $\sigma$ = 12.8. It must be emphasized that this last item of analysis pertains strictly to the companies' present boards of directors and not necessarily to the rest of their organizations or to earlier boards.

Emulation in corporate structure and particularly in boards of directors can be a very dangerous practice. Since hereditary and environmental differences cannot be ignored, it would be imprudent to recommend that Union Carbide remodel its board on the DuPont model. On the other hand, some attention should probably be given to the more prominent factor differences. For example, questions should be asked about the real value of asset impact and special economic service factors as board membership criteria. At Union Carbide there seems to be evidence that a serious reappraisal is in progress. The "President's Office" is one manifestation of such rethinking on the role of directors.

# GENERAL ANILINE AND
# FILM CORPORATION

There are those who say that the public interest would be best served by having governmental agencies designate some or all the outside directors. American industry has had very little experience with this approach although some states do impose restrictions on the composition of bank or insurance company boards. For example New York's Banking Law, Section 7001 (4) states, "No more than one-third of the directors of any bank or trust company with a capital stock of two million dollars or more, or of any industrial bank, shall be active officers or employees of the corporation." New Jersey law provides for state-designated members serving on mutual life insurance company boards. Prudential Life Insurance has six such "public" representatives.

Quite recently the U.S. Senate passed a bill to establish a non-commercial public television system. This bill would allow, "Federal chartering of a corporation for public broadcasting, headed by 15 directors. The President [of the United States] would pick nine of the directors, who in turn would choose the other six."[1] Even at this early, planning stage there was concern as to how a public television corporation could be insulated from political pressures. ". . . Discussion showed that directors of a public broadcasting corporation might have to watch their step politically. Conservative Sen. Thurmond (S.C.) said he opposed the bill . . . and warned

1/ *Wall Street Journal,* May 18, 1967.

that the corporation could be 'captured by a small clique with ideological bias.' "[2]

There are instances abroad of government participation in board-room deliberation, for example, Great Britain's coal and steel industries. Great Britain's steel industry was first nationalized after World War II and then, in 1953, returned to private ownership. It was nationalized again in 1967. The new government-owned National Steel Corporation includes 14 companies accounting for 90 percent of Britain's steel production. The entire industry is "divided into four or five regional boards, in which the *workers* will have a voice. As many as 3 of the 14 to 16 directors of each board will be drawn from the ranks of shop employees, technicians or middle management."[3] The remainder of each board will presumably consist of a few top executives, some public figures, and a majority of career politicians. These unconventional boards will run a 24-million long-ton, $3.5 billion industry.

Germany's continued experiment with codetermination is another well-known example. In this instance, German law provides for a tripartite structuring of certain boards. In a typical eleven-man board, for example, five directors would be selected by the stockholders, five would be named by the union, and the eleventh director would be chosen by the other ten.

One of the best U.S. illustrations of the government running an industrial company through its appointed directors occurred at General Aniline and Film Corporation between 1942 and 1965. This company was incorporated in 1929 under the sponsorship of I. G. Farbenindustrie Aktiengesellschaft, one of the world's largest chemical companies. In 1942, with the United States at war with Germany,

> the [U.S.] Secretary of the Treasury, under an Executive Order delegating authority to the President of the United States under the Trading With the Enemy Act, determined that 459,448 Common A and 2,050,000 Common B shares of the company were the property of nationals of a foreign country. As designated in Executive Order No. 8389 these

2/ *Ibid.*
3/ *Business Week,* May 6, 1967, p. 68.

shares were declared to be vested in the Secretary of the Treasury, to be held, used, administered, liquidated, sold or otherwise dealt with in the interest of and for the benefit of the United States.[4]

On April 24, these shares were transferred to the Alien Property Custodian. On October 14, 1945, they were again transferred, this time to the Attorney General of the United States. These two blocks of stock represented a 98 percent controlling interest in the company. In the years following seizure, there were a number of legal maneuvers by the supposed former owners to regain title to the stock. In March, 1965, the U.S. government divested itself of the stock through public sale. Sale of the seized stock, converted into 11,166,438 new shares, was handled by a syndicate headed by First Boston Corporation and Blyth and Company. The Federal Government received nearly $330 million in this sale. At present there are in excess of 100,000 owners of the company's stock.

In the 23 years during which government-appointed directors ran the company, there was an amazing turnover of both chief executives and directors—eight chief executives during this period and more than 60 directors. Tenure averaged around five years per director and chief executive.

The "instant" director turnover is evident in the following spot check of directors:

| Year | Officer | Outside | Carried over from prior board |
|------|---------|---------|-------------------------------|
| 1950 | 2 | 14 | 0 |
| 1955 | 4 | 12 | 2 |
| 1960 | 3 | 13 | 1 |
| 1967 | 5 | 12 | 1 |

In other words, within each of the 5-year periods, there was a virtual turnover of the whole board of General Aniline. This was the consequence of partisan politics. Both the Republican and Democratic parties used appointment to the company board room as a reward for political services. (Initially, under the Truman administration there was even a battle between two bureaus of the government for control of the board.) After the Eisenhower ad-

4/ *Moody's Industrial Manual, 1967,* p. 1971.

ministration's continued practice of patronage, the final political structuring of the board occurred in 1961 under the Kennedy administration. The Democrats ousted every nonemployee director and replaced them almost entirely with politically loyal individuals. From a directorate dimension point of view, there was little rationale, on the 8-factor basis, for selecting these particular individuals. "Ross D. Siragusa was an old friend of Joe Kennedy's and William Peyton Marin was the principal lawyer of the Kennedy enterprises. One of the new directors was a prominent Democratic lawyer [Charles F. Preusse] ; another was a prominent judge [Albert Conway] ; two were prominent Democratic fund raisers [Snyder and banker Thomas J. Shanahan]."[5] In addition to having its board stacked with political friends of the party in office, General Aniline also permitted political considerations to affect its choice of executives, outside counsel, auditors, and advertising firms.

This experiment with "public" directors running an enterprise proved to be a dismal failure. Despite gains in both sales and net income during government operation, General Aniline lagged far behind its chief competitors. The extent of the lag is brought out in a comparison with Dow Chemical and Monsanto.

In 1942, the three concerns were quite comparable. Between 1942 and 1965 General Aniline's sales grew by approximately 400 percent, its net income by 220 percent. But in the same period, Dow Chemical expanded sales by 1400 percent, net income by 1100 percent. Even more striking was Monsanto's remarkable growth: over 2000 percent in sales and 2300 percent in net income. There seems to be no defense or justification for General Aniline's comparative crawl while two other chemical manufacturers were making such tremendous progress.

|  | *1942* | | | *1965* | | |
|---|---|---|---|---|---|---|
|  | *Sales (millions)* | *Net income (millions)* | *Em-ployees* | *Sales (millions)* | *Net income (millions)* | *Em-ployees* |
| General Aniline | $43 | $4 | 8,200 | $ 215 | $ 13 | 8,140 |
| Dow | 78 | 9 | 14,000 | 1,176 | 108 | 33,800 |
| Monsanto | 69 | 5 | 18,600 | 1,468 | 123 | 56,200 |

5/ *Fortune,* "General Aniline Goes Private," Irwin Ross, Sept., 1963, p. 129.

The indictment is even more severe when it becomes known that the government-appointed directors inherited "a vast stock of patents (perhaps 3,900 in all), and these enabled the new managers to maintain their competitive position and even to expand to a degree. At the present time, General Aniline has a portfolio of about 1,500 U.S. patents."[6]

As partial explanation, *Fortune* comments,

> The board members were often ill-acquainted with the chemical industry, and tended to feel that conserving the assets the Attorney General had temporarily entrusted to them was their main responsibility. Back in 1953, President Jack Frye confessed to a senatorial committee, "One of the problems of this company is that, due to the ownership situation, the management, the boards of directors, and all concerned are extremely cautious about making expenditures. In trying to avoid mistakes, they actually move more slowly than do their competitors."[7]

FIGURE 17.  General Aniline and Film, 1942 to 1965 (Composite)

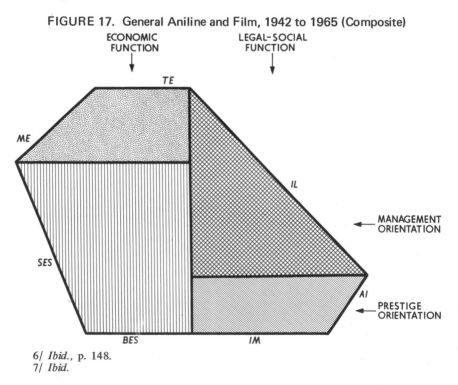

6/ *Ibid.*, p. 148.
7/ *Ibid.*

As in all such instances, credit or blame must ultimately be placed with the company's board of directors. Long-run corporate success is inextricably linked to the character of the board. The board's character, in turn, is determined by the caliber of its members and leaders. General Aniline's unique 1942 to 1965 board structure is shown graphically in Figure 17. Product acceptance

TABLE 15. General Aniline and Film Corporation, 1942 to 1965, 1967

|  | 1942 to 1965 | 1967 |
|---|---|---|
| *Factor* | | |
| Technical Expertise | 10 | 13 |
| Management Experience | 10 | 18 |
| Special Economic Service | 20 | 17 |
| Broad Economic Sophistication | 11 | 16 |
| Image | 14 | 12 |
| Asset Impact | 6 | 6 |
| Interlock | 29 | 12 |
| Owners' Equity | 0 | 6 |
| | | |
| *Acceptance* | | |
| Product | 20 | 31 |
| Peer | 31 | 33 |
| Public | 20 | 18 |
| Personal | 29 | 18 |
| | | |
| *Orientation* | | |
| Management | 49 | 49 |
| Prestige | 51 | 51 |
| | | |
| *Function* | | |
| Economic | 51 | 64 |
| Legal-Social | 49 | 36 |

was obviously not a paramount consideration. In most modern outside-type directorates, while the technical expertise lines tend to be short, management experience is generally important. Recognition of this latter factor is manifest in the increasing emphasis being placed on top corporate executives being selected as outside directors. At General Aniline, however, there were seldom more than two or three well-known businessmen on the board at any one time. The emphasis was on second- or third-echelon political figures. As a consequence, the corporate dimensions indicate an emphasis on special economic service and interlock. This results in exaggerated peer acceptance and personal acceptance sectors. The heavy stress on SES is a consequence of political and economic reciprocity. Interlock is excessively large because of the significance of political affiliation as a prerequisite for board membership. In this context, interlock at General Aniline is in marked contrast to the type of interlock found in so many other enterprises run by outside directors. The complete absence of owners' equity in the graphic presentation of Figure 17 results from the 98 percent government ownership.

Contrary to expectation, there was fairly little emphasis on public acceptance at General Aniline. Selection of politicians and political friends did not lead to the use of many publicly known and influential people as General Aniline directors.

Subsequent to the public sale of the government's 98 percent stock holdings, the board has been somewhat reconstituted. The relative shift in factor emphasis is apparent in both Table 15 and in a comparison of Figure 17 with Figure 18. Note that in the

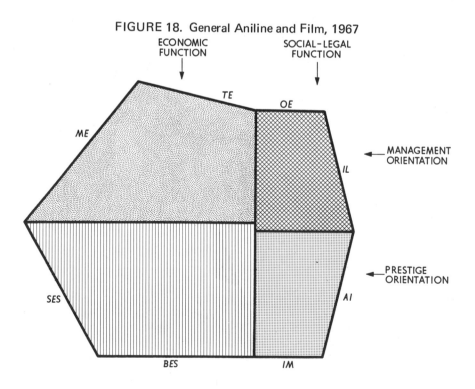

FIGURE 18.  General Aniline and Film, 1967

new, 1967 board, more emphasis is placed on management experience and broad economic sophistication. Interlock in the political context has been significantly reduced. While special economic service has also declined, the change is relatively minor. Probably the most obvious consequence has been the increased emphasis in the new board on product acceptance.

It is probably not possible—or it is at least premature—to conclude that any given set of directorate dimensions is optimal. Nevertheless, it is impossible to ignore the fact that the government-appointed boards at General Aniline were the epitome of ineffectiveness. Consequently, the conclusion might be drawn that the role of the federal government in appointing directors in business enterprises should be minimized—at least until more, and more favorable, evidence is available. To conclude this is not in any way to deny government's legitimate function as a referee on the business scene. It would, however, seem to rule out the government's exercising its public defender's role to the extent of influencing or even passing upon the selection of individual directors in the private sector of our economy.

# GREAT ATLANTIC AND PACIFIC TEA COMPANY

Institutional investors—including foundations and pension funds—are potentially *the* most significant force pertinent to directorate structuring and corporate control. To date, however, most foundations and pension funds have been passive participants in boardroom proceedings. There are, of course, some exceptions, most of them being foundations set up by company founders—entrepreneurs with the specific objective of keeping corporate control in the founding family through the mechanism of the foundation. In a number of these instances, the foundation, while owning a significant portion of the company's stock, has no real voting power. For example, the Ford Foundation in early 1967 owned 38,916,666 shares of Class A, nonvoting stock of the Ford Motor Company. While this block of stock has been considerably whittled down from the Foundation's initial endowment, it still represents approximately a $2 billion equity in Ford Motor Company. But this ownership interest has no official say, through voting privileges, in Ford Company policy making, even though several of the Foundation's trustees, including Benson Ford and Henry Ford II, are also company directors. (There is, then, an indirect influence exerted by the Foundation upon the corporation and, presumably, the Foundation's equity interests are quite diligently guarded.)

This relative noninterference in company affairs by a Foundation which is a major stockholder appears to be the rule. Direct ac-

152

tion to protect the major stockholders' interests occurs only when the company's future seems to be in jeopardy.

Developments at the Great Atlantic and Pacific Tea Company within the past few years corroborate this thesis. The John A. Hartford Foundation, set up in the early 1950's to engage in medical research, currently owns 8,360,850 A&P shares, or 33.69 percent of the outstanding stock. (This ownership position has decreased somewhat from the Foundation's original 40 percent of the company's stock.) The Foundation was set up through bequests from two of the founder's sons, John A. and George L. Hartford. George H. Hartford, the company's founder, died in 1917 and left each of his five children equal shares in the company's stock. All stock was put into a trust, however, and the power to vote it was vested in John A. and George L. Hartford. From 1917 to 1951 the brothers ran the company almost in the manner of a partnership, but after John's death in 1951, the control pattern began to change markedly and the board of directors, previously a legal figment, began to take a more active role. This change in top-level structure and function was accentuated further after 1957 when George L. Hartford died.

With the death of George L. Hartford, the voting trust set up by the founder came to an end. At this point the Foundation had a 40 percent ownership interest; most of the remainder of the stock was owned by ten Hartford heirs. The heirs' interest was soon decreased through public offerings so that at the present time members of the family own less than one fourth of the company's stock. Meanwhile, the Foundation's voting power was given to Ralph W. Burger, a long-time confidant of the brothers, John and George. Mr. Burger had for many years served as the company's secretary. Ultimately he became its chief executive and chairman. He resigned these official posts in 1963 but continued as head of the John A. Hartford Foundation.

With the dissolution of the voting trust in 1957, significant changes were made in the directorate structure. "There never has been an open fight between the family and Ralph Burger for control, but the heirs have been badgering and pushing Burger on a number of issues. Early in the game [1958] the heirs succeeded in enlarging the board with six outside directors. Fourteen members drawn from the company's management made up the rest of the board."[1]

In 1963, the company announced, "that the board had been expanded from 20 to 25 members, and that all five new ones come from outside the company. . . . Three of the new directors represent members of the Hartford family."[2]

Evidently changing the board structure did not placate all the Hartford heirs. In particular, George Huntington Hartford II, who in 1958 owned about 10 percent of the company's stock, continued to be interested in further changes in the board's composition and policies, though on the occasions when he had been nominated to board membership, he was resoundingly defeated. In the 1966 meeting a stockholder nominating Mr. Hartford stated, "He deserves a place on the board more than the five lawyers we have now."[3]

A subsequent attempt to elect him to the board was made at the 1967 annual meeting, ". . . the first A&P annual meeting George Huntington Hartford II ever attended."[4] At this session Mr. Hartford contended that David Sher, an attorney who represented his interests on the board, had been asked to resign. This contention was vigorously denied by the board chairman, Melvin W. Alldredge, who stated, "I was told that Mr. Sher was not standing for re-election, that's all I know."[5] While Mr. Sher was *not* one of the management nominees for re-election in 1967, Mr. Hartford *was* duly nominated for a board seat. Although at that time he owned 78,281 shares and was trustee for another 39,479 shares, he received only 65,074 votes in the balloting. The 17 management-designated nominees each received a minimum of 20,450,-890 votes.

In a postmeeting comment, Mr. Hartford,

> objected to a situation whereby a "foundation controls this company." His reference was to John A. Hartford Foundation Inc., which owns 8,360,850 A&P shares, or 33.69 percent of the company's outstanding common.

1/ *Fortune,* "Pinch 500,000,000,000 Pennies," March, 1963, p. 106.
2/ *Business Week,* March 28, 1963.
3/ *Wall Street Journal,* June 22, 1966, p. 4.
4/ *Wall Street Journal,* June 21, 1967, p. 4.
5/ *Ibid.*

Mr. Hartford charged that the "foundation controls the company and that Ralph Burger completely controls the foundation. Because of this," he said, "the company is hamstrung. Mr. Jay [president] and Mr. Alldredge [chairman] are not free men."

Mr. Burger, president of the foundation, retired in early 1963 as chairman and president of A&P.

Told of Mr. Hartford's allegations, Mr. Alldredge, apparently annoyed at the remarks, said, "the foundation has 10 trustees and Mr. Burger holds only one vote. Mr. Burger has no active interest in the company," he declared.[6]

In the 1967 meeting the board was reduced from 21 to 17 members; 11 officer-directors and 6 outside directors. It had been reduced from 22 members the previous year. This compares with a board of 25 members in 1963, 20 in 1962, 14 in 1957, 11 in 1956 and 7 in 1950. Fluctuation in board size in this instance might be interpreted as a manifestation of instability in stockholder control and directorate objectives.

The 1967 reduction in size seems to reflect a consolidation in control by the present promanagement forces and relegation to the sidelines of the disgruntled Hartford heirs. This consolidation has been facilitated by the relative decrease in A&P stockholdings by Hartford family members. The best example is Mr. George Huntington Hartford II. While only a few years ago he owned about 10 percent of the outstanding stock, currently, chiefly through several rather large public offerings of some of his holdings, he owns or is trustee of less than 1 percent of the common stock.

The recent changes also portend a new and more forceful role to be taken by the Hartford Foundation. During the 1958 to 1967 period of directorate flux, the company was outperformed by most leading food merchandisers. A summary view of sales performance is shown in Figure 19 and Table 16. Data of this sort, however, must be interpreted with caution. At first glance it does appear that A&P's sales have grown at a slower pace than its major competitors—but a part of the seemingly better performance by its competitors is illusory. All of A&P's growth has been internal, that

6/ *Ibid.*

is, through reinvestment of retained earnings. On the other hand, *all* of its six biggest competitors have been active in acquiring components through merger. Consequently, the upward-sloped growth curves for A&P's six competitors, as shown in Figure 19, should actually be flattened somewhat.

This, of course, does not give A&P's directors straight A's. The record, particularly since 1958, has been less than phenomenal. It

FIGURE 19. Sales growth, 1950 to 1967, leading merchandising firms

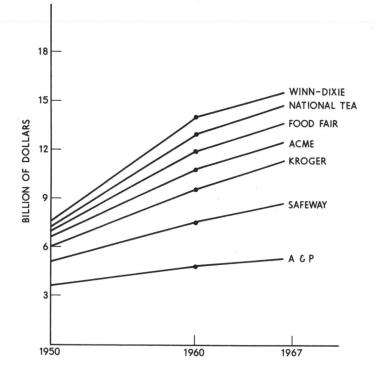

is very possible that the major changes in directorate dimensions have had a debilitating effect upon what previously had been a very dynamic merchandising firm.

The addition by 1963 of 11 outsiders, none of whom had any experience in merchandising food products, could have been a mistake. Inclusion of five lawyers probably accentuated intra-board bickering, and adding several "professional" directors seems to have been of no great help to the company.

TABLE 16. Percentage increase, 1958 to 1966 leading merchandising firms

|  | *A&P* | *Safeway* | *Kroger* |
|---|---|---|---|
| Sales | 7.4 | 50.0 | 49.0 |
| Net Income | 4.3 | 79.0 | 32.0 |
| Assets | 34.0 | 57.0 | 57.0 |
| Invested Capital | 45.5 | 74.0 | 59.0 |

The effects of the radical change from a board run by two men to a mixed board of directors is shown graphically in Figures 20 and 21. The 1950 board was preponderantly management-oriented. Both product acceptance and personal acceptance received major emphasis. Figure 21 shows the directorate dimensions just after the June, 1967, reduction in board size from 21 to 17 members. Previously, the board, chiefly through inclusion of nine outsiders, had a considerably different pattern. The 1967 change put much greater stress on special economic services, broad economic sophistication and asset impact. (These factors were very incidental in the earlier board.) Changes in relative factor importance are graphically evident in the relative decline in prod-

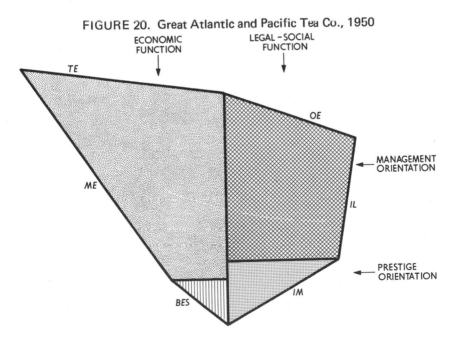

FIGURE 20.　Great Atlantic and Pacific Tea Co., 1950

uct and personal acceptance sectors and the remarkable increase in peer acceptance. In the same manner, management orientation declined while prestige orientation was accentuated.

The analysis on an authoritarian-equalitarian basis is somewhat handicapped because of a lack of information about some of the board members. Figure 22 uses judicious estimates to fill the gaps. The conclusion, despite data limitations, is obvious: in 1967 the

FIGURE 21.  Great Atlantic and Pacific Tea Co., 1967

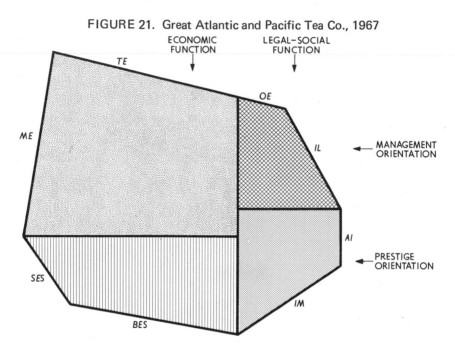

company experienced a significant shift away from the previously authoritarian board. This was not necessarily due to the addition of outsiders, however. It was much more the result of upgrading of its officer directors. This type of graphic modification, incidentally, is almost invariably associated with the transfer of power from owner-entrepreneurs to any form of broader control, whether predominantly officer director or outside director in character.

What, then, should be the role of a foundation, pension fund, or any other large institutional investor in structuring a particular company's directorate dimensions? The somewhat parallel examples of the Ford Motor Company and the Great Atlantic and Pacific Tea Company bring the question into clearer focus. In both instances (despite Mr. Hartford's allegations), the respective foundations seem to take a minimal role. In both cases, management is endorsed by the foundations. However, management at Ford includes three very competent and active members of the founder's family who have influence in Ford's management, its board, and the Ford Foundation. At A&P, the founder's heirs have no role in management or the Foundation and only a very minor representation on the board. At A&P there has been, and continues to be a very intimate contact between the corporation and the Foundation, as witnessed by the facts that prior to his retirement as company chairman, Mr. Burger served as head of both organizations and that he continues to hold the top post in the Foundation. In addition, A&P's chairman, president, and treasurer, together with an outside director, Mr. Schiff of Kuhn, Loeb & Co., serve as Foundation trustees. Finally, several retired A&P officials are trustees.

This near identity of Foundation trustees and present or past directors of the company provides an excellent example of a new version of interlock. In this new version, the third- and fourth-

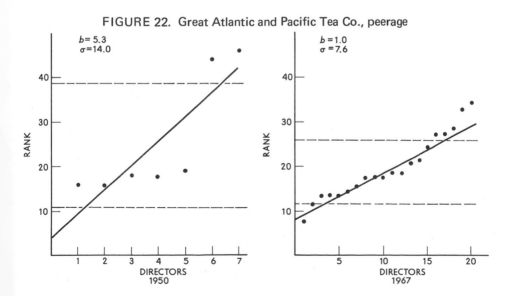

FIGURE 22.  Great Atlantic and Pacific Tea Co., peerage

generation descendents of the founder are superseded as the control force by working executives. This gives the Foundation much more of a public character, and reduces nepotistic influence to practically zero.

In structuring A&P's directorate dimensions, the impact of this new form of interlock is extremely difficult to appraise. In the conventional interlocks, a man's family, social, political, or business contacts can quite readily be identified as the interlocking forces. At A&P, however, the Foundation currently seems to be emphasizing technical competency, managerial proficiency, and long-term company service as the requisites for selecting specific individuals for board membership. (For example, among the eleven officer-directors are A&P's five presidents of regional divisions.)

Opponents of this near-identity of corporate officials and foundation trustees stress the conventional self-perpetuation-of-management argument. However, there seems to be nothing wrong in a management perpetuating itself as long as the organization continues to be effective. In fact, the ability of any management to build the best possible succession is one of the hallmarks of managerial excellence—and at A&P there does seem to be considerable stress on the movement of competent and dedicated lower-level managers to top echelon posts. If the John A. Hartford Foundation fosters this democratic advancement of talent—not only to top executive positions but even to the company's board room and ultimately to the Foundation's trusteeship—there should be minimal objection from either private or institutional investors who hold A&P stock. There is no guarantee that a complete cleavage of Foundation and company policy makers would produce better results and, actually, since the Foundation's long-term interests are identical with the company's long-term aspirations, there is considerable logic in the overlap of directors and trustees. Both bodies are working for mutually compatible goals.

# MONTGOMERY WARD AND COMPANY

Despite the much-publicized increase in outside directorships, this is not exclusively a one-way trend. There seems to be a growing sentiment in a number of predominantly outside-type directorates for more meaningful officer-director representation. Montgomery Ward and Company provides an interesting example.

During his 24-year tenure as Montgomery Ward's chief executive officer, Sewell Avery was the epitome of the autocratic tycoon. While "boss of Montgomery Ward, he had four presidents and 40 vice presidents exit suddenly."[1] For almost a quarter of a century, his personality and his convictions played *the* significant role in shaping the company's board of directors, its policies, and philosophy.

Mr. Avery began his executive career as president of United States Gypsum. "Convinced in the 1920's that the U.S. economy was headed for a depression, [he] so prepared U.S. Gypsum to weather it that the company was able to show a profit every year of the '30's. This performance so impressed J. P. Morgan & Co. that the banking firm asked Avery to take over an ailing Montgomery Ward in 1931. Avery quickly put his rough brand of rugged individualism to work at Ward, in three years turned a $9,000,000 loss into a $9,000,000 profit."[2]

As a bank-appointed chief executive of a large merchandising firm, Avery rigidly adhered to the conviction that the directors

1/ *Time,* Nov. 14, 1960, p. 102.
2/ *Ibid.*

should be predominantly non-officers of the company. His ten-man board included only two, at the most three, company officers, among whom were the chairman and president. For more than a quarter century, Ward was a classic example of a firm with an almost completely outside-director board. In the composition of its board, lawyers and financiers were usually in the majority. The 1950 board, for example, included only three individuals who were not lawyers or bankers.

Up to the start of World War II, Montgomery Ward managed to compete quite effectively even with the dominant merchandising firm, Sears, Roebuck. The early favorable comparison on a sales volume basis is clearly evident in Figure 23, with the point of competitive departure somewhere in the mid-1940's. In the past quarter century, however, Montgomery Ward sales have grown by only about 250 percent, while Sears, Roebuck has increased its sales volume by almost 1000 percent. More than chance is responsible for this disparity.

While Sewell Avery's rough, tough, ruggedly individualistic actions have been frequently mentioned as causal factors for Montgomery Ward's slippage, there has been virtually no citing of the firm's board of directors' structure or of its performance record. "Management" has, indeed, been severely indicted; Avery, himself, was ousted as chief executive in 1955. Louis E. Wolfson's abortive attempt at takeover was another manifestation of disquietude. More recently, the resignations in the early 1960's of John Barr as chairman and Paul Hammaker as president further emphasized the vulnerability of management and officer directors. Up to this point the nonofficer directors seemed to have been held blameless.

In a sense, this exoneration-through-silence of the outside directors may be justified for it seems that at least since 1931 the outside directors have abdicated their presumed functions. For over a quarter century, the board was only a ratifying agency. During that time, Montgomery Ward's destiny was completely and exclusively in the hands of one man—Sewell Avery. While Avery as the strong-man type performed admirably during the Depression-crisis years, he apparently had difficulty in adapting to changing circumstances. In fact, his most publicized blunder, the excessive accumulation of cash in anticipation of a post-World War II depression, seems to have been a consequence of relying on his

FIGURE 23.  Sears, Roebuck and Montgomery Ward sales, 1937 to 1967

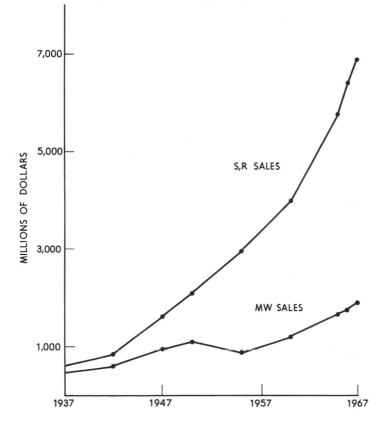

memories. He had been extremely fortunate in maintaining liquidity at U.S. Gypsum just prior to the Depression; the same tactics proved a failure after World War II, when history stubbornly refused to repeat itself.

Rumblings of discontent reached audible proportions by the early 1950's, and Louis E. Wolfson's proxy fight stressed the bungling of Avery's management. Although Wolfson succeeded only in having three of his cohorts elected to Ward's board, it was his fight that ended Avery's career in 1955.

Early in the 1960's the restiveness became even more apparent. Serious questions were asked about the adequacy of legal-financial types as Montgomery Ward's top executives and directors. *Business Week* stated, "There is nothing new in the argument that

Ward needs a 'real merchant' in the top administrative post. When Louis E. Wolfson was seated on the Montgomery Ward board after a bitter proxy fight, he objected to the naming of Barr [a lawyer] as president instead of a merchandising man."[3]

A veteran Ward's employee was quoted as saying, "It seems fundamental that a merchant runs a mercantile organization and that the merchandising department dominates the company. But the operating or fiscal end has always run Ward. They haven't had a real merchandising manager since Frank M. Folsom [a vice president who left in the 1930's]."[4]

After the turbulence of the 1950's Montgomery Ward's board was reconstituted to an extent. The former ten-man board, including two officers, was expanded to twelve, of whom five were officer directors. Unfortunately, this modification seemed to overlook the possibility that the previous board's composition might have been at least partially responsible for the company's poor position with respect to its competition. That is, lawyers and bankers still constituted about half the board. Although the presidents of a railroad, an oil company, and a museum were on the board, the reasons for the inclusion of these "outsiders" were not too clear. "Challenged at the turbulent annual meeting [1961] to explain the dearth of outside merchandising talent on his board, Barr replied that one restrictive factor was federal laws against interlocking directorships. 'We do business nationwide,' said Barr, adding that his directors were men chosen for their business experience and reputation for prudent management."[5]

A basic change in organization philosophy seems to have taken place late in 1961 when Robert E. Brooker was named Montgomery Ward's president. This shift in thinking was reaffirmed in 1965 when John Barr left the company, and in 1966 when Edward Donnell was named president and Brooker was elevated to chairman. Both Brooker and Donnell had been long-time employees and executives at Sears, Roebuck. With their elevations, for the first time in nearly 40 years both chairman and president at Montgomery Ward were working executives with technical grooming in the mercantile business. In addition, Ward hired four other vice

3/ *Business Week,* May 21, 1955, p. 34.
4/ *Business Week,* June 24, 1961.
5/ *Ibid.*

presidents and about 400 employees from Sears, Roebuck. Presumably, this new group was instrumental in changing many of Ward's merchandising practices.

More significantly, the change ushered in a redesigning of management—including even the board of directors. "Brooker, again following the Sears' pattern named four regional vice presidents, *gave them added stature by making them company directors,*

TABLE 17.  Montgomery Ward directorate dimensions

|  | *1950* | *1967* |
|---|---|---|
| *Factor* | | |
| Technical Expertise | 6 | 24 |
| Management Experience | 20 | 33 |
| Special Economic Service | 12 | 9 |
| Broad Economic Sophistication | 18 | 12 |
| Image | 12 | 9 |
| Asset Impact | 14 | 6 |
| Interlock | 14 | 3 |
| Owners' Equity | 4 | 6 |
| | | |
| *Acceptance* | | |
| Product | 26 | 57 |
| Peer | 30 | 21 |
| Public | 26 | 15 |
| Personal | 18 | 9 |
| | | |
| *Orientation* | | |
| Management | 44 | 66 |
| Prestige | 56 | 36 |
| | | |
| *Function* | | |
| Economic | 56 | 78 |
| Legal-Social | 44 | 24 |

assured them a free hand, and decreed they had to perform or get out."[6] The present board includes ten officer directors, and five nonemployees. (The latter group includes only two bankers and not a single lawyer.) By this transformation, Montgomery Ward now tends to emulate Sears, Roebuck, not only in personnel and in merchandising practices but also in board structure. Theoretically, Sears, Roebuck has a 24-man board equally divided between officer directors and nonemployee directors. In practice,

6/ *Wall Street Journal,* May 12, 1966, p. 1.

this distinction is not accurate. Only five of the outside directors have no functional, financial, or retiree status in the company. (Similarly J. C. Penney Company's thirteen-man board includes only three bonafide outsiders.)

By a strange coincidence, Sears, Roebuck's highly successful organization, including its board, was structured by an ex-Montgomery Ward employee, Robert E. Wood, who had been fired from Wards in 1924 and then hired by Julius Rosenwald at Sears.

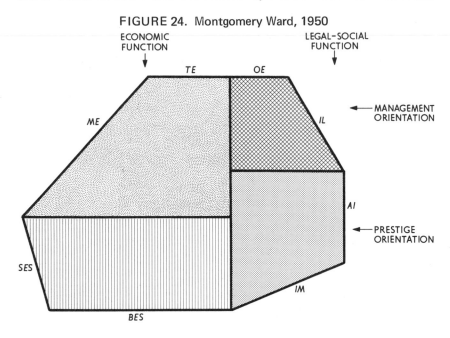

FIGURE 24. Montgomery Ward, 1950

In essence, the Sears' technique has been to decentralize territorially to the point where the five major "territories became administrative dukedoms of a sort. Each is headed by a powerful vice president, and these five constitute one-half of the corporate officers on the board."[7]

This dignifying of a number of key executives with the title, and responsibilities, of director has at least the following positive features:

1) The board has immediate access to vital technical information.

7/ *Fortune,* "Sears Makes It Look Easy," May, 1964, p. 219.

2) The "field" executives on the board serve as checks-and-balances with respect to the "headquarters" officer directors.

3) The corporate course of action is determined by individuals with a competent and continuing interest in company affairs.

4) With minimal banker and lawyer impact, the board is less prone to rest in status quo.

The significance of the organizational and philosophical change at Montgomery Ward is shown graphically in the Figures 24 and

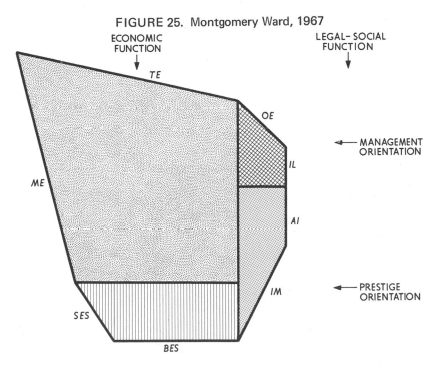

FIGURE 25. Montgomery Ward, 1967

25. The 1950 board of directors as seen in Figure 24 is very similar to the typical bank board. Emphasis is placed on the peer acceptance and public acceptance sectors. Relatively speaking, Ward's in 1950 was equally, or even more so, prestige oriented as versus management oriented.

The radical change in philosophy has resulted in the emphasis shown in Figure 25 on product acceptance, management orientation, and the economic function. At present, directorate dimensions for both Montgomery Ward and Sears, Roebuck are almost

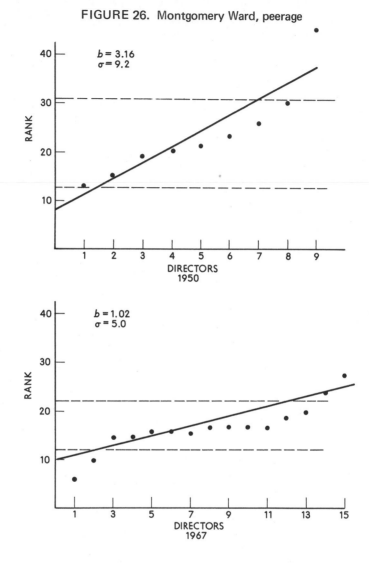

FIGURE 26. Montgomery Ward, peerage

identical, though there are a few notable differences. For one, the Sears' owners' equity factor is far more visible, since its 24-man board together owns nearly 750,000 Sears' shares, while Ward's fifteen-man board owns less than 50,000 shares of its common stock. This is less a matter of inheritance or shrewd investment than it is of attitude toward stock options for executives, however, since a glance at Montgomery Ward's most recent (1967) proxy statement reveals only one executive owning more than 4,000 common shares. In marked contrast, the 1966 Sears, Roebuck's proxy shows 17 of its 24 directors with 20,000 or more shares. The average stock ownership per officer director at Sears, Roebuck is about 52,000 shares; at Montgomery Ward, the average stock ownership per officer director is only 4,700 shares. It is very possible that despite identity in all factors except owners' equity, Montgomery Ward will still have difficulty in catching up with Sears, Roebuck. This would be the case particularly if significant participation in ownership by key executives really *does* enkindle the entrepreneureal spark.

As a final comment on the change at Montgomery Ward to an emphasis on product acceptance, the economic function, and management orientation, it does seem reasonable to assume that "merchants should run a mercantile organization." The relatively sluggish record during the past 20 years at Montgomery Ward is vivid testimony to the inadequacy of control by the lawyers and bankers who once constituted the major portion of the company's board of directors. This of course is far from an indictment of all lawyers and bankers performing as directors. The important consideration is whether or not particular lawyers, bankers, and others, in composite, provide a company with appropriate directorate dimensions. In the past, Montgomery Ward's directorate dimensions have evidently been inadequate in certain vital areas.

# THE HOOVER COMPANY

From its inception in 1908 almost to the present, the Hoover Company has been family-owned and family-run. As late as 1950, ten out of a seventeen-man board were direct descendents or members-by-marriage of the Hoover family. This family impact is very evident in the disproportionately large area of the personal acceptance sector in Figure 27: both the owners' equity and interlock factors are very evident. (Interlock in this instance is a consequence of the 10 members of the Hoover family who in 1950 were serving as members of the board.) While product acceptance was given some prominence, technically trained directors were not very prominent in Hoover's earlier boards. For example, Herbert W. Hoover, Jr., subsequently the company's chief executive and chairman, was made a director of the company in 1945 at age 27, before he had even held a management position. As late as 1963 Mr. Hoover was quoted as saying that "He doesn't want to be bothered with financial details. 'I don't understand a profit-and-loss statement and I don't want to see one. I just want a simple bar chart. If it's up, fine. If it's down, somebody gets chewed.' "[1]

> Hoover does not measure the company or his executives by such customary standards as return on investment or cash flow. "I don't worry about that," he said recently, "as long as we're solvent, I'm not much interested in money." ... He admits to what he calls "philosophical difficulties" with executives who have different ideas. "I tell these sophisticates

[1] *Time,* "Sweeping the World," November 2, 1963, p. 100.

in the financial market," he says with a touch of disdain, "to concentrate on sales and let the money take care of itself."[2]

As might be inferred, Hoover's directors were not chosen for their broad economic sophistication.

In January of 1954, Herbert W. Hoover, Jr., assumed the presidency of the company, in what could be described as a coup.

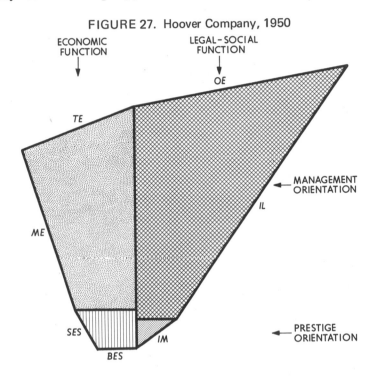

FIGURE 27. Hoover Company, 1950

There was considerable family feuding—particularly on the issue of who was to succeed H. W. Hoover, Sr.—and ownership, although primarily in the Hoover family, was quite fragmented. The results of changes he made in the board during the next decade are shown in Figure 28. While personal acceptance is still prominent, the interlock factor has decreased markedly with the exodus of most of the Hoover family from the board, and product acceptance has

2/ *Fortune,* "Hoover's Well-Vacuumed World," Philip Siekman, June, 1964, pp. 143 to 144.

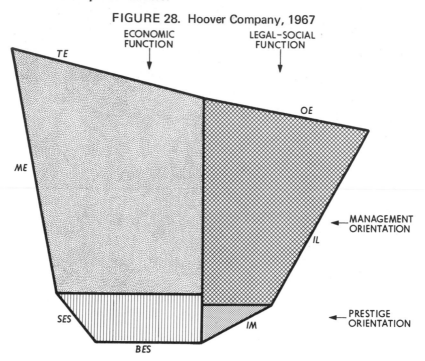

FIGURE 28. Hoover Company, 1967

become the dominant sector. There is even a sign of development in the peer acceptance sector.

In terms of peerage, with the ascendency of H. W. Hoover, Jr., to the chief executive's post, there was a pronounced emphasis on authoritarian control. Both the slope of the peerage trend line and the related standard deviation increased between 1950 and 1967, as can be seen in Figure 29. As partial explanation, in the earlier board, family membership provided a basis for equality. Various segments of the family tended to equalize a board member's stature. But after 1954, Herbert W. Hoover, Jr.'s one-man control transformed the board. "Hoover's rule is described by one of his close relatives as a 'dictatorship of sorts.' He approves of what he calls 'self-discipline' in his executives, a trait he feels is best learned in military service. And he insists that no manager ever be out of the boss's reach."[3] An aide is quoted "you just learn to do what he wants."[4]

3/ *Ibid.*, p. 143.
4/ *Ibid.*, p. 144.

But, as always, statistics must be interpreted cautiously. This caveat applies particularly since the September, 1966, ousting of Mr. Hoover as the company's president, chairman, and chief executive officer. For despite his ouster from the executive posts, Mr. Hoover remains on the board. Thus, while there is no significant change in the 8-factor point value ascribed to him, in all likelihood his effectiveness and directorate-dimension worth as a Hoover director have been drastically reduced. This being so, it might be suggested that Mr. Hoover not be reckoned in the calculations. If he is not, then Hoover Company's 1967 peerage statistics show a major move in the equalitarian direction, the new figures being approximately $b = 1.7$, $\sigma = 5.0$. That such a change has indeed taken place seems to be supported by facts.

The more than 7,000 "public" stockholders own about 20 percent of the voting stock, thirty members of the Hoover family hold another 45 percent, the nonfamily management group owns the remaining 35 percent. Voting stock, however, consists of only 185,048 shares of Class B stock. The remaining ownership interest, represented by 6,399,602 shares of Class A stock, has no voting rights. Herbert W. Hoover, Jr., and his immediate family own 37.3 percent of the voting shares and 7.2 percent of the nonvoting

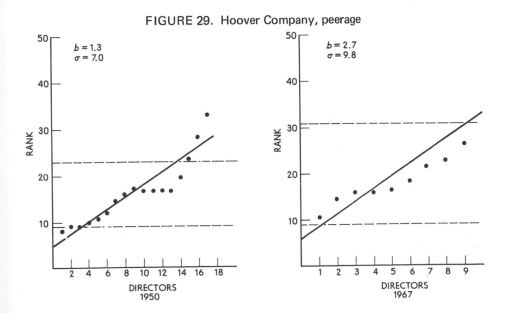

FIGURE 29. Hoover Company, peerage

shares. (The Harter Bank and Trust Company of Canton, Ohio, is the largest holder of Class A nonvoting stock with 1,677,165 shares held in a total of 104 trusts.)

Considering the distribution of Class B voting stock, it seems likely that the Hoover revolt against its chief executive and largest stockholder was an action prompted by the officer directors and at least tacitly endorsed by dissident Hoover family members. The

TABLE 18.  Hoover Company directorate dimensions

|  | 1950 | 1967 |
|---|---|---|
| *Factor* | | |
| Technical Expertise | 12 | 21 |
| Management Experience | 18 | 25 |
| Special Economic Service | 4 | 5 |
| Broad Economic Sophistication | 4 | 10 |
| Image | 4 | 6 |
| Asset Impact | 0 | 0 |
| Interlock | 35 | 18 |
| Owner's Equity | 22 | 14 |
| *Acceptance* | | |
| Product | 30 | 46 |
| Peer | 8 | 15 |
| Public | 4 | 6 |
| Personal | 57 | 32 |
| *Orientation* | | |
| Management | 87 | 78 |
| Prestige | 12 | 21 |
| *Function* | | |
| Economic | 38 | 61 |
| Legal-Social | 61 | 38 |

reason publicly stated for the ouster was that Mr. Hoover had suffered a heart attack. Although he was recuperating from the ailment, "the board felt it in the best interests of the company that he be relieved of his responsibilities."[5]

Almost concurrent with the deposition of the chief executive was a move to equalize voting rights of the two classes of common stock. A proxy statement was issued calling for a special meeting to be held October 28, 1966. The proxy stated that Mr. Hoover, "did not approve of the proposed amendment and did not attend

5/ *Wall Street Journal,* "Who's News," Sept. 14, 1966.

the meeting of the board at which the proposal to amend the certificate of incorporation was approved. . . . Mr. Hoover has advised management that he is opposed to the adoption of the amendment."[6]

Subsequently, there were a number of involved legal maneuvers by both parties. In June, 1967, Felix N. Mansager, current chairman and president of the company, and Mr. Hoover said in a joint statement that an agreement, subject to approval by the United States District Court in Cleveland, had been reached providing for equal voting rights for holders of Class A common stock. The agreement also gives Mr. Hoover a two-man representation on the board, now expanded to 13 members.

The significant point is that a chief executive officer, even with a very substantial ownership interest, is not necessarily secure from the danger of being ousted by a predominantly inside board of directors. Nor is there a guaranteed security in the "loyalty" factor supposedly associated with appointment to the board, since practically all the officer directors had, in this instance, been appointed to their top positions, including board membership, during H. W. Hoover, Jr.'s 12-year tenure as company president. Perhaps the Hoover case is not typical, since it involves strong undercurrents of ownership maneuvering by major stock interests, but it does raise doubts as to the validity of the commonly held belief that officer directors are totally subservient to the chief executive.

6/ *Wall Street Journal,* "Hoover Company Board Plans to Slash Voting Power of H. W. Hoover, Jr.," Oct. 17, 1966.

# GENERAL DYNAMICS CORPORATION

That the federal government must soon give the directorate dimensions of our major corporations closer scrutiny follows not only from the government's obligation to protect public interests but also from the government's role as major customer. In 1967 the top fifty defense contractors received nearly $22 billion in prime contracts from the defense department. Among these prime contractors were most of our leading manufacturing corporations—General Motors, Standard Oil (N.J.), Ford Motor Company, General Electric, Chrysler, Texaco, Mobil Oil, IBM, DuPont, AT&T, and 23 other members of the "Billion Dollar Sales Club." Combined sales of these leading corporations totaled about $133 billion; simple arithmetic shows that more than 16 percent of the combined sales of these manufacturing firms was to the federal government for defense contracts alone.

While a 16 percent of aggregate sales figure is significant, such an averaging procedure tends to obscure even more interesting data. At least 12 of the top 50 prime defense contractors sold two thirds or more of their total output to the government. Lockheed Aircraft, United Aircraft, General Dynamics, McDonnell Douglas, Avco, Kaiser Industries, and Northrop depended upon Federal purchases for about three fourths of their total sales, while even such diversified giants as General Electric, Westinghouse, and RCA had defense sales of 17 percent, 18 percent, and 10 percent, respectively.

The magnitude of defense orders should not obscure the fact

176

that the federal government makes other more routine and more prosaic purchases from industry. Because the U.S. government is the world's biggest customer, it is only reasonable to expect federal authorities to develop a keen interest in productivity, pricing, and policymaking in American industry. The big question is, what should be our government's role in the designation of corporate directors?

Historically, there are precedents for including major customer representation on boards of directors. This practice would fall within the specific economic service category. Practiced on a small scale, it might be termed currying favor, under-table dealing, or reciprocity. In this guise, such indirect dealings are generally considered unethical and, in some instances, they are declared illegal. When conducted on a grand scale, however, the landing of huge government contracts is dignified by being termed "industrial diplomacy."

In most seats of government, lobbying is an accepted, perhaps even a necessary, way of life. The typical lobbyist's activity might involve logic, fast-talk, friendship, or gratuities. In the great majority of cases, it is simply a matter of selling. There is no attempt by the favor-grantor to become part of the corporation's decision-making mechanism. There have, of course, been some notable instances of firms adding individuals to their boards who presumably could secure government contracts. In practically all such instances, these actions were initiated by and for individuals.

When a corporation becomes overly dependent—perhaps almost completely dependent—upon direct sales to the federal government, questions are in order as to its private-enterprise status. And the forces which helped structure its directorate dimensions undoubtedly become quite different from those prevailing when the corporation was in its free-enterprise phase. For example the need for owners' equity as a selection factor diminishes drastically. Asset impact, likewise, becomes less meaningful. So too, image, and even broad economic sophistication, probably have less significance. On the other hand, special economic service and interlock of the political and social variety, most likely gain in importance. These inferences seem to be supported by the description of directorate dimensions for General Aniline and Film Corporation presented earlier.

There is probably a very serious threat to the effective function-ing of our economic system in any large-scale use of "political" boards of directors. On the other hand, there is an equally omi-nous threat in tolerating what sometimes seem to be administra-tive or directorate pay-offs to government officials involved in letting macroscopic contracts.

The past 10-year experience of General Dynamics Corporation corroborates this contention. The company, one of our earlier conglomerates, was initiated in 1947 by John Jay Hopkins. For a decade—up to his death in 1957—Hopkins very successfully ran a one-man show. His board of directors, at one time numbering 32, was hand-picked by Hopkins, and, from all indications, the direc-tors had a very incidental role in managing or even in advising. In the fall of 1956, Hopkins, then suffering from an incurable cancer, made two momentous decisions. First, at the next annual meeting the board was to be reduced from thirty-two members to the more conventional fifteen. Second, he decided to have someone succeed him as chief executive officer.

The logical choice as the new chief executive seemed to be Frank Pace, Jr., who was brought in as executive vice president in 1953. Pace was at one time a high-level political figure. He had served in the Truman Administration first as Director of the Budget and, from 1949, as Secretary of the Army. Presumably Pace's contacts and knowledge as to how Washington's inner cir-cles worked was a much desired asset. However, Hopkins hesitated in selecting Pace because he did not have "any confidence in Pace's ability to do much more than take care of the Washington end of the business."[1] He finally decided not to promote Pace.

Shortly before the 1957 annual meeting, several directors began surreptitious maneuvers. Hearing the rumors, Hopkins could not believe a revolt was imminent. " 'Hell,' " he growled, " 'that's *my* board. I picked every man on it.' . . . But at the end of the final board meeting [April 29] Frank Pace was voted in overwhelm-ingly as president and chief executive officer. . . . The next day April 30, Hopkins went to the hospital. . . . On May 3, Jay Hop-kins was dead."[2]

1/ *Fortune,* "How a Great Corporation Got Out of Control," Part 1, Richard Aus-tin Smith, Jan., 1962, p. 180.
2/ *Ibid.,* p. 184.

Subsequently, Pace was elevated to the chairman's post and an old friend of his, Earl Johnson, was made president. Pace had brought Johnson to General Dynamics in 1956. Johnson had been an associate of Pace's in Washington bureaucracy, serving as Pace's Assistant Secretary of the Army and later as president of the Air Transport Association. Johnson's prior business experience had been limited to 14 years with an investment counseling firm.

The subsequent debacle resulting from poor top management at General Dynamics is well known. Within a three-year period, the company compiled a record $490 million loss. By the end of 1961, owners' equity had slumped to a mere $76 million. In its negative performance, General Dynamics had set a mark unequaled in American business history. (Most of this fantastic loss resulted from the failure of the company's 880 and 990 jet programs.)

Despite its almost catastrophic experience under the leadership of two top-level politicians, General Dynamics seems to be committed to a specific corporate philosophy and a particular structuring in its board of directors. As to structure, in the era of the 32-man board, a 12-man executive committee actually passed upon most of the decisions. This executive committee consisted of the chairman, three bankers, two oil men and five lawyers. In 1967, the eleven-man board consisted of the chairman, four financiers, two oil men, three other industrialists and one lawyer. At no time has the board had an abundance of technically qualified directors.

As successor to Pace, Henry Crown, then General Dynamics' largest individual stockholder (initially 2,064,516 shares of convertible preferred stock) and head of its emergency management committee, "tried to get John A. McCone (subsequently head of the Central Intelligence Agency) and Gen. Lucius B. Clay (later senior partner at Lehman Bros.)."[3] The propensity for government and prestigious types as corporate chief executives and directors was still obvious. The choice of successor for Pace was finally Roger Lewis, executive vice president at Pan American World Airways. In some respects this was a propitious choice. Mr. Lewis as a top executive in a leading airline company could be presumed to

3/ *Business Week*, Dec. 7, 1963, p. 145.

have a fairly decent acquaintance with aircraft and aircraft technology. All the same, Lewis had spent three years in Washington during the Eisenhower Administration as the Air Force's Assistant Secretary for Materiel—in this capacity he was responsible for procurement—and the inference could easily be made that General Dynamics was still committed to currying bureaucratic contact in Washington.

Subsequent developments are not necessarily a condemnation of Mr. Lewis or any other ex-government official assuming a top corporate post. However, the TFX uproar in 1963 cannot be dismissed without comment. The controversy pertained to the contracting for the Tactical Fighter Experimental plane. Both Boeing and General Dynamics were the prime contenders for this multi-billion dollar contract. Boeing was consistently the choice of the government's Source Selection Board and most of the top military leaders, but the Air Council and the civilian secretariat vetoed the recommendation of the military experts and awarded the huge contract to General Dynamics. The cost of the project was initially estimated at $6.5 billion. Later, revised estimates doubled that figure.

An unpleasant aftermath of this controversial contract was the impugning of the characters of two key government officials, Navy Secretary Fred Korth and Deputy Secretary of Defense Roswell L. Gilpatrick.

Members of the Senate Permanent Investigations Committee raised the question of Mr. Korth's apparent conflict of interest in awarding the contract. It was pointed out that Mr. Korth had been president of the Continental National Bank of Fort Worth, Texas. General Dynamics was a customer of that bank. Continental National Bank had made loans to General Dynamics and had participated with Chase Manhattan Bank of New York in a $50 million loan. The company also had a checking account with the bank. Senator McClellan's "TFX investigators, going through the files of Korth's Continental National Bank in Fort Worth, had found a sheaf of letters showing that Korth, from Washington, was continuing to conduct business for the bank, including dealings with new depositors."[4] The Senators questioned why Korth had not

4/ *Business Week,* October 26, 1963, p. 29.

openly disqualified himself from all deliberations just as he had in another controversial contract involving Bell Aircraft. (Korth had been a member of Bell Aircraft's board.) The alleged conflict of interest was quite significant since General Dynamics planned to build the TFX at its Fort Worth, Texas, facilities. The 1700-plane contract meant a fairly steady and long-term use of these facilities, with increased Fort Worth employment and payrolls. The Senate subcommittee hearings took place late in July, 1963. Mr. Korth resigned his post as Secretary of the Navy on November 1.

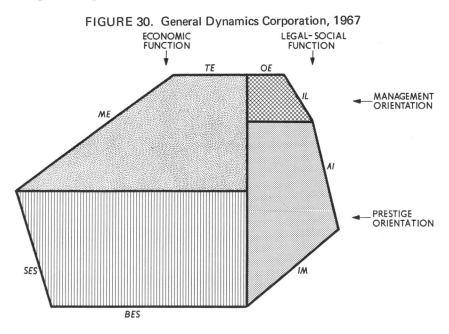

FIGURE 30. General Dynamics Corporation, 1967

This particular conflict-of-interest charge was aggravated by Roswell L. Gilpatrick's involvement. Mr. Gilpatrick had once been Under Secretary of the Air Force and was then Deputy Secretary of Defense. It was pointed out by the investigating senators that Gilpatrick had been a partner in the law firm of Cravath, Swaine and Moore. This firm was paid $110,000 over a two-year period between 1958 and 1961 for Gilpatrick's services as special counsel to General Dynamics. It was alleged that even after Gilpatrick left the law firm of Cravath, Swaine and Moore he continued to receive $21,000 a year from that firm. The senators made another allegation of collusive action by pointing out that one of Gilpatrick's former law partners, Maurice T. Moore, became a director of General Dynamics a month after the Defense Department gave the TFX contract to the corporation.

Mr. Gilpatrick vehemently denied that there was any legal or ethical conflict of interest. He argued that his legal services were restricted to other matters not pertinent to the TFX contract. Senators McClellan and Carl Curtis, however, produced records to show that Gilpatrick:

1. Attended 18 board meetings during the period.
2. Advised on personnel matters involving top management.
3. Investigated other possible acquisitions or mergers as part of a contemplated General Dynamics diversification program.
4. Prepared a special advisory memorandum in August 1960 at the request of Frank Pace, Jr., then board chairman for General Dynamics, on the long-range outlook for the Corvair Division.[5]

Senator Anderson summarized the situation by stating, "It became obvious many months ago that TFX and the Administration's standards of what might be called 'TFX ethics' are shot through with political interest and favoritism. There are facts pointing to a misuse by some of the trusts which repose in public office."[6]

These charges of collusive action and their equally vehement denials can be cause for concern. If even a few of our leading corporations do engage in nefarious back-of-the-scene maneuvers in order to get multi-million-dollar government contracts, then both the philosophy and practice of corporate directors is in jeopardy. This is precisely the sort of questionable activity which gave "free" enterprise of the late 19th century a bad name. If our major corporations do not initiate stringent self-policing in situations of this sort, then it is simply a matter of time before irate citizens and responsive legislators take therapeutic action. Even the very insinuation of this sort of special economic service given corporations by present or former government officials must be eliminated.

5/ *Business Week*, November 23, 1963, p. 33.
6/ *New York Times*, July 29, 1963.

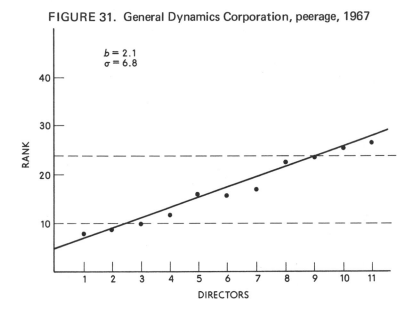

FIGURE 31. General Dynamics Corporation, peerage, 1967

More pertinent to this presentation than the ethical or legal ramifications is the legitimacy of the SES factor, especially when practiced on so grandiose a scale. Reference was made in the Wheeling Steel illustration to the inclusion of major suppliers on a company's board. The ethics of outside counsel holding a board seat and at the same time receiving annual payments ranging up to $1 million can similarly be questioned. Corporate borrowing from banks or investment firms with representation on that company's board is equally reprehensible. The list of special economic services once generally assumed acceptable but currently questionable seems to be growing in length. It could be that the SES factor is on its way out as a significant component in structuring directorate dimensions.

# THE PHILADELPHIA CONTRIBUTIONSHIP AND MUTUAL ASSURANCE COMPANIES

The Philadelphia Contributionship for the Insurance of Houses From Loss by Fire was founded by Benjamin Franklin in 1752. Its counterpart, also headquartered in Philadelphia, the Mutual Assurance Company for Insuring Homes From Loss by Fire, was founded in 1784. These are the country's oldest insurance firms, and as such they provide interesting case studies in survival. Despite the adage "adapt or perish," both companies seem to have refused to alter their policies or practices to conform to changing circumstances. Yet despite their rigid adherence to what most individuals would characterize as antiquated and even archaic business practices, both firms seem to be doing relatively well. Both are earning handsome profits.

> There's no denying their financial strength. For example last year the Contributionship, with $120.5 million of insurance in force, shelled out a mere $110,000 for losses. Net income topped $865,000 while year-end assets exceeded $35 million —an unusually high figure relative to the insurance in force (over half the assets are in common stocks). The balance sheet of Mutual Assurance, which has slightly larger assets, is equally impressive.[1]

1/ *Wall Street Journal,* "Two Ancient Insurers In Philadelphia Flourish Despite Relaxed Ways," Glynn Mapes, Dec. 22, 1967, p. 1.

Undeniably, both firms are small compared with our largest insurance firms. (In the life insurance field, for example, Metropolitan Life with $130 billion of life insurance in force and the Prudential with $122 billion life insurance in force are about 1000 times the size of the Contributionship and Mutual Assurance.) But perhaps it is this disparity that could be THE reason for the significant differences in board structure and function.

At both the Contributionship and at Mutual Assurance, board meetings are more like regal ceremonials than business sessions. The monthly meetings are held in the historic part of Philadelphia, in town houses only a short distance apart: the Contributionship at 212 South Fourth Street and Mutual Assurance at 240 South Fourth Street.

> Following work sessions of an hour or so, board members adjourn upstairs for cocktails and tastefully catered candlelight dinners. A sampling of a recent Contributionship dinner: Oysters, green turtle soup and filet of beef with wine offerings of sherry, Rhine wine, Claret, champagne, brandy and Madeira. . . .
>
> Both firms have maintained wine cellars in their basements for years. Mutual Assurance is noted for having the more extensive wine list, although it suffered a setback last year when several bottles of 1865 Madeira soured and had to be thrown out. "That was a real tragedy," says Daniel D. White, Jr., assistant treasurer, who keeps the cellar stocked.[2]

The remarkable feature about both companies' boards is that the stockholders seem to support their directors as to board-room decorum and company practices. There is no pressure to expand, to diversify, or to conglomerate. In only a single instance, back in 1894, has there been a serious attempt at stockholder revolt. In that instance, "Some policyholders charged the Contributionship was only interested in avoiding risks, maintaining assets and keeping its directors content. The attitude of the board, the dissidents declared, was 'that of a mouse snugly ensconced in a rich old cheese.' However, the old guard was overwhelmingly upheld in a special election."[3]

2/ *Ibid.*
3/ *Ibid.*

These venerable insurance companies are quite unique in their directorate dimensions. Of their combined 24 directors, one third are not listed in *Poors Directory, Who's Who in Commerce and Industry,* or *Who's Who in America.* Whether this is because they are not prominent on the business-social scene or because they insist on aristocratic anonymity, is an unresolved question. Consequently, when these insuring firms are to be measured for directorate dimensions, some judicious extrapolation is imperative.

There is no real parallel instance in large-scale industrial enterprise of a board with comparable dimensions. The closest approximation might be General Aniline and Film's board during the era of government ownership and control. Two factors, special economic service and interlock are identical. The resemblance is particularly noticeable in the exaggeration of the peer acceptance and personal acceptance sectors. Minimizing of the other two sectors is also parallel.

The General Aniline and Film situation during the period 1942 to 1965 was the consequence of a politically-structured board. Selection of specific board members seemed to be a matter of political expediency. In the Contributionship and Mutual Assurance cases, the boards seem to be structured primarily for reasons of social prominence and social acceptability.

These two insurance company boards seem to sit at the apex of what might be termed a social stratification. For quite a few generations, one of the greatest social attainments for the Philadelphian aristocrat, has been an invitation to join either of these boards. Actually, these boards symbolized the genteel Philadelphians' attitude toward boards and directors.

> Philadelphians, *the* Philadelphians, do not live by bread alone; they live by boards. Beyond "work," beyond the railroad, beyond family concerns, beyond even banking and medicine and law, the ultimate goal, the ultimate reward of every good Old Philadelphian is . . . a chair; to be seated on, and as final accolade, chairman of, a board. This is the perfect expression in Philadelphia of the Sedentary, and the real rulers of Philadelphia are not its presidents, who can be hired ("You don't want to bother with people like that"), but its chairmen, who are usually, like poets, born not made. To be

FIGURE 32. Contributionship and Mutual Assurance Companies

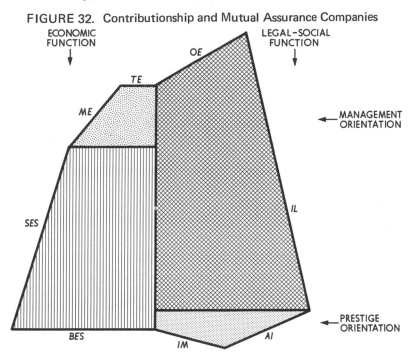

on a good board is reward, recognition, goal. That's where the real prestige and power are, and every aspect of Philadelphia life is securely boarded.[4]

There are few other comparable examples of this rather extreme directorate philosophy. Perhaps the closest approximation can be found in the still very prevalent aristocratic attitude towards boards of directors that is found in Great Britain.

In England, where they have a "profession" known as "company director," the boardroom life is popularly regarded as a cushy sinecure. Said Lord Boothby, a life peer, in a reflective moment: "If you have five directorships it is total heaven, like having a permanent hot bath. . . . No effort of any kind is called for. You go to a meeting once a month in a car supplied by the company, you look grave and sage, on two occasions say, 'I agree,' say 'I don't think so' once, and if all

4/ Nathaniel Burt, *The Perennial Philadelphians,* Little, Brown, p. 219.

goes well you get 500 pounds a year. Multiplied by five directorships, the total sum of 'heaven' is roughly equivalent to
$7,000."[5]

Stratification has been most evident in the succession of directors at both eminent Philadelphia insurance companies.

Biddles have abounded on both boards. Morrises too; one
such succession in the Contributionship has consisted of a
dozen Morrises, with a few Norrises, Whartons and Biddles
snuck in between. Then there are the Ingersolls; they balance
neatly at present, C. Jared being a trustee of the Mutual and
his brother R. Sturgis a director of the Contributionship. If
there is any difference between the Contributionship and Mutual, aside from a feeling of seniority on the part of the
former, it is in the Mutual's high-minded indifference to the
business background of its chairmen; among these have not
only been S. Weir Mitchell, doctor and novelist, but also
Owen Wister, just plain novelist, who was succeeded by Dr.
George W. Norris, just doctor, none of these people being
specialists in insurance.[6]

There is still some evidence of this rigid stratification in the
Contributionship and Mutual Assurance boards in other than family connections. The 16 directors of the combined boards on
whom data is available list a total of 31 university degrees. These
are distributed as follows:

| | |
|---|---|
| University of Pennsylvania | 11 |
| Princeton University | 9 |
| Harvard University | 7 |
| Other | 4 |
| | — |
| | 31 |

Lawyers and bankers are extremely prominent. Residence in
suburban Philadelphia together with a downtown office are indis-
pensable. Club, church, and political party affiliation, while still
noticeable factors, are probably far less prominent today than in
former times. Interlock in Philadelphia area business is quite evi-

5/ *Fortune,* Nov., 1962, p. 109.
6/ Nathaniel Burt, *op. cit.,* p. 150.

dent. Girard Trust Bank has four Contributionship and two Mutual Assurance members on its board. Penn Mutual Life Insurance, Philadelphia Savings Fund, Atlantic Richfield Company, Bell Telephone Company of Pennsylvania, Smith Kline and French, Western Savings Fund, Pennsylvania Company, Philadelphia, Baltimore and Washington RR., Pennsylvania RR., and First Pennsylvania Bank and Trust each have more than two of the prestige insurance company directors on their boards. These 12 companies have a total of 44 Contributionship and Mutual Assurance director contacts with their respective boards. While some inroads have been made, industrialists are still in a distinct minority on the venerable insurance companies' boards.

In some respects it is important to have board models such as those of the Contributionship and Mutual Assurance. While they can be viewed as vestigial remnants, they illustrate a rather important phase in the evolutionary development of boards and public trusteeship.

# STANDARD OIL COMPANY
# (NEW JERSEY)

The structure of the board of directors for the Standard Oil Company (New Jersey) prior to 1966, had for many years been a distinctive one with the membership consisting entirely of officer directors of the company. Moreover these men had served virtually all of their working lives with the organization so that the average length of company service per member was in excess of thirty years. The board was distinctive, too, in the fact that board meetings were convened in formal session at least weekly and the executive committee met daily.

Another distinctive feature, particularly after the 1960 organization realignment following Monroe J. Rathbone's assumption to the chief executive's post, was the emphasis on contact directors. Contact directors, in addition to their functional assignments, had responsibility as top supervisors and advisors for specific geographic regions. The 1960 organization readjustment grouped Jersey's approximately 300 affiliates into six regions, with a contact director for each. In essence this was an epitome of decentralization for operations, however, with a maximum of centralization of policy. According to the company's secretary, John O. Larson,

Jersey supplies its affiliates with coordination, seeing that affiliates act in the best interests of Jersey as well as their own. Jersey serves its companies as banker, executive personnel department, and responsible management consultant. It sets basic policies; has the last word on capital investment

190

proposals; and selects, trains, and evaluates affiliates' officers and directors.[1]

There is no question as to the effectiveness of this board structure, the previous form or the subsequent Jersey top-level organization pattern. The company continues to lead the industry—it is the world's largest industrial firm with assets approaching the $16 billion level. Only General Motors' sales volume exceeds that of Jersey whose approximately 5 billion barrel daily output equals one of every seven gallons of fuel marketed in the free world.

In 1966, with the designation of a new chairman and chief executive officer, Michael Lawrence Haider, the company once again modified its organization structure. For the first time in its then 83-year history, two outside directors were named to the board. This departure from previous practice will, undoubtedly, force a reappraisal of the role to be played in the future by Jersey's directors. "For years the directors have acted as liaison men between top management and operating corporate units. This has been a more time-consuming job than most directorships. Now the outside directors will simply be monthly advisers to top management."[2] In 1967 two additional outside directors were added so that the present board consists of twelve officer directors and four nonofficer directors.

The change in board structure was accompanied by certain modifications in board function. Where formerly all available directors met in weekly sessions—the new board meets for approximately two hours just once a month. Many, if not most, of its duties have been delegated to the executive committee which consists of the chairman, president, and three executive vice presidents. This group meets every Tuesday, Wednesday, and Friday. Another very important policy-making group, the operations review committee, composed of all directors who are employees of the company, meets regularly every Thursday. This group also meets at such other times as necessary. In most respects, this operations review committee is the counterpart of Jersey's board prior to its 1966 reorganization. It would be difficult to imagine any sudden reversal of this group's decisions by either the execu-

1/ *Business Week,* Aug. 6, 1960, p. 51.
2/ *Business Week,* Feb. 12, 1966, p. 34.

tive committee or the board, since the operations review committee's membership includes all twelve of the board's officer directors.

What forces and circumstances prompted this departure by Jersey from its historic board pattern? Obviously, only the surface indications of the real forces and circumstances can be speculated upon in a study of this kind. One of the most compelling factors for this change seems to have been the "spirit of the times." By 1965 Jersey, DuPont, and a very small representation of major companies remained with all-officer type boards of directors. Keith Funston's mandate that all new admissions to the New York Stock Market listing include at least two outside directors on the board could have been a compelling force. Ever spreading public ownership of the company's common stock was probably another factor. The implications of global enterprise, with significantly more complex problems related to international operations, might have had some impact on the decision. Perhaps the most important reason, as stated by Jersey chairman, M. L. Haider, is the hope "that the move will give its board 'an effective outside viewpoint.' "[3] This justification for adding outside directors was reinforced by Mr. Haider in his comment that "their unfamiliarity with the oil business can be useful just because they will ask a question to which we think we've known the answer a long time."[4] It is, of course, much too soon to evaluate the new board's performance. The organizational momentum generated by so dynamic a firm as Standard Oil (New Jersey) could propel the company forward for considerable time even with minimal board-room direction. The consequences, whether plus or minus, will not be evident for at least a few more years.

The significant point for this study is that Standard Oil Company (N.J.), despite an 83-year old board-room tradition, did not hesitate to make a drastic change when it felt there was need for such a change. In summary, the 1966 board-room restructuring has had the following effect upon Jersey's directorate dimensions:

| Year | TE | ME | SES | BES | IM | AI | IL | OE |
|------|----|----|-----|-----|----|----|----|----|
| 1965 | 24 | 22 | 5   | 19  | 12 | 2  | 2  | 14 |
| 1968 | 18 | 22 | 7   | 19  | 14 | 6  | 5  | 10 |

3/ *Ibid.*, Feb. 12, 1966, p. 34.
4/ *Business Week*, Dec. 29, 1967, p. 57.

Technical expertise (TE) and owners' equity (OE) have notice-ably been reduced. Nevertheless, it should be emphasized that Jersey's twelve officer directors have a combined beneficial owner-ship of 151,000 shares of Jersey's common stock, an average per director of 12,600 shares. This means that the twelve officer direc-tors have an average investment of nearly $1 million in the com-pany. This intimate financial tie could be an important reason for the excellence in Jersey's board performance.

On the other hand, special economic service (SES), image (IM), asset impact (AI), and interlock (IL) have gained in importance. It is significant that neither management experience (ME) nor broad economic sophistication (BES) have been substantially affected. Yet, recognition of the need for these factors is one of the chief arguments for including outside directors in most companies. In Jersey's case, both ME and BES seem to be amply abundant in its own top executives. In regard to BES, its twelve officer directors, for example, have a total of thirteen college degrees. They serve in a multiplicity of academic, civic, professional, and philanthropic capacities such as the Council on Foreign Relations, the Business Council, Committee for Economic Development, etc.

The most obvious change in the four sectors is shown graphi-cally in Figures 33 and 34. There has been a shift, although not too pronounced, from product acceptance to public acceptance. Then, too, prestige orientation has grown somewhat at the ex-pense of management orientation.

Measured on the peerage norms, Jersey could be said to have an equalitarian board. This contention holds equally for the previous all-officer-director board which had a standard deviation ($\sigma$) of only 5.0 and a slope or b value of 1.0. The board, at present, is slightly less equalitarian with $\sigma = 7.7$ and b = 1.4. These measure-ments still imply a high degree of peerage and collegiality.

One obvious reason for the high level of peerage is Jersey's enlightened management development philosophy. The systematic development of employee capacities does not cease at the depart-mental or divisional levels. The ultimate in this management devel-opment process is elevation to the board of trustees. A number of deserving candidates are annually promoted to the boards of Jer-sey affiliates. Each year, on the average, one or two of the more outstanding of its personnel are added to the parent company's

FIGURE 33. Standard Oil Company (N.J.), 1965

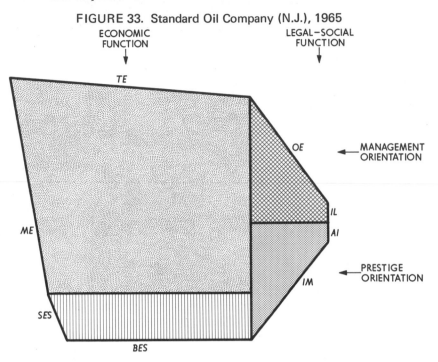

board. This policy was prompted by the realization that, "Over the years Jersey has experienced a steadily mounting need not only for specialists, but for executives of breadth, adaptability, and imagination."[5]

In its attempt to develop promising executive talent, Jersey stresses and accelerates worker mobility throughout its entire organization.

"A young chemical engineer, for example, who has shown managerial promise after six or eight years in a variety of increasingly important jobs with one of our domestic affiliates would be taken out of the affiliate's program and put on the roster of Jersey's executive development coordinator. . . .

"With the sanction of the top management committee, he would perhaps be asked to take an assignment in Europe or Latin America for a few years to assist in the operation of an

5/ Michael L. Haider, "Tomorrow's Executive: A Man for All Countries," *Columbia Journal of Business,* Winter 1966, Vol. 1, No. 1, p. 109.

FIGURE 34. Standard Oil Company (N.J.), 1968

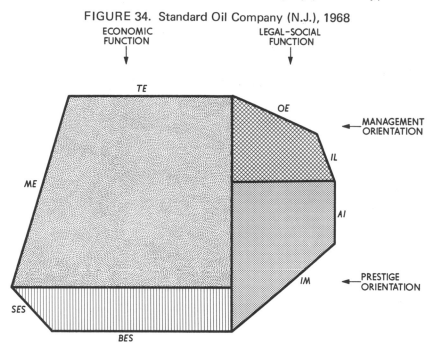

affiliate's refinery. After rising to a management position in some area of that company's activities, he might be sent to one of our new operations—an ammonia or fertilizer plant, for example. . . .

"In time our man might be brought back to the parent company for on-the-job training in employee relations, marketing, production, or some other phase of the business that would help fill out his background. Possibly he would be asked to attend an advanced management course at one of the many colleges and universities to which companies send men to give them a wider perspective on their business and cultural world."[6]

This fairly lengthy quotation was included to point out the essential ingredients in the transformation of a technical expert into a qualified technical generalist. The steps are:
1. Demonstration of competency in a narrow, specialized task.

6/ *Ibid.*, p. 112.

2. Advancement to higher level posts concerned with the same specialty.
3. Lateral movement to another affiliate and perhaps to another country.
4. Lateral movement to an affiliate making a totally different line of products.
5. A transfunctional move into other areas of endeavor.
6. Exposure to peers from other industries through participation in management development programs, seminars, conferences, and other cross-fertilization opportunities.
7. An upward progression through promotion for demonstrated competency.

The ultimate in this transformation at Jersey is election to its board of directors. Prior to 1966 all 15 members were company officers and every officer director was a combination of specialist and generalist. The generalist attributes were, however, immutably rooted in long and successful specialist experience. Even the addition of nonemployee directors to the board, two in 1966 and an additional two in 1967, has not radically changed Jersey's directorate dimensions. The long and diversified technical expertise and managerial experience attained by 12 of its 16 directors gives the company a first quartile ranking for both these factors. The concerted effort to broaden its executives' and its officer-directors' competencies also adds to the company's broad economic sophistication and image factors.

It is in these two latter categories that Standard Oil's development-through-mobility program is most distinctive. The great majority of our major corporations acquire these directorate dimensions by adding nonemployee directors. At Jersey BES and IM have for some time been supplied to a very noticeable degree by the high-caliber men who serve as its officer directors. Some of this acceptance and recognition can be attributed to the eminence of the company itself. However, the major reason for the high ranking of these factors is probably the result of a deliberate optimizing of talents possessed by high-caliber and highly-motivated managers.

This point deserves emphasis. It is through this approach that a board tends to become collegial in character. If, as is highly possible, collegiality will become *the* prominent characteristic of future boards, then Standard Oil Company (N.J.) is well ahead of the great majority of our leading corporations. It comes closest in providing us with a preview of the collegial board.

Jersey's board, even in its restructured form, is also an excellent example of what many of our corporations might be forced to emulate. Assuming that the supply of willing and competent outside directors will not keep pace with demand (for any of the several reasons advanced in earlier portions of this book), then major corporations must develop sources of supply within their own organizations. The probabilities are steadily increasing that the currently popular practice of borrowing other companies' talent to serve in outside director capacities will be subjected to severe scrutiny. If this will be the case, it becomes even more expedient for the leading firms to expand the supply of this scarce directorate talent. Jersey, here too, has pioneered in providing its manpower talent with the maximum opportunities for executive development.

# NEW YORK STOCK EXCHANGE

Seemingly, one of the staunchest proponents for outside director representation on corporate boards is that collective but intangible being known as Wall Street. During his tenure as president of the New York Stock Exchange, Keith Funston insisted on setting at least a minimum of outside representation on every one of the 1,285 companies listed on the Exchange. Under Funston's prodding it was stipulated that every applicant for listing on the Big Board had to have at least two nonofficer directors. With so vigorous a pro-outside director campaign being waged by the world's leading financial institution, it was perhaps inevitable that previously prominent and very successful all-officer-director boards became almost a thing of the past. American Tobacco, Monsanto, Bethlehem Steel, and Standard Oil (N.J.) are some recent converts to the inclusion of outsiders on the board. While it is probably an oversimplification to say that all these formerly "inside" companies have modified their structure because of pressure from Wall Street, it is certainly no mere coincidence.

If Mr. Funston and other Big Board forces have been instrumental, even partially, in instigating such change, it would be enlightening to study the structure of the Big Board's board itself.

Despite the supposed close scrutiny given to financial transactions by federal agencies such as the SEC, the Big Board is basically a self-regulatory body. It has considerably more autonomy and less interference than do any of our major industrial or banking firms. Self-regulation in the New York Stock Exchange "is exercised by several exchange bodies. Foremost is the 33-man board of governors. This consists of the president, three 'public members' he [the president] *appoints,* and 29 governors elected annually by the exchange members. Of these, 21 can be allied members, but 17, or a board majority, are required by the exchange constitution to be seat holders."[1]

In this structuring, the Big Board is almost entirely an "Inside" board. Even if—by stretching the imagination—the three members appointed by the Exchange's president might be viewed as "public members," this still gives at best a 9 percent outside representation. On a typical manufacturing company's board, Keith Funston's two-outsider-minimum norm, means about a 15 percent nonofficer representation. Very many manufacturing firms have between 50 and 90 percent outside-director membership.

Despite this preference for officer directors in the governing body of the Exchange itself, these same Big Board members preach a totally contrary policy for other sectors of our society. It should be noted that in May, 1967, Gustave L. Levy, partner in Goldman, Sachs and Company, was designated to serve as Exchange chairman for the ensuing year. Mr. Levy's firm has, even prior to the classic outside-director endeavors of Sidney Weinberg, been very prominent on the boards of some of our leading enterprises. Levy himself, in addition to his Goldman-Sachs partnership, is a member of fifteen other boards of directors.

It seems inconsistent, then, that the foremost institutional proponent of outside directors, the Stock Exchange, is itself virtually free of the benefits or constraints inherent in outside-director structuring. In this regard, the Big Board does not follow the thrust of its convictions.

Public representation on the boards of investment firms and even on the Big Board itself is probably just as much needed, and perhaps even more so, than it is on boards of industrial firms. It would certainly be specious to imply that in manufacturing industry officer directors need special overseeing by public representatives while member directors on the Exchange's board do not. Considering the relative recentness of the Big Board's respectability, the reverse would more likely be the case.

Until 30 years ago, the exchange operated as a private club, and the little investor was usually at the mercy of manipula-

1/ *Wall Street Journal,* June 1, 1967, p. 17.

tors. . . . One bull device was the pools: speculators pooled their capital, corporate connections and trading talents and then quietly bought stock in a company. They artfully pushed up its value, suddenly sold out and let artificial prices plunge. One such pool in Sinclair Consolidated Oil earned $12,618,000 for Harry F. Sinclair and a group of cronies. Another in Radio, as RCA was then known, netted nearly $5,000,000 for a 70-member syndicate.

The practice was halted only after Congress passed the 1934 Securities Exchange Act and F.D.R. named Joseph P. Kennedy to head the new Securities and Exchange Commission. Ironically, Kennedy, the year before, had made $60,800 on Libbey-Owens-Ford Glass Co., one of the last pools.[2]

Of course it might be argued that while ethical self-policing by the Exchange was a dismal failure in its earlier years, this certainly cannot be said of the current self-policing effected by the 33-man board of governors. But if in recent times the Exchange's Board of Governors has been adequate in structural design, then the Exchange should propose similar directorate patterns for industrial enterprise. Under present circumstances, however, our leading investment firms seem to be staunch proponents of inside control for themselves, but favor outside control elsewhere on the business scene.

Figure 35 is an approximation of the New York Stock Exchange's Board of Governors' directorate dimensions. Some judicious estimating was necessary, since a number of the 33 Exchange Governors are not public figures and biographical data for them is not readily available. The Exchange's Board of Governors' directorate dimensions are remarkably similar to those of the most inside-director type industrial firms. Technical expertise and managerial experience are very prominent, resulting in an exaggerated product acceptance sector. By contrast, the remaining three sectors are quite incidental.

A comparison of dimensions, sectors, and "hemispheres" between the New York Stock Exchange's Board of Governors and the median values for boards of directors of 26 of our largest industrial firms is shown in Table 19. Note that the Stock Ex-

2/ *Time*, "Wall Street. Happy Birthday, Big Board," May 26, 1967, p. 88.

change has considerably higher relative values for technical expertise and management experience, distinctly lower values for broad economic sophistication, image and owners' equity. As a consequence, the Stock Exchange's top policymaking group is far more preoccupied with product acceptance, management orientation and the economic function. Reflection on the way the components of the Stock Exchange think and act will readily substantiate these inferences.

FIGURE 35. New York Stock Exchange

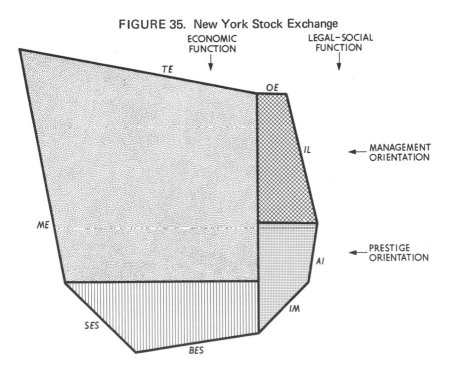

It is, then, a paradox that Stock Exchange members, who are staunch advocates of outside directors for banking, insurance and industrial firms, keep outsiders from taking a more prominent position on the Exchange's policymaking board. The fairly recent proposal to permit investment firms to "go public," has pertinence to this issue. In the event that the general public does eventually get an opportunity to purchase equity in our leading investment firms, then the domination of the Stock Exchange's Board of Governors by Exchange members becomes even more of a para-

TABLE 19. Comparison of New York Stock Exchange and industrial firm directorate dimensions

| | New York Stock Exchange | Average industrial firm | Montgomery Ward, 1967 |
|---|---|---|---|
| *Factor* | | | |
| Technical Expertise | 27 | 13 | 24 |
| Management Experience | 25 | 19 | 32 |
| Special Economic Service | 9 | 9 | 9 |
| Broad Economic Sophistication | 12 | 16 | 12 |
| Image | 5 | 14 | 9 |
| Asset Impact | 6 | 8 | 6 |
| Interlock | 12 | 10 | 3 |
| Owner's Equity | 3 | 11 | 6 |
| | | | |
| *Acceptance* | | | |
| Product | 52 | 32 | 56 |
| Peer | 21 | 25 | 21 |
| Public | 11 | 22 | 15 |
| Personal | 15 | 21 | 9 |
| | | | |
| *Orientation* | | | |
| Management | 67 | 53 | 65 |
| Prestige | 32 | 47 | 36 |
| | | | |
| *Function* | | | |
| Economic | 73 | 57 | 77 |
| Legal-Social | 26 | 43 | 24 |

dox. Note in Table 19 that public acceptance is currently rather an
incidental consideration in the structuring of the Exchange's
Board of Governors.

While directorate dimensions of the Stock Exchange's Board of
Governors are quite different from those of the median large-scale
manufacturing firm, they do approximate the dimensions found in
merchandising company boards (see Table 19). The inference that
might be drawn from this near identity is that enterprises preoccupied with the selling function probably require directorate dimensions quite different from those best suited for manufacturing
firms. However, another inference might also be made from the
fact that the Stock Exchange's directorate dimensions closely resemble those found in firms run or dominated by the founder-
entrepreneur. (The major variances would be in the owners' equity
and interlock factors, since the Exchange's Governors cannot of
course be presumed to be the owners of all the equity encom-
passed within the Exchange's listings.) The resemblance is remarkable in that the Exchange is not exactly a neophyte in the finan-

FIGURE 36. New York Stock Exchange, peerage

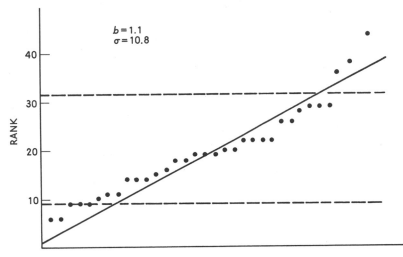

cial game, having celebrated its 175th anniversary in 1967. This leads, then, to the inference that the characteristics deemed essential for top leadership in today's Stock Exchange are quite similar to those requisite for successful entrepreneurship in the industrial sphere a generation ago.

FIGURE 37. Directorate dimensions, average board (Md; Σ = 26 cos.)

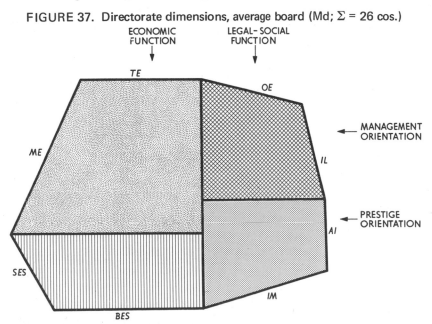

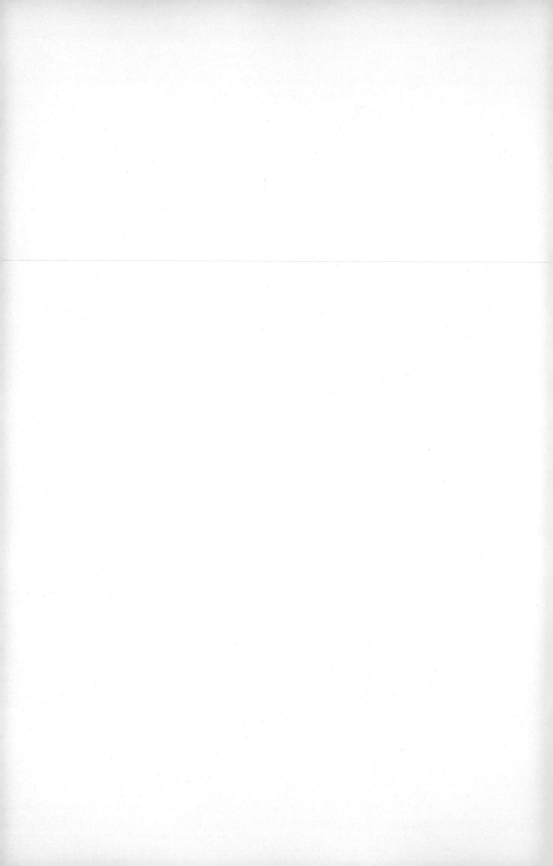

# Part III
## CONCLUSIONS

# BOARDS OF DIRECTORS REDEFINED

As is evident from the preceding Analysis Examples, boards of directors vary in composition, comportment, and competency. No two boards "look alike," nor do they ever perform in exactly the same way. When it comes to economic objectives, value systems, ethical standards, philosophical ideals—you name the norm—there is a tremendous latitude within which boards function. It would be just as wrong to attempt a board-room classification on an either-or basis as it would be to categorize all human beings as either tall or short, good or bad, brilliant or stupid.

Because of the great variance, the conventional designations of "inside" board and "outside" board tend to lose their significance. An inside board, by definition, is one comprised entirely, or almost entirely, of company officers actively engaged in the business. An outside board, while it invariably includes at least one or two company officials, finds most of its members from outside the company. Although this differentiation had meaning in the earlier days of our economy, it is rapidly losing the significance it once had. In particular, it loses meaning when major stockholders who do not hold any other company post except a directorship are called outside directors. Similarly, it would be false to designate as an outsider a director who is a retired or former employee. It is difficult to believe that an officer director who retires was an inside director prior to retirement but is—on his retirement—instantaneously transformed into an outside director. It seems equally ludicrous to lump into a single "outsider" category individuals who have minimal interest, competency, or company association with individuals who are maximal in these respects. Classifying corporate directorates as inside- or outside-type on a simple head count of members is meaningless.

While a more exact classification is needed, it should be fairly obvious from the great diversity in directorate dimensions that any

TABLE 20. Directorate dimension averages of 21 leading companies (condensed)

|  | Median (Md) | Range (R) |
|---|---|---|
| *Factor* | | |
| Technical Expertise | 13 | 3  to 24 |
| Management Experience | 19 | 13  to 33 |
| Special Economic Service | 9 | 2  to 18 |
| Broad Economic Sophistication | 16 | 10  to 19 |
| Image | 14 | 5  to 20 |
| Asset Impact | 8 | 0  to 18 |
| Interlock | 10 | 3  to 18 |
| Owners' Equity | 11 | 4  to 23 |
| | | |
| *Acceptance* | | |
| Product | 33 | 22  to 57 |
| Peer | 25 | 15  to 33 |
| Public | 21 | 6  to 36 |
| Personal | 21 | 8  to 38 |
| | | |
| *Orientation* | | |
| Management | 54 | 37  to 78 |
| Prestige | 46 | 21  to 63 |
| | | |
| *Function* | | |
| Economic | 58 | 44  to 78 |
| Legal-Social | 42 | 24  to 56 |
| | | |
| σ | 8.5 | 5.0 to 12.8 |
| b | 1.8 | 1.0 to  3.8 |

attempt at systematization will have an abundance of deviations and exceptions. This is particularly evident when directorate dimension values for a number of major corporations are compared, as they are for twenty-one major corporations. These data—condensed in Table 20—are shown in more detail in Table 21. Although we can readily determine from the tables averages on either a mean or median basis, there is a remarkable latitude as expressed in the range (R) values. These data corroborate the con-

TABLE 21. Dimensions of 21 firms averaged in Table 20

| Firm | Factors | | | | | | | | Acceptance | | | | Orientation | | Function | | Col. 13 plus Col. 15 |
|---|---|---|---|---|---|---|---|---|---|---|---|---|---|---|---|---|---|
| | TE | ME | SES | BES | IM | AI | IL | OE | Prod-uct | Peer | Pub-lic | Per-sonal | Man-age-ment | Pres-tige | Eco-nomic | Legal-Social | |
| Ford | 13 | 18 | 6 | 16 | 15 | 7 | 11 | 14 | 31 | 22 | 22 | 25 | 56 | 44 | 53 | 47 | 109 |
| Standard Oil (N.J.) | 18 | 22 | 7 | 19 | 14 | 6 | 4 | 10 | 40 | 26 | 20 | 14 | 54 | 46 | 66 | 34 | 120 |
| Wheeling Steel | 12 | 23 | 18 | 12 | 5 | 7 | 13 | 11 | 35 | 30 | 12 | 24 | 59 | 42 | 65 | 36 | 124 |
| Montgomery Ward | 24 | 33 | 9 | 12 | 5 | 6 | 3 | 6 | 57 | 21 | 15 | 9 | 66 | 36 | 78 | 24 | 144 |
| Union Carbide | 8 | 15 | 9 | 17 | 14 | 18 | 12 | 6 | 23 | 26 | 32 | 18 | 41 | 58 | 49 | 50 | 90 |
| DuPont | 14 | 17 | 2 | 16 | 11 | 2 | 15 | 23 | 31 | 18 | 13 | 38 | 69 | 31 | 49 | 51 | 118 |
| General Aniline | 13 | 18 | 17 | 16 | 12 | 6 | 12 | 6 | 31 | 33 | 18 | 18 | 49 | 51 | 64 | 36 | 113 |
| Hoover | 21 | 25 | 5 | 10 | 6 | 0 | 18 | 14 | 46 | 15 | 6 | 32 | 78 | 21 | 61 | 38 | 139 |
| A&P | 17 | 21 | 10 | 15 | 8 | 7 | 8 | 13 | 38 | 25 | 15 | 21 | 59 | 40 | 63 | 36 | 122 |
| US Steel | 6 | 20 | 13 | 17 | 16 | 16 | 9 | 4 | 26 | 30 | 32 | 13 | 39 | 62 | 56 | 45 | 95 |
| General Foods | 10 | 18 | 8 | 18 | 17 | 14 | 8 | 6 | 28 | 26 | 31 | 14 | 42 | 57 | 54 | 45 | 96 |
| B. F. Goodrich | 6 | 19 | 6 | 17 | 19 | 15 | 12 | 6 | 25 | 23 | 34 | 18 | 43 | 57 | 48 | 52 | 91 |
| RCA | 13 | 18 | 9 | 18 | 14 | 5 | 8 | 15 | 31 | 27 | 19 | 23 | 54 | 46 | 58 | 42 | 112 |
| GE | 3 | 19 | 9 | 19 | 17 | 14 | 12 | 7 | 22 | 28 | 31 | 19 | 41 | 59 | 50 | 50 | 91 |
| IBM | 10 | 16 | 9 | 15 | 13 | 10 | 12 | 16 | 26 | 24 | 23 | 28 | 54 | 47 | 50 | 51 | 104 |
| ITT | 8 | 18 | 14 | 17 | 15 | 10 | 6 | 12 | 26 | 31 | 25 | 18 | 44 | 56 | 57 | 43 | 101 |
| Owens-Corning F. | 4 | 13 | 11 | 16 | 20 | 16 | 10 | 10 | 17 | 27 | 36 | 20 | 37 | 63 | 44 | 56 | 81 |
| Sears, Roebuck | 15 | 20 | 4 | 14 | 9 | 9 | 8 | 21 | 35 | 18 | 18 | 29 | 64 | 36 | 53 | 47 | 117 |
| Beth. Steel | 19 | 24 | 6 | 18 | 15 | 11 | 4 | 4 | 43 | 24 | 26 | 8 | 51 | 50 | 67 | 34 | 118 |
| Armstrong Cork | 15 | 22 | 6 | 17 | 13 | 8 | 6 | 13 | 37 | 23 | 21 | 19 | 56 | 44 | 60 | 40 | 116 |
| US Plywood | 20 | 27 | 8 | 16 | 9 | 4 | 3 | 14 | 47 | 24 | 13 | 17 | 64 | 37 | 71 | 30 | 135 |
| MD | 13 | 19 | 9 | 16 | 14 | 8 | 10 | 11 | 33 | 25 | 21 | 21 | 54 | 46 | 58 | 42 | |
| $R_L$ | 3 | 13 | 2 | 10 | 5 | 0 | 3 | 4 | 22 | 15 | 6 | 8 | 37 | 21 | 44 | 24 | |
| $R_H$ | 24 | 33 | 18 | 19 | 20 | 18 | 18 | 23 | 57 | 33 | 36 | 38 | 78 | 63 | 78 | 61 | |

tention that there is no single prescription for the ideal board of directors: *no two boards are identical.*

Nevertheless, a close inspection reveals a centripetal force seemingly drawing these manifestations of diversity closer to the median value. For example, even though the broad economic sophistication values range from 10 to 19, more than four fifths of the companies have values between 16 to 19. A generation ago the range was probably just as great, but in all likelihood there was far less concentration around the median value at that time. This pull toward the "average" is a natural phenomenon. Corporations like individuals appear to be similar in all respects to their neighbors, their associates—and even their competitors. Nonconformity seems to be just as much a reason for concern in corporations as it is among individuals. This, to a great degree, is why corporations tend to approximate other "leading" corporations in policies, philosophy, and even in their public image. Very often the followers cannot explain precisely why they are emulating the leaders. Just as frequently, neither can the leaders explain their actions with sound logic and conviction.

The seemingly popular past quarter-century shifts in directorate dimensions are:

Noticeable increases in:
1) Managerial experience (ME)
2) Broad economic sophistication (BES)
3) Image (IM)
4) Peer acceptance
5) Public acceptance
6) Prestige orientation

Noticeable decreases in:
1) Technical expertise (TE)
2) Special economic service (SES)
3) Owners' equity (OE)
4) Product acceptance
5) Management orientation
6) Peerage trend-line slope (b)
7) Peerage standard deviation ($\sigma$)

Counterbalanced changes in:
1) Asset impact (AI)
2) Interlock (IL)

3) Personal acceptance
4) Economic function
5) Legal-social function

The reasons for these modifications in dimensions can be debated. Perhaps the most judicious explanation is that the corporation and its board of directors have simply adapted as needs emerged. A more cynical explanation would hold that corporations, like consumers, buy the highly-visible, much-advertised products and ideas. An increase in the image factor, for example, is generally assumed to be in the best interests of the stockholders, the company, and the country. There is of course, no objective information to support this contention. Like so many other accepted beliefs, it *is* accepted because it is the popular thing to do—despite the danger that overemphasis on the image dimension may turn an otherwise effective board into a pontificators' paradise.

Recognizing the tremendous diversity in directorate dimensions, it is obvious that no simple either/or classification can be acceptable. (It is the very simplicity of inside-outside designations, and their seemingly mutually exclusive character, which has reduced the usefulness of such labels.) The following classification is an attempt to redefine the role of the board of directors in terms of four conceptual norms:
1) Constitutional boards
2) Consultive boards
3) Collegial boards
4) Communal boards

## Constitutional boards

The board of directors is a concomitant of the concept of the corporation. Chief Justice John Marshall's classic Dartmouth College Case definition of the corporation in the 1819 Supreme Court decision focused attention upon the corporation as a legal entity. More than 300 years ago, first exigency, then precedent, and finally law resulted in the evolution of corporate charters and corporate bylaws. Within these legal prescriptions there invariably was, and is, a provision for a board of directors. It was the need—a legal need—to set at least some minimal rules of the game which led to the mandating of a board of directors for every corporation.

During what might be termed the dawn of free enterprise, two very distinct types of entrepreneurs, the product-oriented and the finance-oriented, resulted in two almost antithetical charter-based or constitutional board structures. The differences in these two early types of boards are quite apparent when they are compared on a scale showing the relative importance of the eight directorate dimensions stressed in this study. Figure 38 shows this comparison.

Note that the finance-oriented entrepreneur, usually function-

FIGURE 38. Relative directorate dimension emphasis in constitutional or charter-type boards

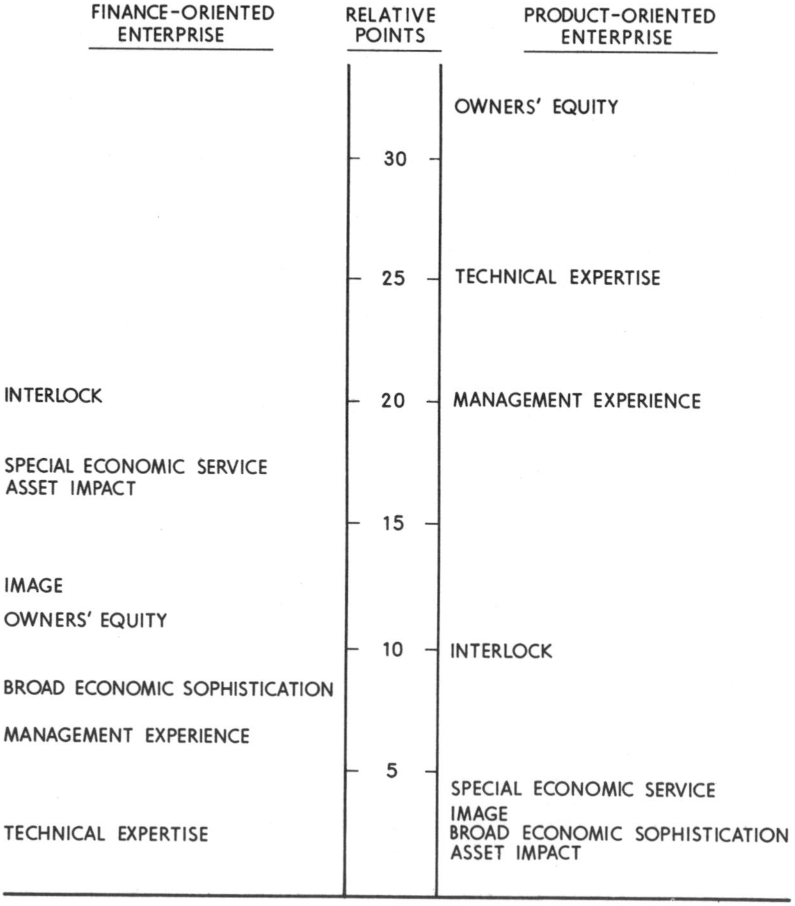

| FINANCE–ORIENTED ENTERPRISE | RELATIVE POINTS | PRODUCT–ORIENTED ENTERPRISE |
|---|---|---|
| | | OWNERS' EQUITY |
| | 30 | |
| | 25 | TECHNICAL EXPERTISE |
| INTERLOCK | 20 | MANAGEMENT EXPERIENCE |
| SPECIAL ECONOMIC SERVICE ASSET IMPACT | | |
| | 15 | |
| IMAGE OWNERS' EQUITY | | |
| BROAD ECONOMIC SOPHISTICATION | 10 | INTERLOCK |
| MANAGEMENT EXPERIENCE | | |
| | 5 | SPECIAL ECONOMIC SERVICE |
| TECHNICAL EXPERTISE | | IMAGE BROAD ECONOMIC SOPHISTICATION ASSET IMPACT |

ing in consort with a syndicate, preferred a board whose members were fairly well interlocked (IL), in the broader sense of the term. Special economic service (SES) and asset impact (AI) likewise rated rather high. Conversely, the finance-oriented entrepreneur's board subordinated technical expertise (TE), management experience (ME) and broad economic sophistication (BES). This emphasis on some dimensions, and subordination of others, was a logical concomitant of the development of the finance-oriented firm. Boards of this type were usually an amalgam put together by a group or syndicate of financiers. This syndicate rarely was a group of peers. Usually, as in all the J. P. Morgan-founded firms, it was led by one strong-willed and usually financially dominant individual. In his quest for associates in order to put together the requisite capital funds and in order to spread the inherent risks, interlock (IL), special economic service (SES) and asset impact (AI) were the dominant factors. Owners' equity (OE), while very important, was less significant, since the syndicate rarely owned even a majority interest in the firm. In marked contrast, technical expertise (TE) and managerial experience (ME) were of minimal importance, since managers and even chief executives were considered "hired hands." In the minds of the syndicate members, these hirelings were of a lower order, incapable of decision making at the board room level.

At the other extreme in this classic dichotomy, were the production-oriented entrepreneurs who generally were also the company's founders or direct descendants of the founder. Quite frequently the product-oriented entrepreneur was also an inventor, a practical engineer, or a salesman. In any event, he was intimately concerned with that company's line functions and spent much of his working day close to the line activities. It is quite understandable that this version of the entrepreneur surrounded himself with technicians and managers. As is evident in the graphic comparison, in addition to owners' equity (OE), technical expertise (TE) and management experience (ME) also rated very high. Antithetically, the dimensions deemed important by the finance-oriented entrepreneur (IL, SES, AI, and IM) are rated very low on the production-oriented entrepreneur's directorate-dimension scale.

Despite their apparent dissimilarities both these pristine forms of enterprise had much in common at the board level. The most significant feature of their similarity was the relative unimportance of the board in corporate decision making. In both cases, the chief executive or his equivalent ran the show, the board of directors was a legal fiction. Law mandated a board for every corporation and the law was observed. Instead of managing and controlling the top policy matters of the company, however, the board was usually an unused appendage. On some few occasions, particularly in the syndical, finance-oriented form of enterprise, a board would be shuffled and reshuffled to reflect changing components of the syndicate. This phenomenon is still quite evident in many of today's moderate-sized firms subject to severe proxy fights. Metro-Goldwyn-Mayer's 1966 to 1967 post-proxy battle realignment of forces demonstrates this phenomenon. Late in 1967, TIME Inc. was allotted one MGM board seat and the Edgar Bronfman group was given two seats. This was a consequence of these two groups acquiring most of the former holdings of the defeated dissident director, Philip J. Levin.

The MGM illustration also indicates that some semblance of the finance-oriented entrepreneur is still active on the business scene. As in prior periods, there is great diversity in the degree to which the controlling syndicate delegates its authority to the board, the chief executive, or some other entity. In some cases, the syndicate seems to interfere even in minor matters. More frequently it appears to abdicate its responsibilities by giving the chief executive almost dictatorial powers.

Similarly, product-oriented entrepreneurship in today's environment manifests considerable diversity. Some family-controlled firms, even where the ownership interest has dwindled to a very low percentage of total equity, are still characterized by top-level arbitrary action. For the most part, however, the owner's control is now almost always tempered by a realization that autocratic control based on ownership is a thing of the past.

It certainly is not a revelation that finance-oriented entrepreneurs and product-oriented entrepreneurs preferred boards with quite different directorate dimensions. Nevertheless, both these differently structured board types moved with equal vigor toward identical ultimate goals with seemingly equal success. There is solid logic to explain this phenomenon.

In the dawn of free enterprise, and perhaps even into its present "morning" or "noon" phase, there was an imperative need for fast, incisive decision making. The remarkable dynamism, the fierce competition, the tremendous technological changes, the rapid growth of mass markets, and similar factors made it imperative that someone at the corporate helm make immediate authoritative decisions. Perhaps these were not always the absolutely best or optimal decisions. Nevertheless, these suboptimal decisions—when made by a dedicated man with the assistance of his expert associates—usually were adequate to maintain a competitive position. If a corporation were so fortunate as to have, in addition to a strong-willed chief executive, one who knew his business, attended to that business, and took calculated risks when necessary, that firm tended to prosper. It made very little difference whether the company's board was of the "inside" or of the "outside" type. Consequently, during the first phase of free enterprise, and even today, in companies with either strong proprietorship or syndical forms of control, the board of directors is all too frequently a figment. It is structured to fulfill a corporation charter requirement. Despite the directorate title, privileges, and pay, boards serving either of the pristine forms of finance or product entrepreneur do not really fulfill many top-level decision-making functions.

This strongly negative conclusion must be placed in its proper evolutionary context. As stated, the earlier era of enterprise was characterized by a ferocious competition and minimal legal or social restraints. Adequate restraints and laws were lacking because there previously had been no need for them. Out of this somewhat chaotic state came the "robber barons," including finance-oriented entrepreneurs, product-oriented entrepreneurs, and all intermediate variants. This was an era characterized by *crisis* management. On the political scene, even in our own democratic country, during periods of crisis and particularly in wartime, the democratic process is considerably abridged. The chief executive then functions primarily as the commander-in-chief. This is a consequence of exigency and expediency. A vital job must be finished with speed, dispatch, and success. Parliamentary procedures are frequently set aside. The niceties of civilized life become of secondary importance. In order to get the big job done, authority is concentrated even to the point of dictatorship.

The initial periods of free enterprise were marked by similar compulsive forces. Despite the stigma attached to the robber barons, these individuals were outstanding and necessary products of their time. They served not in the conventional chief executive capacity but rather as forceful, competent, ruthless, and even despotic commanders-in-chief. Consequently, during the early period of enterprise, virtually all boards of directors were of the constitutional or charter type. Even today, perhaps four out of ten boards of major- and moderate-sized companies serve in the same capacity. They exist to fulfill a legal requirement; their value as decision-making bodies is virtually zero. Even their advisory function potential is minimal.

There is no precise date or time associated with the inception, zenith, or decline of any of the four board-type categories: constitutional, consultive, collegial and communal. It would be misleading, for example, to say that the constitutional or legally-mandated form of directorship began with Chief Justice Marshall's dictum and declined drastically during the mid-20th century. Keep in mind that rudimentary forms of both proprietary and syndical enterprise date back several centuries, and are still evident in today's economy.

Nevertheless, time and evolutionary forces have had a very great impact upon the top-level control structures in all of our leading corporations. As a consequence, the boards of most of these firms have moved beyond the simple charter or constitutional board phase. At present, estimated conservatively, only about 40 percent of our 1000 leading corporations continue to use constitutional boards. Of this number, about two thirds are syndically controlled and one third are of the proprietary type. Approximately 60 percent of the 1000 largest corporations have adopted the consultive board concept. This is a remarkable transformation. At the turn of the century, no more than 2 or 3 percent of major corporations had consultive boards. Even as recently as a quarter century ago, the consultive board category included only about 15 to 20 percent of large-scale industry. (It should be noted that at present less than 1 percent of leading corporation boards have pioneered and advanced to the third evolutionary level—the collegial board.)

## Consultive boards

Moving far out on a speculative limb, it can be contended that both proprietary and syndical or product-oriented and finance-

oriented entrepreneureal endeavors are gradually and impercep-
tibly blending into a single compromise form. From one extreme
point of view, this might be termed mongrelization; genetically, it
could be called hybridization; sociologically (or perhaps theologi-
cally), it could be viewed as ecumenism. Whether this blending
results in improvement or in deterioration remains to be seen.
Nevertheless, board function and board structure have undergone
and continue to undergo change. Completely inside-type and completely outside-type boards of directors (in the conventional sense)
have almost disappeared. Virtually all boards of directors of major
corporations must now be labeled *mixed,* that is, a juncture of the
two extreme types.

These parallel shifts away from the polar extremes reflect attempts at adapting to changing circumstances. Evolution in our
economic system has resulted in significant modifications in the
managerial-crisis mentality. Rules and regulations, even in abundance, have been set forth to reduce the enterpriser's latitude for
action. Public opinion, government legislation, trade-union constraints, international agreements, and even industry self-policing
set ever more rigid parameters. While we do find evidence that a
few 20th century imitations of the "robber barons" succeed, the
breed is disappearing. The top industrial leadership level is more
and more populated with professional executives.

Among the more prominent features of the professional at the
top decision-making level in major corporations are:
1.  More education. Between one fourth and one third of top ex-
    ecutives now have earned masters degrees.
2.  A demonstrated competency in one or more functional fields.
3.  A broad economic sophistication which is manifest in participa-
    tion in high-caliber, high-level, extra-company activities.
4.  A willingness to become "involved" in the corporation's top
    decision-making process even when this requires considerable
    time, study and participation.
5.  An abhorrence of any parallel associations which even insinuate
    conflict of interest or personal aggrandizement.
6.  Availability for considerably more than perfunctory and occa-
    sional board meetings.

These are just a few of the easily discernible characteristics of
the professional manager serving at either the executive or directo-

rate levels. In composite, this means that these professionals when serving as directors can provide the chief executive with valuable consultive services.

On the one hand, this new breed has evolved out of our progressively improving educational system. Equally, or perhaps even more so, this professional type is the product of evolutionary response to need. In the earlier enterprise eras, decision making was far simpler. Lack of rules gave the decision maker greater latitude; wider profit margins meant less penalty in the event of error; technological, market, legal, international, and kindred aspects were all relatively less complex and less demanding. As constraints began to multiply, however, the chief executive began to feel the need for assistance from experts. The span of competence for even the most gifted chief executive could not possibly encompass the steadily increasing number and degree of these constraints. As a consequence, at least half and probably closer to two thirds of all our major corporate boards of directors today stress the use of the consultive process. This does not mean that all directors are peers. Some, at various points in time, are more needed than others. On a typical board, perhaps a third or even half of them might be considered unnecessary. The important feature is that the chief executive, alone, cannot for an extended period of time, guide the corporate destiny. He needs and must have high-caliber assistance.

This phenomenon is increasingly more evident in all three types of corporate ownership: proprietary, syndical, and public. Even the modern counterparts of the product-oriented and finance-oriented entrepreneurs rely more and more upon qualified colleague-directors. The fairly recent innovation of "multiple presidents" in what had typically been predominantly outside-director-type firms run by a single strong executive is an index of this need. This innovative trend is manifest in Westinghouse's former "troika," now redesigned as the President's Council; General Electric's President's Office; Gulf Oil's, The Executive; International Business Machine's, The Corporate Office; Borden's Office of the President; and Union Carbide's, President's Office. In every instance, at least in theory, the chief executive officer supposedly shares his own delegated authority and responsibility with three or four of his top associate executives, a remarkable switch in practice, policy, and philosophy. It is a mark of unconventional—perhaps even desperation—thinking on the part of what was once autocratic-type management to venture into this shared control. Despite the about-face characteristic of this trend, it is a realistic attempt to meet the challenges of a radically changing business environment. (It is significant to note that every instance of the experimental multiple-presidency has resulted in a revamping of that firm's directorate dimensions.)

Although experiments with hydra-headed chief executive positions are laudable, they are rather feeble attempts at getting optimal consultive assistance. A far larger number of progressive firms have restructured their power centers, putting more meaningful emphasis on the executive committee or its equivalent. This follows from a kindred realization that the chief executive's role is expanding much beyond any one man's capabilities.

The executive committee, however, is invariably an integral part of the board. The executive committee exists because the board, as a whole, delegates certain powers to this select group of directors. By contrast, the multiple-presidency concept is a product of the chief-executive office. While the chief executive may seek tacit or routine approval from the board to venture into this experiment, he probably does not need such approval. Neither is it imperative that his fellow "consuls" be members of the board. The chief-executive sharing concept, then, is generally an attempt by a reluctant autocrat to get much-needed consultive assistance.

This seemingly harsh judgment of the one-man dominated, outside-director type of board so common to syndical enterprise should be viewed in context. The same judgment would result from an appraisal of the one-man dominated *inside*-director type of board characteristic of proprietary enterprise. There is as much need—in some cases, more need—in proprietary enterprise for higher-caliber board members who can assist in the consultive and participative capacities. Quite a few product-oriented proprietary boards have taken cognizance of this need, as Ford Motor, Monsanto, Alcoa, Deere, and a host of other companies with strong founder-family interests will reveal. Here too, there has come to be considerably more sharing by a once autocratic chief executive with at least some members of his board.

Formerly, the great majority of inside directors on proprietary

TABLE 22. Directorate dimension relative importance and diminishing difference gap

| Factor | Constitutional boards | | | Consultive boards | | |
|---|---|---|---|---|---|---|
| | (a) Proprietary | (b) Syndical | a − b | $(a_1)$ Proprietary | $(b_1)$ Syndical | $a_1 - b_1$ |
| Technical Expertise | 25 | 4 | 21 | 20 | 10 | 10 |
| Managerial Experience | 20 | 7 | 13 | 22 | 16 | 6 |
| Special Economic Service | 4 | 18 | −14 | 5 | 12 | − 7 |
| Broad Economic Sophistication | 3 | 9 | − 6 | 14 | 19 | − 5 |
| Image | 4 | 13 | − 9 | 9 | 13 | − 4 |
| Asset Impact | 2 | 17 | −15 | 4 | 11 | − 7 |
| Interlock | 10 | 20 | −10 | 11 | 15 | − 4 |
| Owners' Equity | 32 | 12 | 20 | 15 | 4 | 11 |
| | 100 | 100 | | 100 | 100 | |

Note: $(a-b)^2 = 1732$; $(a_1-b_1)^2 = 412$

boards had minimal independence and very few professional management attributes. Today, the opposite holds true. The reason is obvious. So-called outside-type boards can get their talent from outside the organization; reconditioned inside boards must, on the other hand, elevate their own director executives to the level of the high-caliber outsiders already serving on the board. This might be termed peerage-pressure. That is, if both nonemployee directors and officer directors do not have fairly comparable status in all respects, a board will quickly translate existing inequalities into several divergent and perhaps even hostile camps.

In summary, the great majority of large-scale publicly-held American corporations today have consultive boards. Moderate-sized and even small-scale companies still using constitutional or charter boards should give serious thought to ultimate progression into the consultive stage.

At the consultive level, boards of syndical origin tend to increase the significance of technical expertise, management experience, and broad economic sophistication. By contrast, they reduce the relative levels of special economic service, asset impact, interlock, and owners' equity.

Proprietary boards similarly elevate broad economic sophistication and image. There is a slight de-emphasis of technical expertise, and a considerable decline in owners' equity. Most significantly, the "difference gaps" for all eight directorate dimensions contrast sharply for the two types of enterprise in this shift from constitutional to consultive boards (see Table 22). The sum of these "difference gaps" squared $(a - b)^2$, for the hypothetical constitutional board directorate dimensions is approximately 1732. The comparable difference-gap value squared for the hypothetical consultive board directorate dimensions is only 412. This indicates an obvious propensity for the polar opposites to meld into a compromise version, an inference corroborated by observation of the universal trend of both inside-type and outside-type boards to resort to mixed-type boards.

## Collegial boards

The evolutionary progression from proprietary and syndical enterprise using constitutional boards to boards of the consultive type is not of equal momentum or consequence for all companies. Nor is public ownership any guarantee of such a change. Public ownership, however, does appear to be an absolute requisite for any company's board to reach the collegial level. By definition, a collegial board consists of colleagues or near-peers possessing fairly equal rights and responsibilities. Collegial meetings are characterized by discussion, debate, and disagreement. Differences of opinion are resolved by a vote, a majority vote prevailing. Of even more significance, disagreement with the majority or with the chief executive does not mean dismissal from the board. Another characteristic is the frequency of collegial sessions. They must be held fairly frequently or the boards degenerate into ratification boards (the decision-making function then gravitates to some other corporate component). One nearly infallible norm for distinguishing consultive boards from collegial boards is the incidence of board meetings: generally speaking, any board that meets only quarterly or even monthly cannot be given the collegial label. The exception could be that board which meets 10 or 12 times a year but whose executive committee meets weekly or even more frequently.

FIGURE 39.  Hypothetical Collegial Board

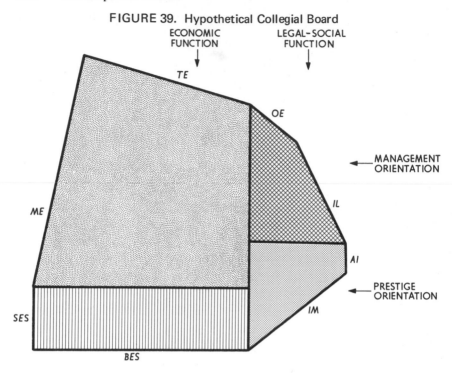

Collegial boards tend to consist of individuals who do not participate on many other boards, though one or two members of a collegial board may be multidirectors. If, however, many or a majority of the board become active in a multiplicity of other activities, the potentially collegial board reverts to either clique control or autocratic centralization.

Whether our larger-scale corporations will move toward collegiality in their board rooms is still uncertain, though it might be argued that there is some negative evidence. For example, Standard Oil Company (New Jersey) had for quite some time a directorate structure which was a close approximation of the collegial board (see Analysis Example). It might be argued that the fairly recent inclusion of four nonemployee directors on Jersey's board is evidence that this leading corporation has had serious doubts as to the practicality of the collegial-type board.

There are also other instances which indicate restructuring in collegially-run organizations. For example, the Chicago Board of

Trade might be considered an epitome of collegiality; although the Board has a staff of 130 employees, the real decision making is vested in an 18-member board of directors. In the past, these men have all been members of the Exchange. The 1402 members of the Exchange elect their directors and the 28 committees on which 150 members of the Board of Trade serve. This was as fine an example of collegiality at the top decision-making level as can be found anywhere.

In September, 1967, the "Directors of the Chicago Board of Trade approved a reorganization plan that would make sweeping changes in the administrative and policy setup of the 119-year-old commodities exchange."[1] The professional staff would be increased; the number of committees would be reduced; three "outsiders" would be added to the previously all-member board. The reason for this change is the time consumption of the nearly interminable meetings which seem to be inherent in collegiality.

While there has been some switching back and forth between collegially-prone and consultive-type boards, there is considerably more evidence of an acceleration in the move from constitutional-board authoritarianism, through consultive-board advising, and into an approximation of collegiality. This is apparent in both the conventionally-termed officer director and nonemployee boards.

In the former category, technically proficient professional managers are proving their right to peerage and collegiality. There is an increasing number of formerly constitutional-proprietary boards adding top executives to the board to serve in more than a perfunctory fashion. The revamping of Kaiser Industries Corporation board after the death of its founder, Henry Kaiser, illustrates this change. Mr. Kaiser, with all due respect to his tremendous contribution to our economy, did not foster collegiality in his board. Soon after his death, his son and successor, Edgar F. Kaiser, increased the board size from nine to fourteen members. The previous six officer director to three nonemployee director balance was then shifted to an eleven officer director and three nonemployee structure. The prime feature of this change was the addition of five presidents and chief executive officers of five affiliated Kaiser companies. These included: "Jack L. Ashby of the 65 percent-

1/ *Wall Street Journal*, Sept. 22, 1967.

owned Kaiser Steel Corp.; Clay P. Bedford, of Kaiser Aerospace and Electronics Corp.; Stephen A. Firard, of Kaiser-Jeep Corp.; Peter S. Haas, of the 39.3 percent-owned Kaiser Aluminum and Chemical Corp."[2]

Kaiser is not an isolated instance. The trend is unmistakable. Geometric increase in corporate size and activity demands an increasingly higher-level type of divisional administrator. While these superbly competent professionals *could* still be termed "hired hands," they are not the compliant "yes-men" typical of many officer directors of two generations ago.

Although there should be relatively little friction in a transition from officer director consultive-type boards to collegial boards, irritation and opposition can be expected in any change from nonemployee consultive-type boards into true collegiality. If a board consisting largely of nonemployee directors is to become collegial, it is imperative that every director becomes intimately involved in that company's affairs. As matters now stand, far too many nonemployee or outside directors make only a pretense of becoming intimately involved in the life of the corporation on whose board they serve. There is no justification for reelecting any director who does not continuously participate with zest and dedication in a corporation's top decision-making mechanism. Certainly no director, inside or outside, who lingers on the corporate periphery can be a meaningful part of a collegial board. Neither can a board with too many perfunctory participants be termed collegial.

There is evidence that a growing number of one-man-run companies, proprietary, syndical, and public, are becoming aware of the need for more involvement by directors. The sharing of the chief executive's responsibilities and authority by three, four, or more key executives is a strong initial step toward collegiality. Where this shared chief-executive role results in a meaningful equality among the group's members, then a measure of collegiality has been attained.

Parallel to the outside-type board's current propensity to structure multiple-chief executives is the inside-board's move toward

2/ *Wall Street Journal*, Dec. 7, 1967.

strong and active executive committees. In almost all cases these consist of four, five, or six of the company's highest ranking executives who also serve on the board. Most of these executive committees meet at least once a week. While most executive committees still function in a strictly advisory capacity, in an increasing number of instances they engage in real decision making in what appears to be a collegial fashion.

Among the more prominent directorate dimension characteristics of the collegial board is a distinct upward trend in management experience and broad economic sophistication. There are equally significant reductions in the importance of special economic service, asset impact and owners' equity. (The result is the hypothetical collegial board with directorate dimensions shown in Figure 39.)

It should be stressed that the era of the collegial board is still in the distant future. Nor is there any guarantee that it will ever become the dominant form of corporate top-level decision making. The most serious obstacles to a more widespread use of collegial boards in business are the slowness and indecisiveness of such group actions. Petty jealousies, preconceptions, and vested positions tend to slow down the collegial decision-making process. All the commonly-heard arguments against committees apply to collegial boards. (Thus, any corporation whose spokesmen have publicly stated anticommittee attitudes, is a long way from collegiality.) Lack of committees, subordination of committees, and frequent overruling by the chief executive of committee-gestated decisions is inversely related to the degree of collegiality found in a given firm.

The greatest uncertainty as to the increased future use of collegial boards stems from our inability to predict the degree to which crisis management will prevail in tomorrow's world of business. If economic forces continue to demand instant board-room response to major problems which are beyond anticipation, then collegial boards will remain a rarity. Only that firm with the foresight to develop its own super-professional executives will be able to attempt collegiality. The remaining firms, through their reliance upon a commander-in-chief type of chief executive, must, by definition, use consultive or constitutional boards.

This uncertainty as to the future incidence of the crisis mentality in corporate management is intimately related to at least three forces:

1. The intensity and course of future social changes.
2. The number and kinds of additional constraints upon economic enterprise that will be forthcoming from these future social changes.
3. The ability and ingenuity of advanced managements to develop techniques to maximize the benefits and minimize the limitations of group decision making.

In a sense, the last condition suggests that tomorrow's board of directors, through collegiality, becomes equivalent to a "composite entrepreneur." With the demise of the individual entrepreneur mandated by social change, the enterprise system must exercise ingenuity in evolving a socially acceptable successor. In theory at least, a collegial board would include the competencies and attributes essential to future top-level effective decision making. Most significantly, since these attributes will be divided unequally among four, five, or twenty board members, the real problem is one of synthesis. Can director individuality be preserved at the same time that these many ingredients are synthesized into a rapidly-responding, decisive, entity? If the vital entrepreneureal attributes cannot be developed and synthesized effectively into a "composite entrepreneur," then the potentially collegial board degenerates into bureaucratic mediocrity.

## Communal boards

In the event that industry fails to structure an adequate replacement for the original entrepreneur, then social needs will give rise to communal boards. There are numerous instances even in today's world economy to support this prediction. In one sense, Marxist revolutionaries and less-violent socialist reformers preached this need for change. Every Utopian movement from Plato's Republic to yesterday's Great Society leans toward the communal solution to organizational needs. Proponents of communal boards assume inequity in constitutional boards, inadequacy in consultive boards, and impossibility in collegial boards.

Great Britain's cyclical swings between private and public ownership of its railroads, steel industry, and coal industry provide immediate illustrations. These swings are logical responses to need: British industry has not been able to produce an adequate consultive board structure. Neither has it developed adequate executive talent to facilitate the effective evolutionary transformation from constitutional to consultive to collegial boards. Society's response, though somewhat slow and seemingly hesitant, is very definite. Unless the remaining private sectors of British industry adequately adapt board structures and functions to meet present and imminent needs, these private sectors must capitulate.

The 1967 nationalization of 14 steelmaking companies illustrates this eventuality. These 14 companies represent 90 percent of British steelmaking capacity. They have current combined sales in the vicinity of three billion dollars. The government-run firm, British Steel Corporation has a board of 20 directors. "The huge new company will be divided into four groups, each headed by a managing director. He will be advised by a board *on which labor unions will be represented* [emphasis added], but he will have executive responsibility for running his group."[3]

In Germany, the British-spawned concept of *Mitbestimungs-recht,* or codetermination, has not produced the anticipated results. Codetermination is the attempt to structure a board of directors so that it consists of stockholder representatives, worker representatives, and one or more government officials. The experiment is still only barely begun, perhaps because German industry has prospered in dramatic fashion. In spite of its authoritarian tradition, Germany's industrial leadership seems to be moving gently but surely toward professionalization. The 1967 switch of the Krupp industrial complex from private ownership and control to public ownership could presage the inception of consultive boards and even of collegial boards.

Rampant nationalism, particularly in newly emerging nations which host major extractive-type industries, may be giving a partial boost to communal boards. For example, early in 1965 the Kennecott Copper Corporation effected a significant agreement with the Chilean government by which it agreed to transfer the business of Braden Copper Company, its Chilean affiliate, to a new

3/ *Business Week,* "Britain Creates Its Own Big Steel," Aug. 5, 1967, p. 30.

Chilean corporation to be known as Sociedad Minera El Teniente S.A. Of the seven directors of this new company, four were to be Chileans.[4]

A comparable move was made recently by another copper producer. "The Union Miniere du Haut Katanga, the large European-controlled mining concern in the former Belgian Congo, elected four Congolese nationals to its 14-man board. The four are the first native Congolese to serve on the board of the Union Miniere. They were nominated by the Congolese Government which controls 17.95 percent of Union Miniere's capital and 24.5 percent of its voting rights."[5] While these illustrations do not necessarily presage a trend, once a national government gets a foothold in corporate control, a reversal of pattern is highly unlikely.

In Communist countries, a great variety of communal boards in industry have proven to be quite workable. Their relative effectiveness is, of course, a debatable matter. Yet, Russia's ability to stalemate so many of the United States' international endeavors is adequate testimony that the Russian political and war machinery has rather effective industrial support. It must be inferred that Russian industry's communal boards, despite their bureaucratic character, are not totally ineffective.

In Yugoslavia, the post-World War II institution of workers' councils is still another example of industry being run by communal-type boards. At the present time there seems to be fairly universal agreement that these communal boards are accomplishing much more than just keeping the Yugoslav industrial mechanism barely functioning.

In our own country, various agencies provide services which, under different circumstances, might be placed in the private sector of industry. The postal system, fire protection, social security, and even education could very well be the province of free enterprise rather than public enterprise. Despite the commonly heard criticisms as to the efficiency of these public service agencies, we have little if any tangible evidence that there is any significant productivity differential.

The important consideration at this point is that if boards of directors of the constitutional, consultive, or collegial varieties lose

4/ *Letter to the Stockholders,* Dec. 30, 1965, Kennecott Copper Company.
5/ *Wall Street Journal,* June 1, 1965, p. 8.

their vigor and fail to satisfy society's needs, then communal boards or some approximation will be instituted. As to the immediacy of such change, much depends upon industry's response. Normally, evolutionary changes of this type are very slow. Barring a cataclysmic or revolutionary reform, the change could cover several generations or even centuries. It can even be put off indefinitely. This last inference is predicated upon future social needs, the intensity with which the public seeks to satisfy these needs, and industry's ingenuity in adapting to changing circumstance.

# DIRECTORATE EVOLUTION

Any attempt to sketch the evolutionary transition from constitutional boards to consultive boards to collegial boards and then, perhaps partially, into communal boards, is bound to be hampered by the necessity for conjecture. We have very few meaningful and available historical documents upon which to base analysis. Then, too, what little evidence is available in documentary form tells virtually nothing about the attitudes, motives, or reasoning underlying boards of directors' actions. Consequently, Table 23 and Figure 40 have all the limitations of semi-subjective estimates.

As is particularly apparent in the graphic portrayal of Figure 40, 250 years ago virtually all organized economic endeavor had top-level direction which approximated the constitutional or charter form. This is the period during which the prototype corporation, first evidenced in the merchant adventurers of the fifteenth century, had evolved into joint-stock companies. The gestation phase was not easy. During the Merchant Adventurers' era, practically all the investing was done by a few wealthy individuals, but in the eighteenth-century joint-stock organizations, thousands of small investors shared ownership. The rash of schemes for fleecing the speculative-minded public resulted in the "bubbles," of which the South Sea Bubble and John Law's scandalous Mississippi Bubble are classic examples.

During this first formative phase of the modern corporation and of boards of directors, most organized endeavor was of the individual entrepreneur type. While much of this early entrepreneurship was unincorporated, most of these small firms ultimately assumed the corporate structure, and it seems desirable to include them in

TABLE 23. Estimated relative importance of basic board types for period 1700 to 2100

| Board type | Year | | | | | | |
|---|---|---|---|---|---|---|---|
| | *1700* | *1800* | *1900* | *1968* | *2000* | *2018* | *2100* |
| Constitutional-proprietary | 99 | 93 | 63 | 17 | 6 | 4 | 0 |
| Constitutional-syndical | 1 | 7 | 35 | 23 | 14 | 11 | 6 |
| Consultive | 0 | 0 | 2 | 59 | 66 | 55 | 33 |
| Collegial | 0 | 0 | 0 | 1 | 12 | 25 | 45 |
| Communal | 0 | 0 | 0 | 0 | 2 | 5 | 16 |
| Total | 100 | 100 | 100 | 100 | 100 | 100 | 100 |

this first historical phase. Because they have been included, however, the percentages for the constitutional-entrepreneur form of top-level control during the 18th and 19th centuries may appear excessively high.

The real expansion of the syndicate-type constitutional board began in the first quarter of the 19th century. It culminated in the era of trusts, of large-scale horizontal integration, and of the "robber barons." Toward the end of that century, it led to the passing of the Sherman Anti-Trust Act, though this legal action did not

FIGURE 40. Estimated relative importance of basic board types, 1700 to 2100

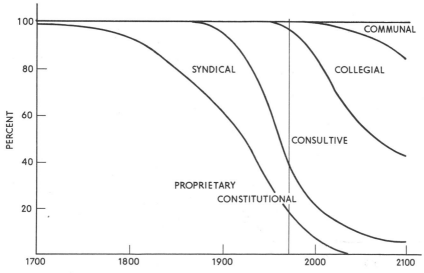

stop the forward momentum of the expansionist philosophy. It continues even to the present in the form of the newer conglomerate corporations. However, in the present pattern, expansion in the conglomerate fashion stresses circular integration or diversification and horizontal integration which transcends national boundaries.

It is tempting to speculate that the merger movement, together with phenomenal growth in scale of operations, gave rise to the consultive-type board, but there is no solid evidence. Yet the two movements seem to run parallel. It may be that the merger movement accelerated the large-scale enterprise phenomenon and this propensity to grow ad infinitum seems to be the basic factor favoring the newer consultive-type board. In the merged large-scale firm, in addition to size, increased product mix and more complicated technology likewise seem to favor a board of experts who can give the chief executive advice.

Whatever the reasons, beginning with the 20th century, constitutional-type boards—both the entrepreneur and syndicate versions—began to decline in relative importance. This is very evident in the downward slopes of both trend lines as shown in Figure 40. At present, about 15 to 18 percent of all boards in major business and industrial enterprise are still of the constitutional-entrepreneur type, and between 22 to 25 percent are of the constitutional-syndicate form. The trends for both these types of control will apparently continue downward.

The phenomenal growth of consultive boards is very evident in Figure 40. Within three quarters of a century this pattern has become the dominant form of top-level control. It will probably continue to grow in acceptance for the next quarter century, chiefly at the expense of the constitutional-entrepreneur structure.

At present, only 1 percent (perhaps fewer) of our major corporations have adopted the collegial-board approach. As indicated in the previous chapter, however, this form will almost certainly become far more popular in the decades ahead. Typical of all change at the board level, the move in this direction will be rather slow, though within the next half century, perhaps as many as one third of all major boards will be practicing collegiality in the board room.

The communal board is only embryonic in American industry

at the present time. It may never become widely used. At present, it might even be said that communal boards do not fit into the American form of enterprise. Consequently, the probability of this board form becoming more commonplace in our system is conditioned by how Americans will view the role of business and industry two or three generations hence. Since this type of speculation is more in the realm of the prognosticating theorist than in that of the empirical theorist, the predictions evidenced in Figure 40 are chiefly given for the sake of stimulating imaginative analysis.

A concomitant of this analysis of evolution in board structure and function is the comparable change which has and is taking place in directorate dimensions. These changes, as has been stressed throughout this study, are simply outward manifestations of inner needs.

## Adaptation to needs: a restatement

Table 24 compares in summary form the rationale for the four basic types of boards. The constitutional board, in both of its variants, serves primarily to fill a legal need. In the beginning of the corporation era, there was a great need for some regulatory body to bring order out of imminent chaos. The body vested by law with both the responsibility and authority to "civilize" and to referee the energetic but sometimes ruthless enterpriser was the board of directors. Understandably such a checks-and-balances device did not always work effectively. Because the decision maker

TABLE 24. Rationale typical of basic types of boards

|  | *Constitutional* | *Consultive* | *Collegial* | *Communal* |
|---|---|---|---|---|
| Reason for Board | Legal | Economic | Socioeconomic | Political |
| Authority Form | Autocratic | Oligarchic | Technocratic | Bureaucratic |
| Decision-Maker | Chief executive | Chief executive plus key executives | The board | Central planning agency |
| Board's Decision-Making Role | Acceptive | Advisory | Definitive | Adaptive |

in these circumstances invariably continued to be the chief executive, he exercised autocratic authority. The board's prime role in such cases seemed to be the passive acceptance and ratification of the chief executive's pronouncements.

Within the past half-century, however, top-level decision-making roles and needs have changed significantly. Causal factors include intensified domestic and foreign competition, geometrically increased complexity in technical aspects, and the more prominent role of unions and government in our economy. Perhaps even more significant is the increasing awareness of the public in all its varied roles as consumer, employee, investor, citizen, voter and taxpayer. As a result, the prime-need emphasis at the board-room level has shifted from the legalistic to the economic.

If a modern chief executive is to be economically successful he must have qualified assistance. He needs assistance and he must delegate. According to nearly every textbook, this assistance will not be forthcoming from threats, domineering, or raw power in any guise. The textbooks stress acceptance, the participative approach, dialogue, consensus, cooperation, and so forth; these terms provide an index of need for consultive techniques. Unfortunately, in too many instances, the transition from the authoritarianism of constitutional boards has generated considerable friction. The chief executive, groomed in and geared to "generalship," could not accommodate his thinking to the refinements of the newer "statesmanship." Some held tenaciously to what might by analogy be termed the regal rights of the chief executive.

The transition was and still is handicapped by a lack of definition and direction. Many well-intentioned chief executives and directors were and are prepared to move—but at what speed and in what direction? While desperately needing counsel and assistance from associate executives, most chief executives are still not sure to what extent the advisory role should be formalized and given status.

At the present time, most chief executives with consultive boards continue to exercise control in the style of a commander-in-chief, though there has been some modification. The industrial "generals" in this category lean more and more on their top staff officers. In some instances this leads to an oligarchic control. But even in this first semblance of group endeavor in directorate decision making, the chief executive invariably retains the right of veto. There are, of course, degree differences in the exercising of veto power. When, in this evolutionary process, the veto gradually gives way to the vote, then the board of directors approaches the third phase—collegiality.

The collegial board can best be described as being technocratic, rather than autocratic or oligarchic. Each director serves because he has a specialized and needed competency. As scale of operation and technological aspects assume still larger proportions, the chief executive has critical need for still more competent colleagues. The "hired hands" who characterized the constitutional phase, and the semi-professionals of the consultive phase will be replaced by near-peers of the chief executive. The essence of collegiality is equality. As long as the "boss" mentality prevails in any organization, collegiality is not a reality.

The use of the term *technocratic* should not be misunderstood. It is not a restatement of technocracy or of James Burnham's managerial revolution, though there are similarities. The prime difference is in scope. The technocrats of a generation ago premised an imaginative but quite limited philosophy and political system for our entire society. The architects of that new order postulated certain needs and need-satisfying systems for a massive and complex polity. Some of their assumptions simply were not in harmony with subsequent times. The technocratic reference in this instance, then, is rigidly restricted to the economic order and to the board of directors.

A significant differentiating feature of collegiality is the process of decision making itself. It is the full board which discusses, deliberates, debates, and decides every major issue. The board as a whole also prescribes the requisite course of action, implements these actions, and ultimately evaluates consequences. Proponents of the earlier types of boards can argue that all boards do just that. Where this is the case, however, then collegiality prevails—though before drawing such a conclusion, the board record must be viewed and studied. If there is no viewable record of debate and dissent, and of minority opinions, collegiality does not exist.

When a board, in consort, through frank discussion and recorded balloting makes the big decisions, the board's decision-making role can be labeled definitive. In this respect, the collegial board differs fundamentally from the constitutional and the con-sultive, whose roles are either acceptive or advisory.

The fourth category of board in this sequence, the communal board, serves a political need. In this instance, the term *political* encompasses much that is ordinarily put into the domain of phi-losophy, sociology, and morality, in addition to economics. Poli-tics then becomes synonymous with polity—the sum total of inter-actions within an organized society.

Political needs in this context are invariably the consequence of inability by any single subdivision of the macropolity to satisfy specific wants of the populace. *If* our enterprise system for any reason lags in servicing the growing needs of our people, then polity takes over from private endeavor. The free enterprise sys-tem as we know it was eased out of mail delivery, fire and police protection, and similar areas. There was a time, not too long ago, when these services were provided by private means. Similar trans-formations are taking place in other sectors. Social security came into being because commercial insurance proved inadequate when measured against changing needs. The field of banking is only a few short steps removed from being government run, and private education at all levels will be an anachronism within two or three generations.

In industry itself, our chronic recourse to war and war prepared-ness is destroying free enterprise in that part of the industrial sector which is intimately connected with national defense. And so it goes. Need determines structure. *If* our enterprise system capitulates, then of course a new system will take its place.

The prime objection to any form of communal-control in our economic system is its super-systematization; all pertinent compo-nents are rigidly fixed within the superstructure; all responses are automatic, predictable, and compliant. Conformity and regimenta-tion prevail. This is the domain of the bureaucrat. While there are quite a few benefits which accompany bureaucratization, the cost in terms of curtailed freedom, reduced motivation, and stifled initiative, is high. Boards of directors operating in a communal atmosphere are basically adaptive in character. They must, by defi-nition, adapt their thinking and doing to the edicts of the central planner. The individual boards and their members do nothing even comparable to what we term top-level decision making.

Here, then, once more, is a statement of what the typical board member serving on one of the basic board types can be characterized as:

| *BOARD TYPE* | *TYPICAL DIRECTOR* |
|---|---|
| Constitutional-proprietary | A top expert but still a hired hand. |
| Constitutional-syndical | A crony, a pal, a business acquaintance of the chief. |
| Consultive-proprietary | A professional manager serving as a full-time executive. |
| Consultive-syndical | A high-image individual. |
| Collegial | A competent and dedicated executive-colleague. |
| Communal | A partisan, a bureaucrat. |

# A SUMMARY AND A QUESTION

The first part of this study stated that a mystique shrouds boards of directors from public view and scrutiny. This mystique seems to go counter to the demand for more information and better understanding characterizing such sectors of our society as politics, education, hospital administration, and even religion. How long can this board room mystique continue in a society where the questioning attitude is so evident?

The need for a better understanding of the role of the director in modern large-scale enterprise was stressed in Part I. One avenue for better understanding is to determine objectively why each individual director on a given board has been selected. By analogy, a quantified summary of the basic reasons for selecting all of a given board's members sets that corporation's directorate dimensions.

In the directorate dimension model developed in Part I, eight specific dimensions are defined, weighted, and used for model structuring purposes. These dimensions are: technical expertise (TE), management experience (ME), special economic service (SES), broad economic sophistication (BES), image (IM), asset impact (AI), interlock (IL), and owners' equity (OE). These eight factors, when quantified, lend themselves to a relatively simple graphing device. When paired, they help to identify boards which are primarily concerned with product acceptance, peer acceptance, public acceptance, or social acceptance. They can also be used to measure boards which stress either the economic function or the legal-social function, as well as those that stress management orientation or prestige orientation.

The critical feature in such a quantitative directorate-dimension analysis is the firm conviction that each director can and *must* be shown to fill a specific need. In order to accomplish this objective, every member on a given board is assigned points ranging from zero to ten for each of the selected directorate dimensions. This rating is based upon information available in proxy statements, annual reports, *Who's Who, Poor's Register,* newspaper and journal articles, and personal evaluations. Each category in the zero-to-ten point allocation is rigidly defined.

Totaling the vertical or column values and translating these values into relative terms provides an excellent gauge of individual directorate-dimensions significance. Tabulating the horizontal or row values shows the relative "weight" of each director.

The first set of relative cumulative values gives an arithmetical basis for comparing boards of directors on a dimension basis both numerically and graphically. Similarly, plotting individual director point values graphically provides an index of peerage. The concept of peerage is a vital concomitant of democracy in industry.

In one sense, this arithmetical analysis is simply an adaptation of job-description and merit-rating principles. The board-room function is divided into eight components. If, in a given case, it is deemed imperative to add, subtract, or modify any of these eight dimensions, such a change can be made rather easily. If objections are raised as to any of the arithmetical analyses made in this study, the plaintiff can make his own evaluation. If a one-man appraisal is considered inadequate, then the obvious approach would be to get an average value through group analysis. The ideal probably would be an evaluation of a particular board's members by that group's peers and near-peers.

The second part of this study consists of analysis examples. The significance of these descriptive analyses is brought out by reference to arithmetical and graphic models. The graphic presentations vividly emphasize the individual differences found in major corporations' boards of directors. No two boards are alike. More significantly, no individual board keeps a given set of directorate dimensions indefinitely. Modifications are constantly occurring as needs and circumstances change.

Because of this heterogeneity, it is not advisable for any firm to model its directorate dimensions after those of any other firm, no matter how successful that other firm might be. There are so many variables and even imponderables that no formula-for-success will invariably survive the acid test of application.

Part III of this study now attempts to reclassify boards of directors on the basis of their fundamental purpose or function. Four classifications are set forth. Initially, practically all boards were constitutional in character. Within the past half-century a new category, the consultive board, has evolved as a consequence of the expanding scale of enterprise, technical and competitive complexities, and sociopolitical evolutionary changes.

A third category, the collegial board, is still in its gestation stage. While very few corporations presently sense the need and inevitability of this board type, there are compelling forces. Assuming a continued democratization in all sectors of society, the collegial board seems to be one logical and effective mode for top-level decision making.

If the trend toward fragmentation of ownership of industry continues, and if democracy prevails economically as well as politically, and if the collegial approach to top-level decision making is found wanting, then the communal board becomes a very real possibility. This form of control is found in quite a few socialist societies. There is, however, no evidence to imply the evolutionary inevitability of this type of corporate control. Neither does placing this category fourth in the sequence imply progression or superiority. This form of control seems to come about largely through default on the part of industrial leaders. Judged on the basis of recent performance in socialistic experiments, communal boards seem subject to serious limitations.

The role of the entrepreneur in developing our industrial system is subject to controversy. Nevertheless, there seems to be almost universal agreement that in past decades it was distinctly the entrepreneur who articulated the significant corporate decisions. In the past, the entrepreneur was rather readily identifiable.

With the passage of time, evolutionary forces have transformed the entrepreneur and his functions. Today in many of our largest corporations it almost seems as if there is no one person who can be singled out and designated as the entrepreneur. Yet, as every student of management must admit, there are no "headless-horsemen" corporations. It is equally obvious, however, that designation as "head" of a corporation is not necessarily synonymous with being the "entrepreneur."

There is conclusive evidence that despite the absence of a readily identifiable entrepreneur, all of the forces associated with that designation continue to propel modern organizations. It seems logical then to assume that industry has found a substitute entrepreneur: the board of directors. If this is so, then it becomes extremely vital that we get to know more about the synergistic process of board-room decision making. It was difficult enough to try to comprehend what propelled the individual entrepreneur. Now we must contend with far more perplexing problems. We must determine what will be the important components in a "composite entrepreneur." Assuming we succeed in this task, then we must contend with the synthesis process. Problems of motivation, integration, and evaluation abound. The question is: Can the entrepreneur's individual spark of genius and his fire of determination be perpetuated by group endeavor?

# A PERTINENT COMMENT

On June 27, 1968, after this text had been set in type, it was announced that a number of interlocking directorates involving 16 major corporations were ending due to antitrust suit threats. This was a consequence of a broader interpretation of Section 8 of the Clayton Antitrust Act by the Justice Department. This latest action is monumental since it goes far beyond the conventional definition of interlock as an association of directors serving on the boards of two companies which directly and substantially compete in the same line of business. The present interpretation goes much further by expanding the interlock concept to include mutual directors of companies which even though they are engaged in similar lines of business, are not *substantial* competitors. Among the 16 firms agreeing to end such interlocks are:

Chrysler Corp. with Continental Oil and Texaco, Inc.
TRW, Inc. with Midland-Ross Corp.
White Motor Co. with Eaton, Yale and Towne, Inc.
General Motors Corp. with Gulf Oil Corp., Mobil Oil Corp., and Standard Oil Co. (New Jersey).
Ford Motor Co. with Standard Oil Co. (Indiana), B. F. Goodrich Co., and Mobil Oil.
Halle Brothers Co. with Gray Drug Stores, Inc.

This present action has tremendous significance for future structuring of boards of directors in large-scale enterprise. Assuming that the Justice Department together with the Federal Trade Commission and other interested governmental agencies go still further in the logical interpretation of Section 8, it will become almost impossible to find competent and willing outside directors. The intensifying trend toward conglomerates will further accentuate this dilemma. Perhaps, as stated so frequently in this text, now is the time for every American corporation to intensify efforts to develop high-caliber officer-directors equal or even superior in all respects to the men who currently serve industry as outside directors. Actually, there is very little by way of alternatives.

# Appendix

# EVALUATIONS OF DIRECTORATE-DIMENSION FACTORS*

TABLE A. Technical expertise (TE) point allocation

| | | Years duration | | | | |
|---|---|---|---|---|---|---|
| *When* | *Type* | 1 to 5 | 6 to 10 | 11 to 20 | 21 to 31 | 31+ |
| 1 to 5 Years Ago | General | 1 | 2 | 4 | 6 | 8 |
| | Special | 2 | 4 | 6 | 8 | 10 |
| 6 to 10 Years Ago | General | 0 | 1 | 2 | 4 | 6 |
| | Special | 1 | 2 | 4 | 6 | 8 |
| 11+ Years Ago | General | 0 | 0 | 1 | 2 | 4 |
| | Spccial | 0 | 1 | 2 | 4 | 6 |

TABLE B. Related management experience (ME) point allocation

| | Years duration | | | |
|---|---|---|---|---|
| *Type* | 1 to 5 | 6 to 10 | 11 to 15 | 16 to 20 |
| Current | | | | |
| Chief Executive | 5 to 7 | 6 to 8 | 7 to 9 | 8 to 10 |
| Chairman | 4 to 6 | 5 to 7 | 6 to 8 | 7 to 9 |
| President | 3 to 5 | 4 to 6 | 5 to 7 | 6 to 8 |
| Vice-Chairman | 2 to 4 | 3 to 5 | 4 to 6 | 5 to 7 |
| Vice-President | 1 to 3 | 2 to 4 | 3 to 5 | 4 to 6 |
| Other | 0 to 2 | 1 to 3 | 2 to 4 | 3 to 5 |
| Past | | | | |
| Chief Executive | 2 to 6 | 3 to 7 | 4 to 8 | 5 to 9 |
| Chairman | 2 to 5 | 3 to 6 | 3 to 7 | 4 to 8 |
| President | 2 to 4 | 2 to 5 | 3 to 6 | 3 to 7 |
| Vice-Chairman | 1 to 3 | 1 to 4 | 2 to 5 | 2 to 6 |
| Vice-President | 1 to 2 | 1 to 3 | 1 to 4 | 2 to 5 |
| Other | 0 to 1 | 0 to 2 | 0 to 3 | 1 to 4 |

* Evaluation of Owners' Equity (OE) was presented on page 93.

## TABLE C.  Special economic service (SES) point allocation

|  | *Type* | | | |
| --- | --- | --- | --- | --- |
| *Degree* | *Buyer vendor* | *Educational, legal, etc., talent* | *Banking connec-tions* | *Government & lobby value* |
| Major frequent | 5 to 10 | 3 to 5 | 5 to 6 | 4 to 5 |
| Major infrequent | 4 to 8 | 2 to 4 | 4 to 5 | 3 to 4 |
| Minor frequent | 3 to 6 | 1 to 3 | 3 to 4 | 2 to 3 |
| Minor infrequent | 1 to 4 | 0 to 2 | 0 to 2 | 0 to 2 |

## TABLE D.  Broad economic sophistication (BES) point allocation

| *Education* | *Points* | *Professional & public recognition* | *Points* | *Publications, addresses, etc.* | *Points* |
| --- | --- | --- | --- | --- | --- |
| DBA-PHD | 2 to 3 | Office holder | | National frequent | 1 to 4 |
| MBA | 1 to 3 | Major | 1 to 4 | Local frequent | 0 to 2 |
| MA, MS | 1 to 2 | Minor | 0 to 2 | National occasional | 0 to 2 |
| Honorary | 0 to 3 | Advisor | | Local occasional | 0 to 1 |
| | | Major | 1 to 4 | | |
| | | Minor | 0 to 1 | | |
| | | Honors | 0 to 4 | | |

## TABLE E.  Image (IM) point allocation

| *Extent* | *News media coverage* | *Honorary posts* | *Social promi-nence* | *Other image affili-ations* |
| --- | --- | --- | --- | --- |
| International | 3 to 10 | 2 to 10 | 1 to 4 | 1 to 5 |
| National | 2 to 10 | 2 to 9 | 1 to 4 | 1 to 4 |
| Regional | 1 to 3 | 2 to 5 | 0 to 3 | 0 to 2 |
| Local | 0 to 2 | 0 to 2 | 0 to 2 | 0 to 2 |

TABLE F.  Asset impact (AI) point allocation

| Asset Representation (millions) | Number of companies | | |
|---|---|---|---|
| | One | Two | Several |
| 0 to    50 | 1 | 1 | 1 |
| 51 to  100 | 1 | 1 to 2 | 1 to 2 |
| 101 to  150 | 2 | 2 to 3 | 2 to 3 |
| 151 to  200 | 2 | 2 to 4 | 2 to 4 |
| 201 to  300 | 3 | 3 to 5 | 3 to 5 |
| 301 to  400 | 3 | 3 to 6 | 4 to 6 |
| 401 to  500 | 4 | 4 to 7 | 5 to 7 |
| 501 to  750 | 4 | 4 to 7 | 6 to 8 |
| 751 to 1000 | 5 | 5 to 8 | 7 to 9 |
| 1001 to 5000 | 5 | 5 to 8 | 8 to 10 |

TABLE G.  Interlock (IL) point allocation

| Level | Type | | | |
|---|---|---|---|---|
| | Club, church, college | Small company | Large company | Institutional |
| Two top executives | 1 to 3 | 2 to 3 | 3 to 5 | 4 to 6 |
| Top executive and other | 1 to 2 | 2 to 3 | 3 to 4 | 4 to 5 |
| Multiple | 1 to 2 | 2 to 3 | 3 to 4 | 3 to 5 |
| Single | 0 to 1 | 1 to 2 | 2 to 3 | 3 to 4 |

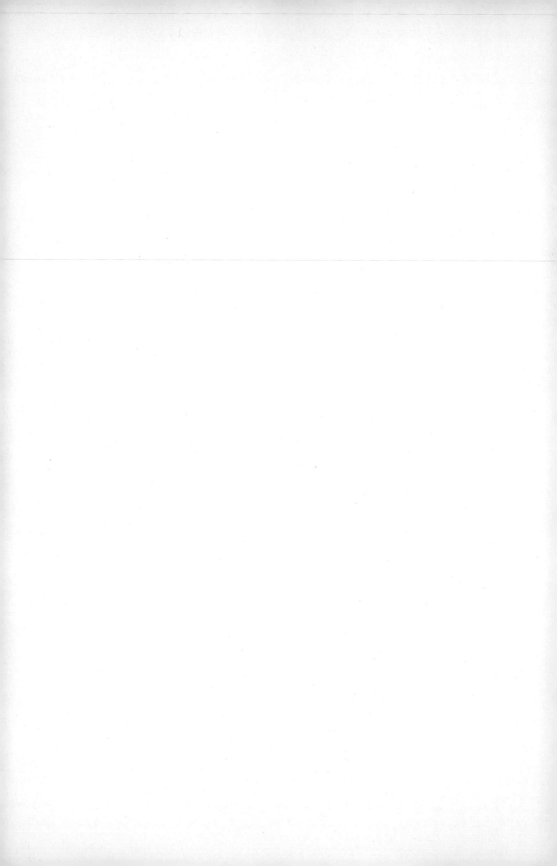

# RECOMMENDED
# READING

# Recommended reading

Feuer, Mortimer. *Handbook for Corporate Directors.* Englewood Cliffs, N.J.: Prentice-Hall, Inc., 1965.
A fine treatise with special emphasis on the legal aspects and implications inherent in directorates.

Juran, J. M., and Louden, J. Keith. *The Corporate Director.* New York: American Management Association, Inc., 1966.
A comprehensive presentation of the responsibilities and duties of the corporate director.

Koontz, Harold. *The Board of Directors and Effective Management.* New York: McGraw-Hill Book Co., 1967.
An excellent analysis of the role of the director. Selected as a 1967 winner of the academy of Management Best Books Award.

*Corporate Directorship Practices.* SBP 103 and SBP 125.
A joint product of the National Industrial Conference Board and the American Society of Corporate Secretaries. The most authoritative collection of data relative to certain directorate topics.

*The Conference Board Record.*
A monthly periodical, published by the National Industrial Conference Board, with quite a number of articles bearing on the subject of directorship.

*Poor's Register of Corporations, Directors, and Executives.*
*The* most authoritative listing showing the board room structure of 31,000 corporations and biographical sketches of 75,000 directors.

*Moody's Investors Service—Industrials.*
Presents a listing of corporate officers and directors together with details of current company performance.

*The Wall Street Journal.*
The best single source of daily reporting of the corporate scene

with very frequent references to directors and boards of directors.

*Business Week.*

An excellent factual presentation with quite a few references to individual executives and companies.

*Fortune.*

Each issue has at least one article which touches on the directorate theme.

Other commendable sources:

*New York Times*
*Forbes*
*Dun's Review and Modern Industry*
*Barron's*
*National Observer*
*Time* (business section)

Last and certainly not the least:

*Company Annual Reports and Proxy Statements.*

Every observer of the corporate scene must peruse (acquaint himself with) as many as possible of these succinct but frequently informative reports by the managements to the owners of American industry.

# INDEXES

# Name Index

# Topic Index

DISCARD